A Sanctioned Project
of
The Arkansas Sesquicentennial Commission

A SELECTION OF RECIPES
Compiled by
SEVIER COUNTY COOKBOOK COMMITTEE
Representing
**DeQueen Band Boosters
Gillham Fire Department
Horatio Camelia Garden Club
Lockesburg Park Committee
Sevier County Historical Society**

Copyright 1985
Sevier County Cookbook Committee
Lockesburg, Arkansas

FIRST PRINTING   SEPTEMBER, 1985   5,000 COPIES
Library of Congress Catalog Card Number 85-50329
International Standard Book Number 0-9614182-0-6

If you wish to order additional copies of **CELEBRATION**,
use the order blanks provided in the back of the book,
or write to:

Sevier County Cookbook Committee
P. O. Box 66
Lockesburg, Arkansas 71846

$13.95 per copy plus $2.25 for postage and handling

All proceeds from the sale of CELEBRATION will be apportioned to the sponsoring organizations to be returned to the communities through the voluntary projects of the organizations.

Front Cover: GILLIAM-NORWOOD HOUSE, at Paraclifta, built in 1840, oldest home in Sevier County, owned by the Gilliam-Norwood family until 1978, now restored by Mr. and Mrs. Jack T. Williams, San Antonio, Texas. Artist: Polly Pate, DeQueen, Arkansas.

Printed in the United States of America
Hart Graphics, Inc.
Austin, Texas

A TASTE OF ARKANSAS

The history of a people is likely told by what they eat. Eating is a social custom as well as a physical function so how food is obtained and prepared offers insights into the life styles of the eaters. We find an interesting analogy in the foods of the pioneer peoples of Arkansas. A woman living near Hot Springs knew poke sallet and cooked it just as did a woman near the Missouri border. Cleo Chism's mother of Ozan picked the sweet wild blackberry — complaining of chiggers — and made her cobbler similar to the one made in Chicot County. Hungry pioneers gathered the meaty scalybark hickory nuts and learned to store them in a pit. The sorrel and the sour dock and even wild strawberry leaves supplied vitamins long before we had a name for such. One woman wrote "I remember Ma telling me of her mother gathering poke sallet, sour dock, lambs' quarter and tender dewberry buds. All were put into a big pot with a chunk of pork." That pork came from pigs fattened on the big white oak acorns which covered the hills and river bottoms; the salt to cure the pork came from the Saline River or another salt works nearby. Since the majority of Arkansas pioneers came from the rural states of the East and South, it is not strange that their ways were alike. They were seeking new homes but kept their country ways, "making do" with what was available.

Indians contributed to the early tables with their samp (hominy), made from the maize they introduced, and the making of hominy became an art of the Arkansas woman, along with her lowly, but tasty, crackling that has astounded many fine palates. Indians also gave us the barbecue and barbecues and fish fries became social events.

According to the memories of some old-timers, many fruits were to be found: berries of all kinds — the blackberry was the favored; plums, mayhaws, even persimmons and pricklypears were eaten and are included in many recipe books today.

Wild game was plentiful in Arkansas. Stories about bear abound. Deer meat was on every table, according to Schoolcraft who traveled in the Ozark country and recorded seeing twenty species of game from quail to buffalo. Rabbit dumplings substituted for chicken and became a gourmet dish; their method of cooking opossum with yams is used today by hardy souls. Even a short study of the foods of our early settlers makes us glow with pride that they could improvise so well and pass down to us a healthy and precious heritage.

Arkansas cooks today, devoted to the past, are not bound by it. We still exchange ideas, happily adopting one another's foods. Arkansas people continue to openly welcome newcomers to our state; their recipes come alive in our kitchens. Traveling, we sample a dish on its home ground; home again, it becomes part of our menu, perhaps with fine shades of difference in the way we put the raw materials together. That is the taste of Arkansas, a reaching for the new while holding tight to the traditions we treasure; this book is a celebration of the culinary smorgasbord produced.

Luise Pride Thompson

ACKNOWLEDGEMENTS

Sevier County Cookbook Committee
Ida Margaret Stone, Chairman

Barbara Anderson	Donna Gallaher	Nina McCoy
Linda Bowden	Cindy Hale	Ilene Smith
Laverne Corbell	Juanita Karr	Suzanne Wray

The committee expresses its sincere appreciation to the following firms and individuals without whom this project would never have been possible: Bailey Discount Building Supply, Inc., David Pate, DeQueen; Bank of Lockesburg, Lockesburg; First National Bank of DeQueen, DeQueen; Gary Green, City Drug, Horatio; North Park Pharmacy, DeQueen; Cindy and Larry Hale, DeQueen; Wanda and Leonard Hampson, Little Rock; Horatio State Bank, Horatio; Lawrence Lewis, Lewis Food Center, DeQueen; Pilgrim Industries of Arkansas, DeQueen; Ilene Smith, Tri-Lakes Insulation, Gillham; Tyson Foods, Nashville.

EDITORS
Ida M. Coulter Stone
Suzanne Allison Wray

FOREWORD
Luise Pride Thompson

ARTIST
Polly Pate

Typists: Leoti Cox, Twyla McWhorter

Proofreaders: Kathy Latimer, Dianne Ross, Laura Thompson

TABLE OF CONTENTS

APPETIZERS 7

BEVERAGES 33

SOUPS AND SANDWICHES 41

EGGS, CHEESE, PASTA, RICE 53

MEATS 69

POULTRY 111

SEAFOOD 155

SALADS AND DRESSINGS 167

VEGETABLES 193

BREADS 219

DESSERTS 249

PRESERVING 341

FOREWORD

The Sevier County Cookbook Committee proudly presents to you a cookbook CELEBRATION *A Taste of Arkansas*. We wish to express appreciation to all Arkansans, residing or transplanted, for the many favorite recipes contributed. We regret we were unable to include all those submitted due to similarity and lack of space. Places of residence are listed only for contributors living outside Sevier County.

This book is part history; in recognition of Arkansas' 150 years of statehood, we take note of the men and women who have guided Arkansas with Heritage Lines, designated by ◇ and listed below recipes donated by members of their families or by their descendants.

Recipes have been kitchen tested and edited for conciseness, readability and procedure. Nothing has been left to guesswork with exact can and package size, pan sizes, oven temperature and yields given. For your information, the following procedures have been used:

Ingredients are listed in the order needed; brand names are used only when thought necessary for the success of the recipe; "divided" following an ingredient indicates it is used more than once in the recipe. Unless otherwise stated, flour is all-purpose and unsifted; rice or pastas are uncooked; soups are undiluted; canned products include liquids unless stated "drained." In fresh produce a rib of celery is one piece of a stalk of celery; a clove of garlic is one piece of a pod of garlic.

Instructions give cooking times though adjustments may be needed for individual ovens; all oven temperatures indicate "preheated." The **Arkansas Razorback** symbol is a guide to the relative time of preparation for a recipe: one little pig for "quick," two for "a bit more time" and three pigs "worth it for the effort."

We hope that you will enjoy the recipes within, do a bit of your own improvising and relish a taste of Arkansas.

Ida M. Coulter Stone
Suzanne Allison Wray
Editors

APPETIZERS

CHEESE STRAWS
Yield: 5 to 6 dozen

1 pound sharp cheese, finely grated	1 teaspoon salt
¼ pound butter, softened	¼ teaspoon cayenne pepper
1¼ cups flour	

Cream cheese and butter, beating until light and fluffy. Combine flour and seasonings; gradually add to creamed mixture, beating well. If necessary, add a few drops of water to form a stiff dough. Divide dough in half; roll out each section to ¼-inch thickness; cut into strips about ⅜-inch by 6-inches. Place on ungreased cookie sheet; bake 10 to 12 minutes at 350°.

Virginia Fouse
Executive Director
Arkansas Sesquicentennial Commission
Little Rock, Arkansas

ANTIPASTO
Yield: 2 quarts.

2 (4-ounce) cans mushrooms	½ cup diced celery
1 (14-ounce) can artichoke hearts	⅔ cup white vinegar
	⅔ cup salad oil
1 (18 to 22-ounce) jar salad olives	½ cup minced onion
	2½ teaspoons Italian seasoning
1 (16-ounce) can ripe pitted olives	1 teaspoon sugar
	½ teaspoon pepper
1 (4-ounce) jar pimento	2 teaspoons garlic salt
½ cup diced green pepper	

Drain liquid from first 5 ingredients; chop finely; add green pepper and celery. In a sauce pan combine remaining ingredients; bring to a boil. Pour hot marinade over all; refrigerate overnight. Serve with crackers. (Freezes up to 4 weeks; in tight container will refrigerate a week or more.)

Jean Smith
Little Rock, Arkansas

HOT ARTICHOKE DIP
6 to 8 servings.

1 (16-ounce) can artichoke hearts, drained, mashed	1 cup Parmesan cheese
	Dash of garlic powder
1 cup mayonnaise	Paprika

Combine all ingredients, mixing until smooth. Pour into a greased 8 × 8-inch baking dish, sprinkle with paprika; bake at 350° for 30 minutes. Serve with crackers.

Ann Coulter Clemans
Little Rock, Arkansas

APPETIZERS / 9

BAKED BEEF DIP
Yield: 12 servings.

½ stick margarine	1 cup chopped black olives, drained
1 tablespoon dried onions	
1 tablespoon minced garlic	1 (4-ounce) can green chilies, drained and chopped
½ cup chopped nuts	
1 (8-ounce) container sour cream	1 (5½-ounce) jar dried beef, finely chopped
1 (8-ounce) package cream cheese, softened	

Over low heat sauté onion and garlic in margarine until softened. Add remaining ingredients; blend well; spoon into greased 1-quart casserole. Bake 30 minutes at 350°; cool. Serve with buttery crackers.

Kay Hale
Bryan, Texas
Sondra Graves

BROCCOLI DIP (Microwave)
Yield: 6 servings.

1 (10-ounce) package frozen chopped broccoli	8 ounces jalapeño pepper cheese
8 ounces garlic cheese, or Velveeta plus garlic salt	1 (10¾-ounce) can cream of mushroom soup

Microwave broccoli in package on HIGH 6 minutes, turning after 3 minutes. In 1-quart dish soften cheese for 1 minute on ROAST (70% power). Combine all ingredients; microwave on ROAST 3 to 4 minutes.

Nancy Jenkins

LOW CALORIE DIP
Yield: 3 cups.

½ cup ripe olives	⅓ cup green onions or chives
⅓ cup carrots	¼ teaspoon salt
⅓ cup radishes	1 pint cottage cheese

In food processor chop vegetables and olives finely. Add remaining ingredients; mix well. Chill. Serve with crackers or chips.

Ilene Smith

CARACAS
Yield: 3½ cups.

1 (14½-ounce) can tomatoes	1 tablespoon Worcestershire sauce
8 to 12 ounces sharp Cracker Barrel cheese, shredded	3 eggs, well beaten
1 (5½-ounce) jar chipped dried beef, shredded	**DO NOT SALT**

Simmer tomatoes until reduced by one-third. Add next 3 ingredients, cooking over low heat, until cheese melts. Add eggs and cook until thick, a very few minutes. Serve immediately with crackers.

Mrs. G. W. Roark

 Governor Charles H. Brough, 1917-1921

SPICY CHEESE DIP
Yield: 3 cups.

¼ cup butter	1 teaspoon cumin
1 tablespoon catsup	¼ teaspoon dry mustard
1 teaspoon Tabasco sauce	½ teaspoon garlic salt
3 tablespoons flour	2 cups milk
1 teaspoon chili powder	½ pound American cheese, grated
1 teaspoon paprika	

In a heavy saucepan, melt butter; add catsup and Tabasco. In a separate bowl, mix flour and seasonings; add to butter mixture (will make a thick paste.) Stirring, slowly add milk, then cheese and cook over low heat until cheese melts. Serve with nacho chips.

Bernice Zachry
Little Rock, Arkansas
Linda Nichols

CURRY DIP
Yield: 2½ cups.

1 pint mayonnaise	1 teaspoon Worcestershire
½ teaspoon Tabasco sauce	sauce
3 teaspoons curry powder	Garlic powder
½ cup catsup	Onion powder

Combine all ingredients, seasoning to taste. Chill. Serve with fresh vegetables.

Myrtle Sims

DILL DIP IN PUMPERNICKEL
Yield: 3 cups.

1½ cups sour cream	2 to 4 ounces chopped dried
1⅓ cups mayonnaise	beef
2 teaspoons dillweed	½ teaspoon celery seed
2 teaspoons parsley	3 tablespoons minced onion

Combine all ingredients; mix well. Chill. To serve, hollow out a round loaf of pumpernickel or light rye bread. Fill hollow with dip; use pieces of bread removed in the hollowing process as dip pieces.

Norma Martine
Little Rock, Arkansas

CHILLED CRAB DIP
Yield: 1 cup.

3 ounces cream cheese, softened	2 teaspoons lime juice
3 ounces crab, flaked	¼ cup chopped pecans
	3 drops hot sauce

Combine all ingredients mixing well; chill. Serve with chips.

Louise S. Burks
Bradley, Arkansas
Theora Carroll Turner
Brinkley, Arkansas

HOT CRAB DIP

Yield: 2½ cups.

1 (8-ounce) package cream cheese	1 tablespoon prepared mustard
1 (6-ounce) can crab meat, drained, flaked	½ teaspoon confectioners sugar
½ cup mayonnaise	2 tablespoons white wine
	Dash Worcestershire sauce

In double boiler blend and heat ingredients. Turn into chafing dish; serve with toast rounds.

Sissy Correll Pride
Friendswood, Texas

GUACAMOLE

Yield: 2 cups.

3 ripe avocados, peeled, mashed	1 (4-ounce) can chilies, finely chopped
1 onion, finely grated	½ teaspoon salt
1 to 2 tablespoons lemon juice	1 clove of garlic, crushed
2 tomatoes, peeled, finely chopped	

Combine all ingredients. Dip may be served at this point and will be chunky. For a smoother texture, process in a blender. Serve with tortilla or taco chips or fresh vegetables.

Diane Fisk
Brazoria, Texas

FRESH FRUIT DIP

Yield: 2 cups.

1 (8-ounce) package cream cheese	1 (7-ounce) jar marshmallow cream

Soften cream cheese; combine with marshmallow cream, blending until smooth. Serve with fresh fruit.

Linda Warren

RED FRUIT DIP
Yield: 1¾ cups.

½ cup mayonnaise
½ cup jellied cranberry sauce
½ cup whipping cream, whipped

Combine mayonnaise and cranberry sauce; fold in whipped cream. Chill. Serve with assorted fruits.

Adrienne Taggart Gillispie

SALSA
Yield: 6 cups.

4 tomatoes, peeled, finely chopped
½ cup minced onion
½ cup minced celery
¼ cup minced green pepper
¼ cup olive oil
3 tablespoons chopped, mild green chilies
2 tablespoons red wine vinegar
1 teaspoon mustard seed
1 teaspoon salt
1 teaspoon ground coriander, or ½ teaspoon garlic salt and ½ teaspoon oregano
Dash of pepper

Combine all ingredients. Cover and chill several hours. Serve as a dip with tortilla chips, or as a mild sauce for other dishes.

Ollie Taggart

SHRIMP DIP
Yield: 2½ cups.

8 ounces cream cheese, softened
1 (4¼-ounce) can small shrimp, drained
1 small white onion, chopped
1 scant cup mayonnaise
Hamburger dill slices, chopped, to taste
Salad olives, chopped, to taste

Combine all ingredients, mixing well. Chill. Serve with chips or crackers. (May also be used as a baked potato topping.)

Vera Wooten Parker
Vivian, Louisiana
Nancy Hedgecock

PARTY SHRIMP DIP
Yield: 5 cups.

1 pint mayonnaise	1½ tablespoons dry mustard
¾ cup chopped onion	1½ tablespoons Worcestershire sauce
1 teaspoon garlic salt	1 cup cottage cheese
½ teaspoon caraway seed	1 pound cooked shrimp, flaked
1 teaspoon dry sherry	
½ teaspoon Tabasco sauce	
½ teaspoon pepper	

Combine all ingredients except shrimp; process in blender; chill, covered, for at least 6 hours. Before serving, fold in shrimp.

Janie Williams
San Antonio, Texas

SPINACH DIP
Yield: 2 cups.

1 (10-ounce) package frozen chopped spinach, thawed, squeezed dry	¼ cup mayonnaise
	1 (2⅝-ounce) package Knorr dry vegetable soup mix
1 (8-ounce) container sour cream	

Combine all ingredients. Chill. Serve with chips.

Molly Stauber Turner
Arkadelphia, Arkansas

TACO DIP
Yield: 7-8 cups.

2 cups jalapeño bean dip	1 cup shredded Mozzarella cheese
1 (1.25-ounce) package taco seasoning mix	1 cup cooked tomatoes, chopped
1 cup sour cream	½ cup sliced olives
½ cup mayonnaise	2 cups chopped green onions
1 cup shredded Cheddar cheese	

Spread jalapeño bean dip on large flat serving dish. Mix taco seasoning, sour cream and mayonnaise; spread over bean dip. Layer remaining ingredients as listed. Serve with chips or crackers.

Mary Sue Steel
Newbury Park, California
Doodle Boykin

TEX-MEX DIP
Yield: 16 servings.

3 ripe avocados, peeled, mashed	1 cup chopped green onions with tops
2 tablespoons lemon juice	2 cups chopped fresh tomatoes
½ teaspoon salt	2 (3½-ounce) cans ripe olives, chopped
¼ teaspoon pepper	
1 cup sour cream	1 (8-ounce) package Cheddar cheese, grated
½ cup mayonnaise	
1 (1.25-ounce) package taco seasoning mix	¼ teaspoon garlic powder, optional
2 (10½-ounce) cans jalapeño bean dip, or 1 (15-ounce) can refried beans	Picante sauce, optional
	Jalapeño peppers, optional

Combine avocados with lemon juice, salt and pepper. In separate bowl, combine sour cream, mayonnaise and taco seasoning. To assemble: spread bean dip on a large shallow serving platter; top with avocado mixture; layer with sour cream mixture. Sprinkle with onions, tomatoes and olives; cover with grated cheese. (If desired, sprinkle with picante sauce and chopped jalapeños.) (Garlic powder, if desired, should be added to avocados.) Serve with tortilla rounds.

Mary Weathersby
Little Rock, Arkansas
Mrs. Stella Lambert
Darla Jones

HOT TUNA DIP

Yield: 3 cups.

1 (8-ounce) package cream cheese
1 (10¾-ounce) can mushroom soup
1 (6-ounce) can tuna, drained, flaked
1 (1-ounce) jar mushrooms, drained, chopped
Slivered almonds, optional

Blend cream cheese with soup over low heat. Add remaining ingredients; blend. Serve hot with chips.

Katherine S. Conner
Newport, Arkansas

AVOCADOS WITH HOT COCKTAIL SAUCE

8 servings.

6 tablespoons butter
6 tablespoons catsup
2½ tablespoons vinegar
2½ tablespoons water
4 teaspoons sugar
2½ teaspoons Worcestershire sauce
½ teaspoon salt
Dash Tabasco sauce
4 ripe avocados
Lemon juice

In sauce pan combine all ingredients except avocados and lemon juice. Heat until butter is melted and sauce is smooth.

Halve avocados; seed and sprinkle with lemon juice. To serve, ladle hot sauce into avocados. May be served as first course or as appetizers.

Janie Williams
San Antonio, Texas

MARINATED BROCCOLI OR CAULIFLOWER
Yield: 4-5 cups.

- 2 bunches fresh broccoli, or 1 head cauliflower
- 1 cup vinegar
- 1 tablespoon dillweed
- 1 teaspoon salt
- 1 tablespoon coarsely ground pepper
- 1 teaspoon garlic salt
- 1-1½ cups safflower oil

Break or cut broccoli into bite size pieces, or break cauliflower into cauliflowerets. Combine remaining ingredients; pour over vegetables pieces, stirring to coat. Marinate in refrigerator overnight. Serve with toothpicks.

June Correll Burr
Ft. Worth, Texas

CRUSTY DILL SPEARS
Yield: about 16.

- ⅔ cup cornmeal
- 6 tablespoons flour
- 1½ teaspoons baking powder
- 1 teaspoon garlic powder
- ½ cup milk
- 2 tablespoons dill pickle liquid
- 1 egg, slightly beaten
- 4 medium dill pickles, cut into spears, or about 16 spears, well drained

In mixing bowl combine cornmeal, flour, baking powder, and garlic powder; stir in milk, pickle liquid and egg. Dip spears in batter to coat. Heat 1 inch oil in heavy skillet (electric skillet 400°). Fry in small batches 2 minutes, or until browned, turning once. Drain on paper towels; serve immediately. May be kept in warm oven up to 30 minutes.

ATKINS PICKLE COMPANY, INC.
Atkins, Arkansas

Atkins of Arkansas supplies hamburger sliced dills to 5 southern states, "pickling up" 4,600,000 hamburgers per week.

CHEESE AND BACON POTATO ROUNDS
Yield: about 32 appetizers.

4 baking potatoes, cut into ½-inch slices	2 cups shredded sharp Cheddar cheese
¼ cup melted margarine	½ cup green onion slices
8 crisply-cooked bacon slices, crumbled	

Brush both sides of potato slices with margarine; place on baking sheet. Bake at 400° 30 to 40 minutes, turning as needed, until lightly browned on both sides. Combine remaining ingredients; top each potato slice with spoonful; bake until cheese is melted. Serve with sour cream.

Donna Gallaher

CHICKEN LITTLE FINGERS
Yield: 12 to 14 appetizer servings.

12 boneless chicken breasts	1 teaspoon salt
1½ cups buttermilk	1 teaspoon pepper
2 tablespoons lemon juice	2 cloves garlic, minced
2 teaspoons Worcestershire sauce	4 cups soft bread crumbs
1 teaspoon soy sauce	½ cup sesame seeds
1 tablespoon Cavender's Greek Seasoning	¼ cup butter, melted
	¼ cup melted shortening

Cut chicken into ½-inch strips. Combine next 8 ingredients; add chicken, coating well; cover; refrigerate overnight.

In large bowl combine bread crumbs and sesame seeds; drain chicken thoroughly; toss in crumb mixture to coat. Place chicken in 2 greased 9 × 13-inch baking dishes. Brush with combined butter and shortening. Bake at 350° 35 to 40 minutes. Serve with Plum Sauce.

Plum Sauce:

1½ cups red plum jam	1½ tablespoons prepared horseradish
1½ tablespoons prepared mustard	1½ teaspoons lemon juice

In small sauce pan combine all ingredients, mixing well. Place over low heat just until warm, stirring constantly. Yield: 2¾ cups.

Lou Carlson

COCKTAIL MEATBALLS

Yield: about 3½ dozen.

1 pound ground round steak	½ cup firmly packed brown sugar
½ teaspoon onion salt	1 (15-ounce) can tomato sauce
¼ cup water	3 tablespoons lemon juice
½ cup fine breadcrumbs	
1 egg	

Thoroughly mix first 5 ingredients; shape into small balls; set aside. In a sauce pan combine remaining ingredients; simmer 3 minutes. Add meatballs, and continue to simmer 45 minutes. Serve in chafing dish set on low heat. Garnish with lemon slices and parsley.

Mona L. Fenton Patterson
Ashdown, Arkansas

OLIVE CHEESE BALLS

Yield: 4 dozen.

8 ounces sharp cheese, grated	Dash chili powder
7 tablespoons margarine	1 (5-ounce) jar stuffed green olives, drained
1 cup flour	

Combine first 4 ingredients, mixing well. Take 1 teaspoon of the cheese mixture; shape into a ball around olive; repeat process. Place on cookie sheet; chill for 2 hours. Bake at 400° 15 minutes, or until golden brown.

Ann Cannon Mays
Shreveport, Louisiana

Olive Beef Variation: Season 1 pound ground beef to taste with salt, pepper, and Worcestershire sauce; wrap as above; cook in batches in oil until brown. Drain; serve in chafing dish.

Evelyn Tradewell

GLAZED HAM BALLS
Serves 8.

3 pounds ground lean ham	¾ cup vinegar
1¼ cups milk	¾ cup water
2½ cups bread crumbs	1½ teaspoons dry mustard
1½ cups brown sugar	

Combine first 3 ingredients and let stand 1 hour. Shape into balls about 1½ inches in diameter; place in a greased 9 × 13-inch baking dish. In saucepan combine remaining ingredients; boil 15 minutes. Pour over ham balls; cover; bake at 350° 30 minutes. Uncover and bake 30 minutes longer. Serve in chafing dish.

Mrs. Alfred B. Bailey
Little Rock, Arkansas

◇   *Governor Carl E. Bailey, 1937-1941.*

MEAT PIES
Yield: 40 pies.

1 pound ground beef	Salt and pepper to taste
1 medium onion, chopped	Cinnamon to taste
2 tablespoons tomato paste	2 (10-ounce) cans flaky
2 to 3 tablespoons lemon juice	biscuits
1 (8-ounce) container sour cream	

Brown meat and onion. Add next 5 ingredients, stirring until blended; chill. Separate each biscuit to make two; roll out on floured board. Place a heaping teaspoonful of cold filling on each biscuit round. Fold over; crimp edges to seal. Place one layer deep on trays; freeze. When frozen, fry in hot oil until golden brown, about 5 minutes. Drain and serve. May be refrozen; will freeze up to 3 months.

Eddith Lewis
Arkadelphia, Arkansas

BEEF AND CHICKEN FONDUE
Yield: 8 servings.

1½ pounds sirloin steak, cut in 1-inch cubes	⅓ cup soy sauce
	⅓ cup sherry
3 whole chicken breasts, skinned, boned, cut in 1-inch cubes	2 cups butter
	2 cups oil

Marinate chicken and beef in soy sauce and sherry 24 hours. To serve, drain; let stand at room temperature 30 minutes. Melt butter in fondue pot; add oil; heat until very hot. Spear cubes with fondue forks; cook to desired doneness; dip into appropriate sauce.

Brown Mushroom Sauce:

2 tablespoons butter	1 teaspoon Worcestershire sauce
2 tablespoons flour	
⅔ cup consomme	½ cup chopped mushrooms
	½ cup sour cream

Melt butter; blend in flour; remove from heat. Slowly stir in consomme; return to heat; cook, stirring, until thick. Blend in remaining ingredients. Serve as dip for beef fondue.

Sour Cream Curry Sauce:

1 cup sour cream	¼ teaspoon sugar
½ teaspoon curry powder	⅛ teaspoon salt
1 teaspoon prepared horseradish	Paprika

Blend first 5 ingredients; chill. Sprinkle with paprika. Serve as dip for chicken fondue.

Josephine Matlock Futrell
Shreveport, Louisiana

SAUSAGE STUFFED MUSHROOMS
Yield: about 2 dozen.

1 pound fresh mushrooms	2 tablespoons chopped parsley
1 pound bulk pork sausage	6 ounces sharp Cheddar cheese, shredded
1 teaspoon minced garlic	

Rinse mushrooms, pat dry; remove stems. Chop stems and sauté with sausage, garlic and parsley until sausage is browned, stirring to crumble. Drain off pan drippings. Stir in cheese, mixing well. Spoon mixture into mushroom caps and place in a 9 × 13-inch baking dish. Bake at 350° for 20 minutes.

Sandra Dunn

CHEESE PETIT FOURS
Yield: 40 petit fours.

2 (5-ounce) jars Old English cheese	Few drops Tabasco sauce
1 stick butter, softened	1 loaf Pepperidge Farm very thin white bread, crusts removed
1 egg	

Beat first 4 ingredients with electric mixer until frothy. To assemble: spread cheese mixture on 3 slices of the bread; stack one on top of the other. Cut twice diagonally to form 4 small triangles; frost tops and sides of each; place on baking sheet 1 inch apart. Repeat process, using entire loaf. Bake at 350° 8 to 10 minutes. Serve as appetizers, or with soup and salad. (Freezes well; freeze, unbaked, on cookie sheet; store in plastic bag. Bake 10 to 12 minutes if frozen.)

Robyn Dickey
Governor's Mansion Secretary
Little Rock, Arkansas

CHEESE PUFFS
Yield: 20 puffs.

1 (10 count) can flaky biscuits	⅓ cup grated Parmesan cheese
¼ cup melted margarine	

Cut each biscuit in half; roll into a ball. Dip each into melted margarine; then roll in cheese to coat. Place about 2 inches apart on baking sheet; bake at 400° until golden, about 8 to 10 minutes.

Cathy Cox

Cheddar Variation: After dipping in butter, sprinkle with grated Cheddar cheese; or roll Cheddar cheese piece inside biscuit and bake.

NUT STICKS
Yield: 48 sticks.

8 slices day-old white bread	¼ cup vegetable oil
½ cup smooth peanut butter	

Remove crusts and cut each bread slice into 6 even strips. Toast crusts and strips at 350° until light brown and crisp. Roll toasted crusts into fine crumbs. Blend peanut butter with oil. Dip toasted strips into peanut butter mixture; roll in crumbs. Lay on waxed paper until dry. Finely chopped nuts may be added to crumbs.

Corene Slaton Latimer
Hooks, Texas

OYSTER CRACKERS
Yield: 1½ cups.

½ teaspoon lemon pepper	½ cup salad oil
½ teaspoon dry dillweed	1 (12-ounce) package oyster crackers
½ (1.6-ounce) package original Hidden Valley Ranch dressing mix	

Combine first 4 ingredients; pour over crackers; stir to coat. Store in airtight container; will keep for weeks.

Nancy Weber
Little Rock, Arkansas
Robbie Rea Tye
Texarkana, Arkansas

DEVILED CHEESE CRACKERS
Yield: 5 dozen.

½   pound sharp Cheddar cheese, grated
1   cup flour
½   cup butter, softened
1   tablespoon Worcestershire sauce
½   teaspoon salt
¼   teaspoon cayenne pepper
1   egg white
2   tablespoons sesame seeds

Combine first 6 ingredients, mixing until dough forms a ball. Form into a log; wrap in waxed paper; chill at least 1 hour. Cut into ¼-inch thick slices; place on baking sheet ½-inch apart; brush with egg white and sprinkle with sesame seeds. Bake 8 to 10 minutes at 375°.

Bonita Crow

CHEDDAR-NUT WAFERS
Yield: about 60 wafers.

½   pound sharp Cheddar cheese, grated
1   stick margarine, softened
½   teaspoon salt
½   cup finely chopped pecans
¼   cup dehydrated minced onion
1   cup flour

Combine first 5 ingredients; add flour and mix well. Divide dough in half; roll each half into a roll about 1½ inches in diameter. Wrap each in waxed paper; chill overnight. Cut rolls into ⅛-inch slices; place on lightly greased baking sheets. Bake at 350° 10 to 15 minutes, or until lightly browned. Remove immediately to paper towels; cool. Store in tight container in refrigerator.

Beverly McWhorter

CHEESE AND SAUSAGE ROLLS
Yield: 16 servings.

16 sausage links	1 cup shredded American cheese
16 bread slices, crusts removed	4 tablespoons butter, softened

Cook sausage links; drain. Roll bread slices flat. Brush one side of each bread slice with butter; spread cheese on the other side. Place sausage on cheese side; roll and secure with toothpick. Bake on greased cookie sheet at 400° for 10-12 minutes or until lightly brown. Slice into thirds and spear with toothpicks. Serve warm.

Mrs. Ken Hughes
Benton, Arkansas

HAM ROLLS
Yield: 24 rolls.

1 (3-ounce) package cream cheese, softened	1 teaspoon prepared horseradish
6 stuffed olives, chopped	¼ teaspoon salt
2 tablespoons whipping cream	Dash white pepper
	6 thin slices cooked ham

Combine all ingredients except ham, mixing well. Spread mixture evenly on each ham slice; roll up and secure with toothpicks. Cover and chill. Slice rolls into 1-inch pieces; serve with toothpicks.

Sandra Dunn

HAM AND CHEESE PINWHEELS
Yield: about 60 pinwheels.

1	(1.37-ounce) packet dry onion soup mix	2	tablespoons chopped ripe olives
1	pint sour cream	6	slices cooked ham
1	(3-ounce) package cream cheese, softened	6	slices American cheese

In bowl blend soup mix, sour cream, cream cheese and olives; chill one hour. Spread chilled mixture evenly on ham slices, top with cheese slices, then more chilled mixture. Roll each prepared ham slice in waxed paper; chill 2 hours. Cut in ½-inch slices and place on Ritz crackers.

Corene Slaton Latimer
Hooks, Texas

HOT PEPPER PECANS
Yield: 1 cup.

2	tablespoons margarine	½	teaspoon salt
1	cup large pecan halves	6	dashes Tabasco sauce
2	teaspoons soy sauce		

Melt margarine in shallow baking pan; spread pecans evenly in one layer. Bake at 300° 30 minutes or until lightly browned, stirring several times. Combine remaining ingredients and stir into toasted nuts; let stand 30 minutes. Drain and cool on paper towels. Store in tightly covered container; will keep for months.

Beverly McWhorter

ORANGE PECANS
Yield: 1 pound.

2 cups sugar	1 tablespoon grated orange rind
¾ cup orange juice	3 cups pecan halves

In saucepan cook sugar and orange juice to soft-ball stage (236 to 240°). Turn off heat; add orange rind and pecans. Stir with wooden spoon until mixture turns cream color, about 5 to 7 minutes. Remove from heat; pour onto cookie sheet. When cool, break apart.

Lois Thomas

Sugar Nuts: Cook 1 cup sugar, 1 teaspoon cinnamon, ½ cup milk to soft ball stage; add 1 teaspoon vanilla and 3 cups pecans; stir until well coated; cool on waxed paper.

Wanda Cowling
Foreman, Arkansas

ARTICHOKE HEART SPREAD
Serves 12.

1 (14-ounce) can artichoke hearts, drained, finely chopped	6 ounces Parmesan cheese, freshly grated
1 cup mayonnaise	2 or 3 dashes Tabasco sauce
	Pinch cayenne pepper
	Salt to taste

Blend all ingredients thoroughly. Pour into a buttered 8-inch square baking dish, or quiche pan, and bake at 350° 30 minutes. Serve hot with assorted crackers.

Wilma Thornton
Sheridan, Arkansas

◇ Ray Thornton, President, University of Arkansas
U. S. Congressman, 1973-1979

BOURSIN CHEESE
Yield: 1 pound.

2 (8-ounce) packages cream cheese, softened	2 teaspoons chopped chives, or green onion tops
2 teaspoons dillweed	2 cloves garlic, crushed
2 teaspoons basil	Lemon-pepper seasoning
2 teaspoons caraway seed	

Cream together thoroughly the first 6 ingredients. Shape into a ball and roll in lemon pepper seasoning to coat. Wrap in waxed paper and chill several hours. Serve with toast rounds or crackers.

Suzie Taggart Lancaster
Longview, Texas

DRIED BEEF CHEESE SPREAD
Yield: 2½ cups.

2 (8-ounce) packages cream cheese, softened	4 to 5 green onions with tops, finely chopped
2 tablespoons milk	1 cup chopped pecans, optional
1 (2½-ounce) jar dried beef, diced	

Blend cheese with milk; add remaining ingredients. Chill. Serve with crackers.

Debbie Gallaher Fisk

GARLIC CHEESE ROLLS
Yield: 3 cheese rolls.

2 pounds Velveeta cheese, softened	¾ teaspoon garlic powder
1 cup chopped pecans	Chili powder

Mix cheese, pecans, and garlic powder thoroughly. Shape into three 1½-inch diameter rolls; coat with chili powder. Wrap in waxed paper, then foil and chill thoroughly to "season" about 2 days.

Vivian V. Keeney
Alleene, Arkansas

"PLAINS SPECIAL" CHEESE RING

Yield: 1 cheese ring.

1 pound sharp cheese, grated	Black pepper
1 cup finely chopped nuts	Dash cayenne pepper
1 cup mayonnaise	Strawberry preserves, optional
1 small onion, finely grated	

Combine cheese, nuts, mayonnaise, onion, and seasonings; mix well. Press into an oiled 4-cup ring mold; chill until firm. Unmold on serving plate; fill center with strawberry preserves. Can be served as a compliment to a main meal or as an appetizer with crackers.

Rosalynn Carter
Plains, Georgia

CHEESY-BACON SOUR CREAM SPREAD

Yield: 2½ cups.

1 (8-ounce) container sour cream	¼ cup wheat germ
½ cup mayonnaise	1 tablespoon chopped green onion tops
1 cup shredded Cheddar cheese	¼ teaspoon salt
2 to 4 slices bacon, cooked and crumbled	¼ cup chopped toasted almonds, optional

Combine all ingredients, blending well. Chill. Serve spread on toasted rye bread rounds. Garnish with the almonds, if desired.

Mona L. Fenton Patterson
Ashdown, Arkansas

◇ *In 1835 Tillman Patterson was paid $250 to build in Washington, Arkansas, a new Hempstead County courthouse, later the Confederate State Capitol of Arkansas.*

MONTEREY JACK CHEESE SPREAD
Yield: 2 French loaf halves.

8 ounces Monterey Jack cheese, shredded	2 sticks margarine, softened
8 ounces Monterey Jack cheese with jalapeños, shredded	2 bunches green onions with tops, chopped
	Garlic powder to taste
	Black pepper to taste
2 cups mayonnaise	1 loaf French bread

Combine first 7 ingredients, mixing thoroughly. Split bread loaf lengthwise. Spread cut surface of both halves freely with cheese mixture. Place on cookie sheet; bake at 400° until bubbly and slightly brown. Cut into serving pieces; serve hot.

Vera Wooten Parker
Vivian, Louisiana
Joyce Gore

CHEESE LOGS
Yield: 2 cheese logs.

2 (8-ounce) packages cream cheese, softened	1 teaspoon sugar
	1 (.07-ounce) packet dry Italian salad dressing mix
2 tablespoons flour	
2 tablespoons sour cream	1 (2-ounce) jar chopped pimentos

Combine all ingredients, mixing thoroughly. Shape into 2 logs. (Logs may be coated as desired with chopped nuts, parsley, chili powder, or paprika.) Wrap in plastic wrap; chill. Freezes well. Serve with assorted crackers.

Glennda Refeld Fread
Almyra, Arkansas

CHEESE ROLL
Yield: one large roll.

1 pound American cheese, softened	½ teaspoon salt
1 (8-ounce) package cream cheese, softened	⅛ teaspoon red pepper
	¼ cup chopped nuts
¼ teaspoon sugar	Chili powder
10 stuffed olives, finely chopped	Paprika

Combine first 7 ingredients, mixing well. Shape into a long roll 1½-inches in diameter. Coat thoroughly with chili powder and sprinkle with paprika. Wrap in waxed paper; chill. Cut in slices for crackers.

Annie Faye Sharp

CHICKEN PECAN LOG
Serves 20.

2 (8-ounce) packages cream cheese, softened	1½ cups minced, cooked chicken
1 tablespoon A-1 steak sauce	⅓ cup minced celery
½ teaspoon curry powder	½ cup chopped pecans, toasted

Combine first 3 ingredients; beat until smooth. Add chicken and celery. Shape into logs, coat with pecans, wrap in waxed paper and chill 4 hours; slice. Serve with Ritz crackers.

Ceci Bettell

SHRIMP MOLD
Serves 20.

2 tablespoons unflavored gelatin	1 cup chopped celery
	1 cup mayonnaise
¼ cup cold water	2 tablespoons lemon juice
1 (10¾-ounce) can tomato soup, undiluted	1 tablespoon Tabasco sauce
	1 tablespoon grated onion
1 (8-ounce) package cream cheese, softened	½ cup chopped stuffed olives
	2 cups chopped shrimp

Soften gelatin in cold water. Heat tomato soup; add dissolved gelatin; cool slightly and beat in cream cheese. Chill until partially thickened. Add remaining ingredients; pour into greased ring mold; chill overnight. Unmold onto lettuce-lined plate; serve with crackers.

In Memory of Mabel Gallaher

CUCUMBER SPREAD
Yield: 2 cups.

1 large cucumber, peeled, seeded	2 tablespoons powdered sugar
3 tablespoons chopped onion	2 or 3 drops green food coloring
2 (8-ounce) packages cream cheese, softened	

In food processor or blender, puree cucumber and onion. Cut cream cheese in 1-inch chunks; add to mixture, blending well. Stir in powdered sugar and food coloring. Chill for several hours to set and for flavors to blend. Use as a dip or for sandwiches.

Mozelle Loyd Nall
Little Rock, Arkansas
Jimmy Huskey

◇ Mrs. Ethel Nall, Postmistress, Lockesburg, 1920-1957.

SALMON BALL
Serves 20.

1 (16-ounce) can red salmon	½ teaspoon salt
1 (8-ounce) package cream cheese	Dash Cayenne pepper
2 tablespoons lemon juice	Dash Worcestershire sauce
3 teaspoons grated onion	¼ teaspoon liquid smoke
2 teaspoons prepared horseradish	3 tablespoons minced parsley
	½ cup chopped pecans

Drain salmon; remove skin and bones; flake. Cream the cheese; add lemon juice, onion, horseradish, seasonings and liquid smoke; stir in salmon. Form into a ball. Combine parsley and pecans on sheet of waxed paper; roll ball in mixture until well coated. Chill overnight. Serve with crackers.

Martha Rea Bankston
Shreveport, Louisiana

BEVERAGES

SPRING TONIC
Yield: 1 quart

3 tablespoons Epson salts	2 tablespoons brown sugar
1 tablespoon cream of tartar	1 quart boiling water
	1 cup lemon juice

Dissolve first 3 ingredients in boiling water; cool; add lemon juice. Drink 2 ounces of tonic before each meal.

Pearl Steel

◇ *Custer Steel, County Judge, Sevier County, 1931-1935.*

ALMOND BUTTER BEVERAGE MIX

Yield: 5 cups.

4 cups brown sugar	½ cup powdered non-dairy creamer
1 cup butter, softened	1 teaspoon cinnamon
⅔ cup Amaretto, or 1 tablespoon almond extract in ½ cup water	1 teaspoon allspice

With electric mixer, beat all ingredients until well blended. Keep refrigerated in tightly covered container; will keep 1 month. To serve, spoon 1 tablespoon mix into a mug; add 6 ounces hot liquid—coffee, wine, cocoa, or milk; stir; serve immediately.

Donna Pass
Longview, Texas

EXOTIC COFFEE

Yield: 25-30 cups.

1 cup instant coffee flakes	⅔ cup dry milk powder, or coffee creamer
⅔ cup sugar	½ teaspoon cinnamon

Mix thoroughly; store in airtight container. To serve, use 1 to 2 teaspoons mix to 1 cup boiling water.

Ann Terry May
Ashdown, Arkansas

HOT CHOCOLATE MIX

Yield: 75 cups.

2 pounds Nestles Quik	25 ounces dry milk powder
1 pound coffee creamer	1 teaspoon salt
1 pound powdered sugar	

Sift ingredients together; store in airtight container. To serve, add 1 tablespoon mix to 1 cup boiling water.

Bonnie Cunningham
Nashville, Arkansas
Elaine Carter
Berniece Stinnett

CINDY'S COFFEE
Yield: 3½ quarts.

1 pint milk	1 quart vanilla ice cream, softened
2 quarts strong coffee, cooled	½ pint whipping cream, whipped
2 teaspoons vanilla	Nutmeg
½ cup sugar	

Combine first 4 ingredients; blend well. To serve, place ice cream in punch bowl; pour in coffee mixture; lightly mix. Top cups with whipped cream and nutmeg sprinkles.

Cindy Coulter Hale

OLD-FASHIONED EGG NOG
Yield: 2 quarts.

6 eggs, separated	¼ cup sugar
½ cup white corn syrup	1 pint vanilla ice cream, softened
½ pint half and half	Nutmeg
¼ cup dark rum	

In mixing bowl beat egg yolks until thick and lemon colored; add syrup and half and half, beating well. Stir in rum; cover; chill 1 hour. In large bowl beat egg whites until foamy; gradually add sugar, beating until stiff peaks form. To serve, pour chilled mixture into punch bowl; fold in egg whites; then fold in ice cream. Sprinkle with nutmeg.

Brenda Wray

DOTTIE LOU'S TEA
Yield: about 6 quarts.

8 tea bags	1 (12-ounce) can frozen lemonade
3 quarts boiling water	1 (32-ounce) bottle ginger ale, chilled
¾ cup sugar	

Pour boiling water over tea bags; cover; steep 10 minutes. Combine brewed tea, sugar, and lemonade; chill. To serve, combine chilled mix and ginger ale; pour over crushed ice.

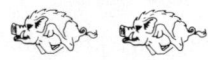

Dottie Lou Norwood

SPICED PERCOLATOR PUNCH

Yield: 30 cups.

9 cups pineapple juice
9 cups cranberry juice
4½ cups water
1 cup brown sugar

4½ teaspoons whole cloves
4 cinnamon sticks
¼ teaspoon salt

Pour juices and water into a 30-cup electric percolator. Place remaining ingredients in percolator basket. Perk through complete cycle of percolator.

Janie Williams
San Antonio, Texas

SPICED APPLE CIDER

Yield: 5 quarts.

1 gallon apple cider
½ cup brown or white sugar
1 (16-ounce) can frozen orange juice
2 cups pineapple juice

½ cup lemon juice
4 sticks cinnamon
20 whole cloves
½ teaspoon nutmeg, optional

In large kettle combine all ingredients; simmer 1 hour; cool; keep refrigerated; will store 2 weeks. Reheat to serve.

Alison Correll Hargis
Little Rock, Arkansas
Myrtle Sims

SPICED PEACH PUNCH

Yield: 2 quarts.

1 (46-ounce) can peach nectar
1 (16-ounce) can frozen orange juice
1 (3-ounce) can frozen orange juice

½ cup firmly packed brown sugar
3 cinnamon sticks, broken
½ teaspoon whole cloves
2 tablespoons lime juice

In a sauce pan combine nectar, orange juice, sugar, and spices tied in cheesecloth bag; heat slowly, stirring constantly, until sugar dissolves; simmer 10 minutes. Remove spice bag; stir in lime juice; serve hot.

Mrs. Charlie Loftin
Ft. Hood, Texas

HOT SPICED TEA
Yield: 4½ quarts.

4 cups hot water	4 tea bags
2 cups sugar	13 cups boiling water
2 sticks cinnamon	½ cup lemon juice
2 teaspoons whole cloves	1½ cups orange juice

In a sauce pan combine first 4 ingredients; simmer 5 minutes; set aside. Steep tea bags in boiling water 4 minutes; remove tea bags. Combine fruit juices, spice mixture, and tea; serve hot.

Naomi Hale

FRUIT FLIP PUNCH
Yield: 1½ gallons.

9 cups water	2 cups lemon juice
9 mint leaves	2 cups cherry juice
3 cups sugar	2 cups pineapple juice
2 cups orange juice	4 cups brewed tea

In a sauce pan simmer water with mint leaves 5 minutes; remove mint; add sugar; boil 5 minutes; cool. Combine cooled syrup with remaining ingredients; mix well; let stand 1 hour; chill. Serve cold.

Chanie Doss Needham
Mabelvale, Arkansas

RASPBERRY FIZZ
Yield: 6 servings.

1 (10-ounce) package frozen raspberries, partially thawed	½ cup vodka
½ cup orange juice	1 (10-ounce) bottle lemon-lime carbonated beverage

Process raspberries and orange juice in a blender until smooth; stir in remaining ingredients; serve at once over crushed ice.

Sissy Correll Pride
Friendswood, Texas

CITRIC ACID PUNCH

Yield: 2 gallons.

4 teaspoons citric acid crystals*	1 cup lemon juice
6 cups sugar	1 (46-ounce) can unsweetened pineapple juice
2 quarts boiling water	2 quarts ginger ale, chilled
2 quarts cold water	

Dissolve crystals and sugar in boiling water; add cold water and fruit juices; chill. To serve, add ginger ale to chilled mixture; serve over crushed ice. (*Purchase at drug store.)

Beth Coulter Weast
Austin, Texas

EASY PUNCH

Yield: 20-25 cups.

1 (3-ounce) package cherry gelatin	1⅓ cups bottled lemon juice
1½ cups hot water	1 tablespoon vanilla
1¾ cups sugar	1 tablespoon almond extract
1 (34-ounce) can pineapple juice	2½ quarts water

Dissolve gelatin in hot water; add sugar; stir to dissolve. Add remaining ingredients; stir; chill.

Jean Rea
Dallas, Texas
Holly Bush

◇ Thomas King, County Judge, Sevier County, 1886-1890.

LIME LIGHT PUNCH

Yield: 50-60 servings.

4 cups sugar	1 (12-ounce) can frozen lemonade
6 cups water	
1 (46-ounce) can unsweetened pineapple juice	5 or 6 bananas, mashed
	4 (28-ounce) bottles lemon-lime carbonated soft drink, chilled
2 (12-ounce) cans frozen orange juice	

Dissolve sugar in water; add juices and bananas; freeze in large freezer containers or milk cartons. To serve, thaw to mush consistency in refrigerator; pour into punch bowl; add lemon-lime drink.

Mollie Stauber Turner
Arkadelphia, Arkansas
Mary Ann Graves Mayo
Petrolia, Texas
Marie Bush

MEXICAN PUNCH

Yield: 2 gallons.

2½ quarts brewed tea	1 (7-ounce) can grape juice
2 cups sugar	1 (16-ounce) can frozen orange juice
1 (46-ounce) can unsweetened pineapple juice	
1 cup lemon juice	3 quarts water

Combine all ingredients, blending well; chill before serving.

Eleanor Turner
Mary Lou Taylor
Lynn Daniels

PINK PARTY PUNCH
Yield: 1 gallon.

1 (.15-ounce) package unsweetened strawberry drink mix	1 (12-ounce) can frozen orange juice
1 (.15-ounce) package unsweetened cherry drink mix	1 cup sugar
	1 quart water
1 (16-ounce) can frozen lemonade	1 quart ginger ale, Sprite, or 7-Up, chilled

Combine first 6 ingredients; mix well; chill. To serve, stir mix well; pour into punch bowl; add ginger ale or carbonated drink.

Louise Hill
Linda Culp
Lois Smith

STRAWBERRY BREAKFAST SHAKE
Yield: 3 cups.

½ cup cooked oatmeal, chilled	2 cups milk
½ cup frozen strawberries	½ teaspoon vanilla
2 to 4 tablespoons sugar	

Process all ingredients in a blender 1 minute; serve cold.

Imogene Cox

SUNSHINE SHAKE
Yield: 3 cups.

2 cups orange juice, chilled	1 egg
1 banana, cut in chunks	1 tablespoon honey

Process all ingredients in a blender until smooth; serve at once.

Novadeen Revels

SOUPS AND SANDWICHES

SOUTHERN BEAN SOUP
8 to 10 servings

2 cups dried navy or great northern beans	1½ pounds ham, butt end
12 cups water	Salt and pepper

Soak beans in water to cover 6 hours or overnight; drain. Place beans and ham with water in a large pot; season to taste; cover and cook slowly until ham is done. Remove ham; cut off meat and dice; return to soup. Simmer, covered, until beans are very soft and soup has thickened.

Coulter Hoppess
Bryan, Texas

◇ *Joe T. Robinson (1902-1937), the last U. S. senator in the nation elected by a state legislature, also holds the unique record of being congressman, governor, and senator-elect all within 14 days.*

MILLIE WOOD'S BEAN SOUP
6 to 8 servings.

1	meaty ham hock	2	tablespoons catsup
2	quarts water	1	teaspoon seasoned salt
2	cups great northern beans		Pepper to taste
2	small hot peppers, seeded	½	cup evaporated milk
1	medium onion		

In large pot bring ham hock in water to a boil; add remaining ingredients except milk; reduce heat. Simmer gently, stirring occasionally, until beans are tender and mixture thickens, about 3 hours. Add milk; turn off heat; let stand 10 minutes.

Marie Sanders
Mary Dickinson

BROCCOLI SOUP
6 servings.

1	(10-ounce) package frozen chopped broccoli	1½	tablespoons flour
		2	cups half and half
½	cup chopped onion	1	teaspoon salt
1¼	cups chicken broth	½	teaspoon basil
3	tablespoons melted butter		Dash cayenne pepper

In a sauce pan bring first 3 ingredients to a boil; simmer over low heat 5 minutes. Make a paste of butter and flour; gradually add to mixture, stirring constantly; add remaining ingredients; cook until hot; do not boil.

Lois Taggart
Alvin, Texas

UNIVITH SOUP
4 servings.

1	potato, sliced	1	tablespoon melted butter
1	onion, quartered	1	teaspoon salt
1	cooking apple, cored, quartered	1	teaspoon curry powder
		1	banana, sliced
1	celery heart with leaves	1	cup heavy cream
2	cups chicken broth		

In a sauce pan cook all ingredients except cream until tender; puree mixture in a blender; add cream. Serve hot or cold.

Jeannette Rockefeller
Seattle, Washington

CREAM OF CAULIFLOWER SOUP
8 to 10 servings.

6   cups water
1   large cauliflower, in large flowerets
Salt and pepper to taste
2   cups grated American cheese
1   cup milk
1   cup cream
¼   cup butter
⅓   cup flour
½   cup cold water

In large sauce pan bring water to a boil; add cauliflower; cook until crisp-tender, 5 to 10 minutes. Add next 5 ingredients; heat, stirring, until cheese melts. Make a paste of flour and cold water; gradually add to hot mixture, stirring constantly. Cook only until soup is consistency of heavy cream; serve immediately.

Brenda Posey

CHEESE SOUP
6 to 8 servings.

2   (14-ounce) cans chicken broth
½   cup finely chopped carrots
½   cup finely chopped onions
6   cups water
1   pound Velveeta cheese, cubed
⅔   cup flour
⅔   cup melted butter

Bring first 4 ingredients to a boil; add cheese; stir until melted. Make a smooth paste of flour and butter; gradually add to soup, stirring constantly; simmer 15 to 20 minutes.

Patricia Humphries
Benton, Arkansas
Vondell Van Bebber
Hot Springs, Arkansas

CHICKEN CORN SOUP
6 servings.

1	(3-to 4-lb.) chicken	3	cups corn kernels
1	rib celery with leaves, chopped	2	cups raw noodles
		⅛	teaspoon pepper
1	onion, chopped	2	tablespoons chopped fresh parsley
2	teaspoons salt		
3	quarts water	2	hard-boiled eggs, chopped

Cook chicken with next 5 ingredients until tender; remove chicken from broth; bone; cut into bite-size pieces. Cool broth; skim and discard fat; return meat to broth with corn, noodles, and pepper. Bring to a boil; cook gently 10 minutes, or until noodles are done. Garnish each serving with parsley and egg.

Linda Bowden

CLAM CHOWDER
8 servings.

3	(8-ounce) cans minced clams, drained, liquid reserved		Salt and pepper
		2	cups boiling water
		¼	cup flour
4	slices bacon, chopped	4	tablespoons butter
2	onions, chopped	2	cups milk
2	cups diced potatoes	1	cup light cream

In a Dutch oven, fry bacon crisp; drain; set aside. In bacon drippings sauté onions until tender; add clam liquid, potatoes, and water; season to taste; simmer 10 to 15 minutes, or until potatoes are tender; add clams; simmer 5 minutes. In separate pan cook flour in melted butter 1 minute, stirring constantly; add milk and cream; cook over low heat, stirring, 5 minutes; add to clam mixture; blend. Chill to blend flavors; reheat; do not boil. Top servings with bacon bits.

Pete Fisk

CRAB-CORN CHOWDER
6 to 8 servings.

5 slices bacon, chopped	1 10¾-ounce) can cream of mushroom soup
1 cup chopped onion	2 cups milk
2 cups chopped potatoes	1 (6-ounce) can minced crab
½ cup water	Salt and pepper
1 (16-ounce) can cream-style corn	
1 (16-ounce) can whole kernel corn, drained, liquid reserved	

In large sauce pan fry bacon crisp; drain; set aside. In bacon drippings sauté onion until limp; add potatoes, water, and reserved corn liquid; simmer until potatoes are tender. Add remaining ingredients; season to taste; heat thoroughly. Top servings with crumbled bacon.

Mrs. Burton K. Walker, Jr.
Ashdown, Arkansas

◇ *E. B. Kinsworthy, Arkansas Attorney-General, 1895-1899.*

EASY GUMBO
6 to 8 servings.

3 tablespoons oil	Salt and pepper
1 green pepper, chopped	2 cups sliced okra
1 small onion, chopped	¼ cup minced fresh parsley
4 to 6 cups chicken stock	1 to 2 cups cooked chicken or shrimp
1 (16-ounce) can tomatoes	
1 bay leaf	

In large pot simmer green pepper and onion in oil until soft; add next 3 ingredients; boil gently 30 minutes; season to taste. Add remaining ingredients; simmer 10 minutes, or until okra is tender. Serve in bowls over hot rice.

Mary Ann Schreit
Paragould, Arkansas

LENTIL SOUP

6 to 8 servings.

1 pound lentils	2 quarts water
6 slices bacon, cut up	2½ teaspoons salt
1 large onion, diced	½ teaspoon pepper
1 large carrot, shredded	¼ teaspoon thyme
1 rib celery, chopped	2 bay leaves
2 potatoes, grated	
1 meaty ham hock, or 2 cups diced ham	

Soak lentils overnight in cold water; drain. In a Dutch oven fry bacon crisp; drain; set aside. In bacon drippings, sauté onion, carrot, and celery until onion is soft; add drained beans and remaining ingredients; bring to a boil; simmer over low heat, covered, until beans are tender, about 2 hours. Stir occasionally. Serve hot, topped with bacon bits.

Sharie Mathis

ONION WINE SOUP

6 to 8 servings.

¼ cup butter, melted	1 tablespoon vinegar
5 large onions, chopped	2 teaspoons sugar
5 cups beef broth	1 cup light cream
½ cup celery leaves	1 tablespoon minced parsley
1 large potato, sliced	Salt and pepper
1 cup dry white wine	

Combine onion with melted butter; mix well; add next 3 ingredients; bring to boiling; cover; simmer 30 minutes. Puree mixture in a blender; return to pan; blend in wine, vinegar and sugar; bring to boiling; simmer 45 minutes. Stir in remaining ingredients, seasoning to taste. Heat thoroughly but do not boil.

Nancy Reagan
The White House
Washington, D. C.

OYSTER STEW
4 to 6 servings.

¼ cup finely diced celery with leaves
¼ cup finely diced green onions
4 tablespoons butter

2 (8-ounce) cans oysters
4 cups milk
Salt and pepper
1 (12-ounce) box oyster crackers

In a sauce pan, sauté celery and onions in butter over low heat until tender; add oysters with liquid; heat through; add milk and season to taste; heat thoroughly; do not boil. Serve with crackers.

June Correll Burr
Ft. Worth, Texas
Sue McDonald

POLISH MEATBALL SOUP
6 to 8 servings.

1 pound fresh or frozen cut green beans
4 quarts plus ¼ cup water, divided
1 medium onion, chopped
1 rib celery, chopped
1 pound ground beef

2 medium potatoes, cubed
1 teaspoon salt
1 teaspoon pepper
4 tablespoons vinegar
1 teaspoon allspice
2 tablespoons flour

In large pot in 2 quarts water, cook beans, onion, and celery 10 minutes. Shape beef into small balls; add to beans with 2 quarts water, potatoes, spices, and vinegar; simmer 2 hours, or until vegetables are tender. Make a paste of flour and ¼ cup water; stir into soup; simmer 10 minutes; serve.

Eleanor Jemiolo

MICROWAVE POTATO SOUP

4 to 6 servings.

1   small onion, chopped
3   large white potatoes
4   cups milk, divided
3   tablespoons butter

2   teaspoons instant chicken bouillon
Salt and pepper
Tabasco sauce

In a large bowl microwave onion until soft; set aside. Microwave potatoes until done; skin and dice. In a blender process ⅔ potatoes with 2 cups milk until smooth. Add to onion with remaining potatoes and milk, butter, bouillon, and seasonings to taste. Heat in microwave until thickened, stirring often.

Ann Allison Birge
Little Rock, Arkansas

POTATO SOUP

8 to 10 servings.

4   cups cubed potatoes, in ½-inch cubes
1   cup diced celery
1   medium onion, chopped
½   cup minced fresh parsley
4   cups chicken broth

¼   cup melted butter
¼   cup flour
2   teaspoons salt
½   teaspoon pepper
4   cups scalded milk
1   cup grated Cheddar cheese

In a sauce pan bring first 5 ingredients to a boil; reduce heat; cover; simmer 20 minutes, or until tender; process in a blender until smooth; set aside. In a heavy pan cook flour in butter 1 minute, stirring; add seasonings and milk; cook, stirring constantly, until slightly thickened; add potato mixture; mix well; heat. Add cheese; stir until melted.

Gerry Robison

SQUASH SOUP
6 to 8 servings.

5 or 6 yellow squash, thinly sliced	1 teaspoon sugar
1 large onion, thinly sliced	1 cup milk
½ stick margarine	1 (13-ounce) can evaporated milk
1 teaspoon salt	1 (14½-ounce) can chicken broth

In large skillet sauté vegetables in margarine over low heat about 30 minutes; add salt and sugar. In a blender puree half the squash mixture with ½ cup milk; repeat process. In a sauce pan combine squash puree and evaporated milk. Whip chicken broth in blender 15 seconds; add to squash mixture; bring to a boil. Serve hot.

Florence Phillips Turner
Baton Rouge, Louisiana

SPICY TORTILLA SOUP
4 to 6 servings.

½ onion, chopped	1 cup water
2 cloves garlic, chopped	4 cups chicken broth
1 tablespoon oil	1 teaspoon cumin
1 (16-ounce) can stewed tomatoes, pureed	½ teaspoon pepper
2 (8-ounce) cans tomato sauce	Monterey Jack cheese, grated
	Tortilla chips

In large pot sauté onion and garlic in oil until tender; add remaining ingredients except cheese and chips; simmer 20 to 30 minutes. To serve, place chips and cheese in serving bowls; ladle soup into bowls; serve immediately.

Mothers' League
Longview, Texas

BARBECUED SHREDDED BEEF
10 to 12 servings.

3 pounds chuck roast	1 teaspoon dry mustard
1 to 2 cups water	Dash of cayenne pepper
3½ teaspoons salt, divided	3 tablespoons vinegar
2 tablespoons shortening	3 tablespoons sugar
1 cup chopped onion	3 tablespoons Worcestershire sauce
2 teaspoons paprika	1 clove garlic, minced
1 teaspoon pepper	1 (16-ounce) can tomato paste

In a Dutch oven cook roast, water and 3 teaspoons salt over low heat, covered, until very tender. In a pan sauté onion in shortening until tender but not brown; add remaining ingredients; simmer over low heat 20 minutes. Trim fat from cooked meat; shred meat. Deglaze Dutch oven; add all roast liquid to sauce with shredded meat. Cover; simmer very slowly 30 minutes, thinning as needed with water. Serve on toasted buns.

Floy Cannon

PINEAPPLE-BARBECUED BEEF SANDWICHES
4 servings.

1 (15½-ounce) can unsweetened pineapple tidbits, drained, liquid reserved	2 teaspoons prepared horseradish
4 tablespoons Worcestershire sauce	¼ teaspoon garlic powder
2 tablespoons soy sauce	1 pound top roast or flank steak
2 teaspoons Dijon mustard	1½ cups catsup
	4 French rolls, split, toasted

In a shallow pan combine reserved juice, Worcestershire and soy sauces, mustard, horseradish, and garlic powder; marinate meat in mixture 1 hour, turning once. Remove meat; pour marinade into a sauce pan; add catsup; bring to a boil; simmer 5 minutes; set aside. Broil meat 6 inches from heat about 4 minutes on each side; slice diagonally. To serve, place meat slices on rolls; spoon warm sauce over meat; top with pineapple.

Sissi Slabaugh
Valiant, Oklahoma

MAMA NINA'S PIMENTO CHEESE
8 to 10 servings.

4	tablespoons sugar	½	cup vinegar
4	tablespoons flour	½	teaspoon salt
2	cups milk	1	pound cheese, grated
4	egg yolks	1	(4-ounce) can pimentos, chopped

In a double boiler combine first 3 ingredients. In a bowl beat egg yolks with vinegar; add to milk mixture; cook, stirring constantly, until mixture thickens; add remaining ingredients; mix thoroughly. Refrigerate in covered container.

Nina Whitmore Dildy
Nashville, Arkansas
Marjorie Whitmore
North Little Rock, Arkansas

CHEESEBURGERS TO GO
8 servings.

6	tablespoons chopped onion	2	cups grated Cheddar cheese
1	pound ground chuck	8	hamburger buns
2	teaspoons prepared mustard		Butter

In a heavy skillet sauté meat until brown; add onions; cook until soft; drain. Add mustard and cheese; mix well. Spoon onto buttered buns; wrap buns in foil; freeze. To serve, heat frozen buns 20 to 25 minutes at 400°.

Carol Craun
Jewell Breedlove

BEEF SANDWICHES
6 servings.

1	pound ground beef	6	sesame seed buns
1	(8-ounce) can baked beans	2	large tomatoes, sliced
1	large carrot, shredded	3	dill pickles, sliced lengthwise
Salt and pepper			

In a skillet sauté beef until it loses color; drain; stir in beans and carrot; season to taste. Spoon mixture onto buns; top with tomato and pickle slices; close buns; wrap for freezing; freeze. To serve: heat 2 minutes in microwave on HIGH, or 20 minutes at 350° in oven.

Shelley Helms

HOT HAM SANDWICHES
8 servings.

1	stick butter, melted	8	buns
2	tablespoons prepared mustard	1	pound ham, thinly sliced
½	teaspoon Worcestershire sauce	1	(8-ounce) package sliced cheese, Swiss, Cheddar, or American
1	teaspoon finely chopped onion		
1	tablespoon poppy seeds		

In a bowl, combine first 5 ingredients; mix well; spread on buns. Layer slices of ham and cheese in buns; wrap for freezing; freeze. To serve, heat in foil 20 minutes at 350°.

Jen Oliver
Little Rock, Arkansas

MAYTIME MUFFULETTA MIX
Yield: 2½ pints.

1	(15-ounce) jar salad olives, drained, chopped, with 1 teaspoon liquid	1	(3¼-ounce) jar capers, drained, chopped
1	(6-ounce) can pitted black olives, drained, chopped, with 1 teaspoon liquid	3	carrots, grated
		3	ribs celery, coarsely chopped
½	cup finely chopped onion	2	tablespoons olive oil
		1	teaspoon Italian herb seasoning

Combine all ingredients; mix well; store refrigerated in glass jar; will keep for several weeks. Makes 6 to 8 sandwiches: Split round Italian rolls; spread with mustard and mayonnaise; layer with sliced meat (ham, salami, etc.), cheese slice topped with generous amount of mix. Secure bread halves with toothpicks; place on baking sheet; heat at 400° until cheese melts.

Cindy McCoy
Shreveport, Louisiana

EGGS, CHEESE, PASTA & RICE

BACON SPAGHETTI
4 servings

5 slices bacon, cut in small pieces	4 cups cooked spaghetti or noodles, drained
1 onion, chopped	Salt and pepper
2 cups canned tomatoes	

Fry bacon; drain; set aside. Sauté onion in pan drippings; add tomatoes; simmer 5 to 10 minutes. Add bacon and spaghetti; season to taste; heat through.

In memory of Patti Flanagin Mitchell
Ann Mitchell Taylor
Newport, Arkansas

◇ *After the fall of Little Rock to federal troops September 10, 1863, Governor Harris Flanagin (1862-1864) moved what remained of the state government to Washington, Arkansas.*

BREAKFAST CASSEROLE
10 servings.

2 pounds pork sausage	½ pound fresh mushrooms, sliced
1 dozen eggs	
2 (10¾-ounce) cans mushroom soup	2 cups grated Cheddar cheese

Crumble and fry sausage; drain well; spread in bottom of a 9 × 12-inch baking dish. Lightly scramble eggs, spread over sausage; pour soup over eggs. Cover; refrigerate overnight. Set out for 30 minutes; add layer of mushrooms; sprinkle with cheese. Heat at 325° for 25 to 30 minutes.

Alison Correll Hargis
Little Rock, Arkansas
Dot Williams

24-HOUR OMELET
10 to 12 servings.

1 loaf bread, crusts removed	8 eggs, beaten
1 stick butter, melted	2 cups milk
1 (8-ounce) package cream cheese, cut in chunks	½ teaspoon dry mustard
	1 tablespoon chopped chives
3 cups grated Cheddar cheese	Dash of cayenne pepper

Tear bread into pieces into a greased 9 × 13-inch baking dish; pour butter evenly over bread; crumble cream cheese over bread, then sprinkle with grated cheese. Combine remaining ingredients, mixing well; pour over cheese; cover; refrigerate overnight. Bake, covered, at 325° for 1 hour, or until set, removing cover last 10 minutes of baking time.

Sue Gilliam
Elkhart, Kansas

SAUSAGE AND EGG CASSEROLE

4 servings.

3 cups grated Cheddar cheese, divided	1 pound bulk sausage, browned, drained
1 (4-ounce) can green chilies, chopped, divided	4 eggs
5 slices bread, buttered, toasted, cubed	2 cups milk
	¼ teaspoon pepper
	¾ teaspoon salt
	¾ teaspoon chili powder

Layer ½ cheese into a greased 7 × 11-inch baking dish; layer in order over cheese ½ chilies, bread cubes, sausage, remaining cheese and chilies. Beat eggs well; combine with remaining ingredients; pour over top. Cover; refrigerate overnight. Bake, uncovered, at 350° for 1 hour, or until lightly browned. Cool 10 to 15 minutes before serving.

Mary Ann Gilliam Nash
Shreveport, Louisiana

◇ Great-granddaughter of Robert C. Gilliam, builder of Gilliam-Norwood House.

BREAKFAST TACOS

6 servings.

¾ pound sausage	1 cup shredded Monterey Jack cheese
2 potatoes, cooked, diced	
6 eggs, slightly beaten	Picante sauce
12 flour tortillas	

In skillet crumble and brown sausage; drain; add potatoes and eggs; scramble over low heat until eggs are done. Place a few spoonfuls of mixture on a warmed tortilla; sprinkle with cheese; season to taste with picante sauce; roll up like a burrito.

Stan Fisk
Brazoria, Texas
Sharon O'Neal

SUPPERTIME EGGS

4 servings.

- 2 tablespoons butter
- ½ cup chopped onion
- ½ cup chopped green pepper
- 8 eggs, beaten
- ¼ cup milk
- 1 teaspoon seasoned salt
- ½ teaspoon basil
- ¼ teaspoon seasoned pepper
- 1 (3-ounce) package cream cheese, cubed
- 1 medium tomato, chopped
- 2 to 4 slices bacon, cooked, crumbled

In large skillet sauté onion and pepper in butter until tender; combine next 5 ingredients; pour over skillet mixture; sprinkle with cheese and tomato. Gently push spatula completely across bottom and sides of skillet to form large soft curds; cook until eggs are thickened throughout but still moist. Serve sprinkled with bacon crumbles.

Carmie Henry
Little Rock, Arkansas

◇ Rev. John Henry established the first Methodist Church in Arkansas near Old Washington.

ZUCCHINI OMELET

4 servings.

- 3 medium zucchini, thinly sliced
- 1 medium onion, grated
- 3 tablespoons olive oil
- 4 eggs, beaten
- 3 tablespoons milk
- ½ cup grated Parmesan cheese
- Salt and pepper

Sauté zucchini in oil until brown. Combine remaining ingredients; fold in zucchini. Pour into a hot, lightly greased 9-inch skillet; brown gently on bottom over medium heat until set, but still soft. With wide spatula, fold omelet in half; cook 1 minute longer; turn out onto a hot platter.

S-C Seasoning Company, Inc.
Harrison, Arkansas
Maxine Williamson Vilanova

CRAB QUICHE
6 servings.

4 eggs, slightly beaten	Dash of cayenne pepper
2 cups cream, or half and half	1 cup finely chopped onion
1 teaspoon salt	1 tablespoon butter
8 ounces Swiss cheese, finely grated	1 (6½-ounce) can lump crab meat
Dash of nutmeg	1 (9-inch) unbaked pie shell

Combine first 6 ingredients, blending well. Sauté onion in butter until transparent; add with crab to mixture; blend; pour into pie shell. Bake 10 minutes at 450°; reduce heat to 325°; cook until set, 20 to 25 minutes.

Hillary Rodham Clinton
Little Rock, Arkansas

OLIVE QUICHE
12 servings.

1½ cups whipping cream	¼ pound Swiss cheese, shredded
½ cup buttermilk	¼ cup chopped green onion tops
3 eggs, slightly beaten	
½ teaspoon salt	
Dash of black pepper	6 ounces pitted, ripe olives
¼ to ½ pound bacon, cooked, crumbled	2 (8-inch) unbaked deep-dish pie shells

Heat cream and buttermilk; whisk in eggs and seasonings; gently fold in remaining ingredients. Pour into pie shells; bake at 375° for 35 minutes, or until custard is set in center and golden brown.

Mothers' League
Longview, Texas

SPINACH QUICHE

6 servings.

1 (10-ounce) package frozen spinach souffle, thawed	½ cup sliced mushrooms
2 eggs, beaten	¾ cup Italian sausage, or bacon, cooked, crumbled
3 tablespoons milk	¾ cup grated Swiss cheese
¼ cup chopped onion	1 (9-inch) unbaked pie shell

Combine all ingredients, blending well. Pour into pie shell; bake at 350° for 35 minutes, or until set and golden brown.

Martha Rea Bankston
Shreveport, Louisiana

CHEESE GRITS

6 servings.

2 cups quick cooking grits	1 stick margarine, softened
8 cups boiling salted water	3 eggs, beaten
1 pound Velveeta cheese, cubed	1 tablespoon Tabasco sauce

Cook grits 5 minutes in boiling water; remove from heat. Add next 2 ingredients, stirring until melted. Fold in eggs; add Tabasco. Pour into greased 2-quart casserole; bake 30 minutes at 400°.

Betty Blackwood

Garlic Cheese Variation: Substitute 2 (8-ounce) packages garlic cheese, grated for Velveeta.

Mildred Baucom Penney
Houston, Texas
Beth Coulter
Little Rock, Arkansas

HOT CHEESE STRATA
12 servings.

12 slices bread, crusts removed
6   slices American cheese
4   eggs
2½ cups milk
Salt

Make sandwiches with bread and cheese. Arrange in 9 × 13-inch pan, fitting sandwiches so that the inner surface of pan is covered. Beat eggs, milk and seasonings; pour over sandwiches; let stand 1 hour. Bake in 350° oven for 40 minutes, or until puffed up and brown. Serve plain or with currant jelly.

Fay Hillsberry
Laverne Liggin

CORNBREAD SOUFFLE
6 to 8 servings.

2   eggs, well beaten
½   cup oil
1   cup self-rising cornmeal
1   cup sour cream
½   teaspoon salt
1   (17-ounce) can cream-style corn

Combine all ingredients, mixing well; pour into a well-buttered 1½-quart casserole; bake at 350° 45 to 50 minutes.

Anna L. Gallaher Farris
Memphis, Tennessee

EASY CHILIES RELLENOS
4 to 6 servings.

1   pound Mozzarella cheese, grated
2   (4-ounce) cans chopped green chilies
4   eggs, separated
3   tablespoons flour

Layer a lightly greased 9- or 10-inch pie plate with grated cheese; add layer of chilies; repeat layers. Beat egg whites until stiff; beat in flour; fold in beaten egg yolks; spread evenly over top; bake at 300° for 40 minutes. Serve with Picante sauce.

Jimmy Hooker

WITH-IT DEVILED EGGS
Yield: 24 stuffed halves.

1 dozen eggs, hard-boiled	2 teaspoons Worcestershire sauce
⅓ cup Land O' Frost ham, minced	4 tablespoons salad dressing
1 tablespoon lemon juice	2 dashes Tabasco sauce
1 tablespoon prepared hot mustard	1 teaspoon salt

Cut eggs in half; remove yolks; reserve whites. Mash yolks; combine with remaining ingredients. Refill whites; garnish with additional minced ham and parsley.

Doris Jones
Crawfordsville, Indiana
Land O' Frost of Arkansas, Inc.
Searcy, Arkansas

FETTUCCINI WITH HAM, PEAS & CHEESE
4 servings.

4 ounces cooked ham, cut in thin strips	1 cup heavy cream
¼ cup butter	Fresh ground black pepper
1 cup frozen, tiny green peas	1 (12-ounce) package fettuccini, cooked, drained
½ cup pimentos, cut in thin strips	½ cup grated Parmesan cheese

In skillet sauté ham in butter over medium heat 1 minute; add next 2 ingredients; sauté 1 minute. Stir in cream; season with pepper; cook over low heat, stirring constantly, until slightly thickened. Pour sauce over fettuccini; toss to coat; sprinkle with Parmesan cheese. Serve immediately.

Betty Willich
Oklahoma City, Oklahoma

PASTA FAZULI (Pasta With Beans)
8 to 10 servings.

1	pound dried pinto beans	1	tablespoon chopped parsley
2	quarts water	1	tablespoon flour
Salt to taste		4	ounces tomato sauce
4	tablespoons oil	1	(16-ounce) package spaghetti
1	teaspoon dried rosemary		
3	cloves garlic, minced		

Soak beans overnight; drain. In a large Dutch oven cook beans slowly in water; just before they are tender, add salt. In deep sauce pan sauté rosemary in oil over low heat until rosemary turns color, about 3 minutes. With slotted spoon, remove as much rosemary as possible; add garlic and parsley to oil; brown lightly. Stir in flour; cook, stirring, several minutes until roux is smooth; add sauce; blend well; add mixture to beans. Cook spaghetti until almost done, about 8 minutes; drain; add to hot beans. When spaghetti is added, there should be at least 1 inch of liquid covering beans; spaghetti will absorb this. Allow to sit off heat, covered, 10 to 15 minutes before serving.

Janie Dickinson

MACARONI-HAM CASSEROLE
6 servings.

1	(7½-ounce) package macaroni and cheese dinner	1	(10½-ounce) can cheddar cheese soup
1	cup chopped celery	¼	cup milk
¼	cup chopped onion	1	(6¾-ounce) can ham, diced
¼	cup chopped green pepper	¼	cup diced ripe olives
2	tablespoons margarine	2	tablespoons chopped pimentos
2	tablespoons flour	¼	cup grated cheese

Prepare macaroni according to package directions. In skillet sauté next 3 ingredients in margarine until tender; blend in flour; gradually stir in soup and milk; cook until thick, stirring often. Combine all ingredients except cheese; pour into a greased 2-quart casserole; top with grated cheese; bake 25 minutes at 350°.

Mrs. Willie Gibson

DELUXE MACARONI AND CHEESE
6 to 8 servings.

1	(7-ounce) package elbow macaroni, cooked, drained	¾	teaspoon salt
2	cups small curd cottage cheese	⅛	teaspoon pepper
		8	ounces sharp cheese, shredded
1	cup sour cream	1	tablespoon minced parsley
1	egg, slightly beaten	¼	small onion, grated
¼	cup chopped pimentos	¼	teaspoon paprika

Combine all ingredients, mixing well; pour into a greased 2-quart casserole; bake at 350° 30 minutes.

Marian Matlock
Arkadelphia, Arkansas

GREEN NOODLES
6 to 8 servings.

½	pound green noodles, cooked	1	(16-ounce) container sour cream
2	tablespoons chopped onion	½	cup white wine
1	(3-ounce) can mushrooms		Curry powder to taste
1	tablespoon butter	2	tablespoons chopped parsley
2	(10¾-ounce) cans mushroom soup		Pinch of oregano, salt, pepper and paprika
2	(6½-ounce) cans tuna, chicken or crab		

Brown onions and mushrooms in butter. Combine all ingredients; pour into a greased 3-quart casserole; bake at 350° 45 minutes.

Mary McKean Meier
Oklahoma City, Oklahoma

◇ *J. W. McKean, first state senator from Sevier and Miller counties, 1836.*

PIZZA CASSEROLE
6 to 8 servings.

⅓ cup margarine	½ teaspoon basil
1½ cups chopped onion	1 teaspoon fennel, optional
2 (8-ounce) cans tomato sauce	1 (8-ounce) package spaghetti, cooked, drained
½ pound fresh mushrooms, chopped	1 (4-ounce) package thinly sliced pepperoni
1 large clove garlic, minced	8 ounces grated Mozzarella cheese
½ teaspoon oregano	4 ounces grated Swiss cheese

In a sauce pan sauté onion in margarine about 6 minutes; add tomato sauce, mushrooms, garlic, and spices; mix well. In a buttered 9 × 13-inch baking dish, layer half the spaghetti, cover with half the sauce. Dot with ½ pepperoni slices; sprinkle with ½ both cheeses. Repeat layers. Bake at 350° until heated through, about 25 to 30 minutes.

Eleanor Reeder Berry

ARKANSAS RICE CASSEROLE

From a speech by Senator David Pryor, Congressional Record, March 22, 1984.

Mr. President, I think it is time at this point, with regard to this particular agriculture bill that is before the Senate, to talk about a very, very famous recipe for Arkansas Rice Casserole, six servings. First, one cup of rice, uncooked. Then, Mr. President, one cup of water.

By the way, this is very serious. This is a very fine casserole made with rice.

One can (10½-ounces) of beef consomme. One can (4-ounces), sliced mushrooms, drained. One-fourth cup or one-half stick of butter. One bell pepper, sliced. One jar or 2 ounces of chopped pimento. One onion, diced. One teaspoon of salt.

Mr. President, to properly make Arkansas Rice Casserole as delicious as it should be, preheat oven to 375° F. Mix together and pour into a 9 × 12-inch greased baking dish. Cover and bake for 1 hour. And it freezes very, very well.

BAKED RICE
4 servings.

1 (14½-ounce) can beef consomme
1 (14½-ounce) can beef bouillon
1 stick butter, softened
1 tablespoon Worcestershire sauce
1 tablespoon minced onion
1 teaspoon salt
1 teaspoon pepper
1 cup rice

Combine all ingredients; pour into a greased 2-quart baking dish. Cover and bake at 350° for 1 hour, or until rice is tender and moisture absorbed.

Olivia Romine

CURRIED RICE
8 to 10 servings.

3 cups cooked rice
2 tablespoons curry powder
Salt and red pepper to taste
2 large onions, sliced in thin rings
3 bell peppers, sliced in rings
1 (28-ounce) can tomatoes, drained, liquid reserved
1½ sticks butter

Combine first 3 ingredients, mixing well. In a greased 2-quart baking dish, layer ½ rice, onion and pepper rings, and tomatoes; dot with butter. Repeat layers; pour ½ reserved tomato juice over top. Bake at 350° for 45 minutes, or until mixture bubbles and is "crispy" on top.

Louise McCulloch Daggett
Marianna, Arkansas

◇ Phillip Dodridge McCulloch, U. S. Congressman, 1st Congressional District, 1893-1903.

DIRTY RICE DRESSING
6 to 8 servings.

2	tablespoons flour	½	pound chicken giblets, chopped
2	tablespoons oil		
1	cup chopped onion	2	teaspoons salt
1	cup chopped celery	¼	teaspoon pepper
½	cup chopped green pepper	¼	teaspoon red pepper
2	cloves garlic, minced	1	cup chicken broth
½	pound lean ground beef	3	cups hot cooked rice
½	pound ground pork	1	cup sliced green onion tops

In large heavy skillet, stirring constantly, brown flour in oil to a caramel roux; add next 4 ingredients; cook over low heat until tender. Stir in meats, giblets and seasonings; cook until meat loses its color. Blend in broth; cover; simmer 25 minutes. Stir in rice and onion tops; cook 5 minutes. Mixture should be slightly moist.

Gwen Alter
DeWitt, Arkansas
Rick Hamilton
Texarkana, USA

INDIAN COUNTRY CASSEROLE
8 servings.

1	cup Arkansas rice	1	(12-ounce) can Mexicorn
2	(10½-ounce) cans French onion soup	¼	cup chopped pimentos
		½	cup chopped green peppers
1	(4-ounce) can sliced mushrooms	1	stick butter, melted

Combine all ingredients, blending well; pour into a greased 2-quart casserole; cover. Bake at 350° for 60 to 70 minutes, or until rice is tender and liquid is absorbed, stirring once after 30 minutes.

Sonya Honeycutt
1985 Arkansas Miss Fluffy Rice
Cash, Arkansas

GREEN CHILI RICE
12 servings.

4 cups cooked rice	Salt to taste
2 (4-ounce) cans green chilies, chopped	¾ pound Monterey Jack cheese, cut in 2-inch strips
2 (16-ounce) containers sour cream	1 cup grated Cheddar cheese

Combine first 4 ingredients, mixing well. In a 2-quart casserole, alternate layers of rice mixture and Monterey Jack cheese, beginning and ending with rice; sprinkle grated cheese on top. Cover; bake at 350° for 30 to 40 minutes, or until cheese melts. Freezes well.

Freda Bartlett

FRESH LEMON RICE
6 to 8 servings.

4 tablespoons butter	1½ teaspoons salt
2½ cups Arkansas rice	Pinch of white pepper
½ cup dry white vermouth	4 teaspoons lemon rind
4½ cups chicken broth	¼ cup minced fresh parsley

In a skillet, over medium heat, melt butter; add rice; stir until all grains are coated, about 2 minutes. Add next 4 ingredients; bring to a boil; reduce heat; cover; simmer 20 minutes, or until all liquid is absorbed. Toss with lemon rind and parsley; serve hot.

Gay White
Little Rock, Arkansas

◇ *Governor Frank White, 1981-1983.*

SHRIMP FRIED RICE
4 servings.

4	green onions, sliced	1	(4½-ounce) can small shrimp, drained
2	tablespoons margarine		
3	slices bacon	1	(8-ounce) can water chestnuts, drained, sliced
2	eggs, beaten		
1	cup cooked rice	1	tablespoon soy sauce
1	(4-ounce) can sliced mushrooms, drained		

Sauté onion in margarine; set aside. Fry bacon until crisp; drain; crumble; set aside. In bacon drippings, over low heat scramble eggs, shredding into thin strips as they cook. Stir in remaining ingredients except bacon; heat through. Sprinkle with bacon bits.

Jimmie Lou Fisher
Little Rock, Arkansas

◇ *Treasurer, State of Arkansas, 1981-1987.*

BAKED PASTA, CHEESE AND CHICKEN
6 servings.

¼	cup butter, melted	1½	cups leftover chicken or drained canned chicken, diced
¼	cup flour		
1	teaspoon salt		
⅛	teaspoon pepper	1	(8-ounce) package ziti (large pasta), cooked, drained
1	teaspoon dry mustard		
2	cups milk	1	large ripe tomato, cut in wedges
¼	cup chopped pimentos		
¼	cup chopped green pepper		
1½	cups grated Cheddar cheese, divided		

In a medium sauce pan combine first 5 ingredients; stir until smooth; gradually stir in milk; bring to boiling, stirring; add pimentos and pepper. Reduce heat; simmer 1 minute; stir in 1 cup cheese, chicken and pasta. Pour into a buttered 2-quart shallow baking dish; sprinkle remaining cheese on top; bake 20 minutes at 350°. Garnish with tomato wedges.

Kathy Beyette
Fort Worth, Texas
Shelley Helms

To beat egg whites successfully, always have them at room temperature; use a clean, dry bowl and beaters. A single egg white increases its volume to ½ cup, but 3 egg whites will increase to 2⅔ cups.

Egg yolks should always be tempered by mixing them with a little hot liquid before incorporating them into a hot sauce. Unless the sauce is bound by flour, don't let it boil again after adding the yolks or they will curdle.

Beat egg whites in metal (stainless steel or copper) or glass bowl; never in plastic bowl.

To sour milk add 1 tablespoon white vinegar or lemon juice to 1 cup milk; let stand at room temperature 10 to 15 minutes.

When substituting cornstarch for flour, use only half as much.

MEATS

FRIED VENISON STEAK
6 to 8 servings

3 to 4 pounds venison steaks	2 cups wheat flour, or rolled crackers
¼ pound butter	½ cup boiling water
Salt and pepper	1 tablespoon currant jelly

"Cut a breast of venison into steaks; make a quarter of a pound of butter hot in a pan; rub the steaks over with a mixture of a little salt and pepper; dip them in wheat flour, or rolled crackers and fry a rich brown. When both sides are done, take them up on a dish and put a tin cover over; dredge a heaping teaspoonful of flour into the butter in the pan; stir it with a spoon until it is brown, without burning; put a small teacupful of boiling water into it, with a tablespoon of currant jelly dissolved into it; stir it for a few minutes, then strain it over the meat and serve. A glass of wine, with a tablespoon of white sugar dissolved in it, may be used for the gravy, instead of the jelly and water."

THE WHITE HOUSE COOKBOOK
Published 1908
Submitted by Pam Jester

BEEF BURGUNDY
4 to 6 servings.

2 pounds chuck steak, cut in bite-size pieces	¼ teaspoon thyme
2 tablespoons oil	1 cube beef bouillon, crushed
½ cup chopped onion	¾ cup water
2 tablespoons flour	½ pound fresh mushrooms, sliced
1½ teaspoons salt	1 cup red wine
¼ teaspoon pepper	

In a skillet brown meat and onion over medium heat (300°). Stir in flour and seasonings; add water; stir until slightly thickened. Add remaining ingredients; cover, and simmer 2 hours, stirring occasionally. Serve over wild and brown rice, or noodles.

Margaret F. Cherry
Williamsburg, Virginia

 Governor Francis A. Cherry, 1953-1955.

BRAISED BEEF
6 servings.

2 pounds lean stew meat, cubed	2 (8-ounce) cans tomato sauce
1 cup flour	1 cup water
2 tablespoons oil	½ cup red wine
1 medium onion, minced	1 teaspoon MSG
1 clove garlic, minced	½ teaspoon oregano
1 (8-ounce) can sliced mushrooms	Salt and pepper to taste

Dredge meat in flour. In a large skillet sauté meat, onion and garlic in oil. Add remaining ingredients; cover and simmer until meat is tender. May also be baked in a 2-quart covered casserole at 325° for 2 hours.

Mrs. J. D. Ross

FRENCH BEEF CASSEROLE
4 to 6 servings.

1½ pounds lean beef, cut in 1½-inch cubes
4½ tablespoons flour, divided
Salt and pepper to taste
2 tablespoons butter
2 tablespoons bacon drippings
1 (16-ounce) can tomatoes, drained, reserve juice
1 (6-ounce) can whole mushrooms, drained, reserve liquid
1 pound carrots, cut in 2-inch chunks
2 green peppers, cut in squares
1½ cup sliced celery
3 tablespoons minced onion
1 teaspoon dried basil
1 teaspoon dried tarragon

Dredge meat with 1½ tablespoons flour; salt and pepper to taste. In a skillet, brown meat in butter and bacon drippings; remove with slotted spoon and place in a 2 to 3-quart casserole. Add remaining flour to the fat in the skillet; stirring, add reserved liquids; stir and cook until thickened; pour over meat in casserole. Add tomatoes and mushrooms to dish; cover and bake at 325° 1 hour. Remove from oven; add remaining ingredients; cover and bake 1 hour longer. Serve over rice.

Anna Lou Gallaher Farris
Memphis, Tennessee
Peggy Gallaher Briggs
McMinville, Tennessee

BEEF ROULADES
12 servings.

4 pounds round steak, thinly sliced
4 cups herb-seasoned stuffing mix
½ cup shortening
2 (10¾-ounce) cans cream of mushroom soup
1 cup water

Prepare stuffing according to package directions. Cut steak into 12 pieces; pound with meat hammer. Place ⅓ cup stuffing on each piece of steak; roll up; fasten with toothpick. In a large skillet, brown in shortening; place in a Dutch oven. Combine soup and water; pour over browned rolls; cover and simmer 1½ hours or until tender, stirring occasionally. Uncover and cook until gravy is desired consistency.

Frances Emerson Yates
Texarkana, Arkansas

GRILLADES
6 to 8 servings.

4 pounds lean beef, or veal, rounds, ½-inch thick	⅔ teaspoon thyme
½ cup bacon drippings, divided	1 cup water
½ cup flour	1 cup red wine
1 cup chopped onion	3 tablespoons salt
2 cups chopped green onions	½ teaspoon black pepper
¾ cup chopped celery	2 bay leaves
1½ cups chopped green peppers	½ teaspoon Tabasco sauce
2 cloves garlic, minced	2 tablespoons Worcestershire sauce
2 cups chopped tomatoes	3 tablespoons chopped parsley
½ teaspoon tarragon	

Pound meat, cut in serving-size pieces, to ¼-inch thickness. In a Dutch oven brown meat well in 4 tablespoons bacon drippings. As meat browns, remove to warm platter. Add remaining bacon drippings and flour to pan; stir and cook over low heat to a dark-brown roux. Add next 5 ingredients; sauté until limp. Add tomatoes, tarragon and thyme; cook 3 minutes. Add water and wine, stirring well to blend. Return meat to pan with seasonings and sauces; stir; reduce heat. Cover and simmer; for veal, cooking time approximately 1 hour; for beef, 2 hours. Remove bay leaves; stir in parsley; cool. Let stand several hours, or overnight in refrigerator. Reheat; more liquid may be added; serve over garlic grits, or rice.

Rita Formby
Shreveport, Louisiana

ALL-PURPOSE CREOLE SEASONING
Yield: 4 cups.

26 ounces salt	1 (1-ounce) bottle pure garlic powder
1 (1½-ounce) box ground black pepper	1 (1-ounce) bottle chili powder
1 (2-ounce) bottle ground red pepper	1 ounce Accent

Mix all ingredients well; store in a tightly covered container. Use like salt. For a seafood seasoning, use half the above mixture, and add 1 teaspoon powdered thyme, 1 teaspoon bay leaf, and 1 teaspoon basil.

Margaret Wall

BEEF / 73

CUBE STEAKS DIANE
4 servings.

1 pound cube beef steaks	1 tablespoon Worcestershire sauce
½ teaspoon pepper	1 teaspoon Dijon mustard
3 tablespoons butter, divided	1 tablespoon cornstarch
¼ cup thinly sliced green onions	1 tablespoon chopped fresh parsley
½ cup beef broth	

Sprinkle steak with pepper. In a heavy 12-inch skillet heat 2 tablespoons butter over high heat; add steaks; cook 1 to 2 minutes on each side until browned and cooked to desired doneness; remove and keep warm. Reduce heat; add remaining butter and onions; cook until onions are limp. In a small bowl combine remaining ingredients; stir into skillet with any juices from the beef; cook, stirring constantly, until sauce thickens slightly. Pour over steaks. Serve with noodles or rice.

Lois Taggart
Alvin, Texas

BRAISED SHORT RIBS
6 servings.

6 pounds lean, meaty beef short ribs, cut in serving pieces	1 bay leaf
	1 teaspoon ground cloves
	½ teaspoon garlic powder
½ cup flour	1 large onion, thinly sliced, separated into rings
Salt and pepper to taste	
1 cup beef broth	

Place ribs in a large Dutch oven; sprinkle with flour, salt, and pepper. Roast, uncovered, at 450° for 25 minutes. Remove meat from pan; pour off fat; reduce oven heat to 325°. Return meat to pan with beef broth and crumbled bay leaf; sprinkle with seasonings; smother with onion rings. Cover; bake 1½ to 2 hours, or until meat is tender.

Jeannette Rockefeller
Seattle, Washington

 Governor Winthrop Rockefeller, 1967-1971.

BEEF INTERNATIONALE
6 to 8 servings.

- 2 pounds round steak, cut in thin strips
- 2 tablespoons margarine
- 2 medium onions, thinly sliced
- ½ cup chopped green peppers
- ½ cup water
- 1 (10¾-ounce) can cream of mushroom soup
- ½ cup salad dressing
- ½ cup sliced fresh mushrooms
- Salt and pepper to taste
- 1 (8-ounce) package noodles, cooked, drained, tossed with 1 tablespoon paprika

In a skillet brown meat in margarine; add onion, peppers, and water; cover, and simmer 45 minutes, adding more water if necessary. Add soup, salad dressing, and mushrooms; season to taste; heat, stirring occasionally. Spoon over noodles.

Rebecca Stevens

HUNGARIAN GOULASH
4 servings.

- 1 pound round steak, cubed
- ½ cup sliced onion
- 1 clove garlic, minced
- 1 cup water
- ½ cup catsup
- 1 tablespoon Worcestershire sauce
- 2 teaspoons brown sugar
- 1 teaspoon salt
- 2 teaspoons paprika
- ½ teaspoon dry mustard
- Dash black pepper
- 3 tablespoons chopped bell pepper
- 1 (15-ounce) can whole kernel corn
- 1 tablespoon cornstarch
- 2 tablespoons water

In a large skillet brown beef cubes; add onion and garlic; cook, stirring, until onion is tender. Add next 8 ingredients; simmer, stirring occasionally, until beef is tender. Add bell pepper and corn; stir; cover and simmer 15 minutes. Blend cornstarch and water; add to meat mixture; cook and stir 5 minutes, or until sauce thickens and begins to boil. Serve over hot noodles.

Ed Gallaher

SWEET AND SOUR ROAST
8 to 10 servings.

5 to 6 pounds beef roast
1 teaspoon salt
2 teaspoons pepper
1¼ cups flour, divided

3 tablespoons oil
1 cup sugar
1 cup vinegar

Salt and pepper roast; dredge in 1 cup flour. In a skillet brown well in oil. Place roast in a covered roasting pan; deglaze skillet with ½ cup hot water; pour over roast; cover and roast at 375° for 2 hours. Combine sugar, vinegar, and ¼ cup flour; pour over roast. Add vegetables, if desired, at this point. Bake an additional hour, basting often with pan juices.

Ronny and Diane Ross

BEEF STROGANOFF
6 to 8 servings.

½ cup flour
Salt and pepper to taste
1 pound round steak, cut in thin strips
6 tablespoons margarine, divided
¼ cup chopped onion

1 cube beef bouillon, crushed
4 tablespoons flour
2 tablespoons catsup
1¼ cups water
1 (10¾-ounce) can cream of mushroom soup
1 cup sour cream

Combine flour, salt and pepper in a paper sack; shake meat in mixture until well coated. In a skillet brown meat in 3 tablespoons margarine; remove; set aside. Add onion to pan; sauté until limp. Add remaining margarine, bouillon, flour, and catsup; stir until well mixed. Gradually add water, stirring; cook and stir until thickened. Add soup and meat; simmer until meat is tender, about 30 minutes. Stir in sour cream; heat through; do not boil. Serve over rice.

Sandra Sue Staggs
Texarkana, Arkansas

SHISH KEBABS

4 to 6 servings.

1 to 2 pounds round steak, ¾-inch thick	1 pound whole fresh mushrooms
3 bell peppers	1 (16-ounce) bottle Italian dressing
3 onions	

Cut steak into 1 to 1½ inch cubes. Cut peppers into squares; quarter onions and separate into pieces; stem mushrooms. Combine all ingredients in a large bowl; mix well to coat; marinate 1 hour. String meat and vegetables alternately on skewers. Broil, or charcoal grill, basting with marinade, until meat is done. Serve over rice or noodles.

Teri Dabney
Texarkana, Arkansas

SMOTHERED STEAK

8 to 10 servings.

1 cup plus 4½ tablespoons flour, divided	1 onion, sliced
1 teaspoon salt	Worcestershire sauce, to taste
1 teaspoon pepper	3 cups water
3 to 4 pounds round steak, cut in serving-size pieces	1 (10¾-ounce) can cream of mushroom soup

Combine 1 cup flour with salt and pepper; dredge meat in mixture. In a skillet in hot oil, brown meat quickly on both sides; remove. Arrange browned meat alternately with onion slices in a greased 3-quart casserole. Sprinkle generously with Worcestershire sauce. Blend remaining flour with water and soup; pour over meat. Bake, covered, at 350° for 1½ hours.

Helen Powell

OLD-FASHIONED SWISS STEAK
8 servings.

1	cup flour	3	carrots, sliced
¾	tablespoon dry mustard	1	(4½-ounce) can mushrooms
3	pounds round steak, cut in serving-size pieces	1	cube beef bouillon, crushed
¾	cup chopped onion	1½	cups hot water
6	tablespoons margarine	3	tablespoons brown sugar
1	(16-ounce) can stewed tomatoes	1	tablespoon Worcestershire sauce

Combine flour and mustard; pound into meat. In a skillet sauté onion in margarine; add steak; brown. Place meat in a greased 9 × 13-inch baking pan; top with sautéed onion, tomatoes, carrots, and mushrooms. Combine remaining ingredients; pour over meat. Bake, covered, at 350° for 2 to 2½ hours.

Dennis Coulter
Clinton, Iowa

OVEN BEEF STEW
4 to 6 servings.

2	pounds lean beef, cubed	1	tablespoon sugar
3	or 4 small cooking onions	2	tablespoons instant tapioca, or cornstarch
2	potatoes, cubed	1	(8-ounce) can V-8 juice
3	ribs celery, sliced		Salt and pepper to taste
2	carrots, sliced		
8	ounces fresh mushrooms, sliced, or 1 (4-ounce) can sliced mushrooms		

Place meat and vegetables in a 9 × 13-inch baking pan. Combine remaining ingredients; pour over meat and vegetables. Cover and bake at 275° for 3 to 4 hours, or until meat and vegetables are tender.

Patti Morris
Mrs. Robert Watson

BARBECUED BEEF BRISKET
18 to 20 servings.

9 pounds beef brisket, trimmed	1 teaspoon celery salt
1 (3½-ounce) bottle liquid smoke	1 teaspoon paprika
	½ teaspoon nutmeg
	½ teaspoon garlic salt
Black pepper	½ teaspoon onion salt
Meat Tenderizer	½ cup brown sugar

Place brisket in large roasting pan; sprinkle with liquid smoke, pepper, and tenderizer; marinate 3 hours. Sprinkle with remaining seasonings and sugar; cover and bake at 300° 2 hours. Remove cover; bake an additional 5 to 6 hours at 200°, or until tender. Remove from oven; lift brisket from cooking liquids; reserve liquids for use as sauce. To serve, slice thin diagonal slices.

Glenda Gilliam
Elkhart, Kansas

BARBECUED BEEF ROAST
6 servings.

1 (4 to 5-lb.) rolled rump or sirloin tip roast	6 tablespoons Worcestershire sauce
2 cloves garlic, slivered	3 tablespoons steak sauce
Salt and pepper to taste	2 tablespoons vinegar
½ cup butter, melted	6 tablespoons lemon juice

With point of sharp knife, make several deep gashes in fat of the roast; insert slivered garlic pieces into gashes. Place roast in roasting pan; salt and pepper to taste. Combine butter, sauces, vinegar, and lemon juice, blending well. Baste roast well with sauce; cover and bake at 350°. Cook 2 to 3 hours for rare; 2½ to 3½ hours for medium; or 3 to 4 hours for well done. Baste frequently with barbecue sauce. Roast can also be wrapped in foil and cooked on outside grill.

Cindy Coulter Hale

BEN LOMOND BARBECUED LIVER
Serves 6.

2 to 2½ pounds beef liver
1 medium onion, thinly sliced
1 teaspoon garlic salt
¼ teaspoon pepper
½ teaspoon paprika
1 cup barbecue sauce

Cut liver into ½ by 2-inch strips. Combine ingredients in a crock pot; blend well. Cover and cook on LOW for 7 to 9 hours, or on HIGH for 2½ to 3½ hours.

Ina F. Roberts

FRENCH FRIED LIVER
Serves 4.

1 pound beef liver
1 (8-ounce) bottle French dressing
1 cup flour
Salt and pepper to taste

Cut liver into ½-inch strips 2 to 3 inches long. Marinate strips in French dressing 30 minutes or longer. Combine flour and seasonings. Lift strips from marinade; coat with flour mixture. Fry in deep fat until well browned.

Fern Culp

CHARCOAL-WATER SMOKED BEEF ROAST
16 to 20 servings.

8 to 10 pounds beef roast
½ cup corn oil
2 to 3 tablespoons Cavender's Greek seasoning
2 to 3 tablespoons dry barbecue seasoning

Rub roast with oil; sprinkle with seasonings. Place in a plastic bag; seal; marinate, refrigerated, 3 days. Prepare cooker with 7 to 10 pounds charcoal; 6 to 7 quarts water, and 3 to 4 hickory blocks soaked in water overnight. Smoke 8 to 9 hours.

Dick Coulter
Daingerfield, Texas

◇ *James Coulter, County Judge, Sevier County, 1860-1864.*

LIVER AND ONIONS
Serves 4.

1 pound calves' liver, thinly sliced	3 to 4 tablespoons shortening
½ cup flour	2 large onions, thinly sliced, separated into rings, parboiled
Salt and pepper to taste	

Combine flour and seasonings; dredge liver in flour mixture. In large skillet cook liver in heated shortening over medium heat (electric skillet 350°) until browned; remove. Add drained onions to skillet and stir with pan drippings. Return liver to pan; cover; reduce heat and simmer 5 to 10 minutes, stirring occasionally.

Donna Gallaher

ENCHILADAS
6 servings.

4 cups beef broth	1 clove garlic, chopped
6 tablespoons mild chili powder	1 pound ground beef
¼ teaspoon garlic salt	2 cups shredded Cheddar cheese, divided
1 teaspoon cumin	1 (4½-ounce) can ripe olives, chopped
2 tablespoons cornstarch	12 tortillas
1 tablespoon water	¼ to ½ cup oil
1 onion, chopped	

In a sauce pan bring first 4 ingredients to a boil. Mix cornstarch in water; add, stirring; boil 1 minute; set aside. In a skillet sauté onion and garlic in 1 tablespoon oil until golden; add meat and brown. Add ½ cup reserved sauce, 1 cup cheese and olives; heat. In another skillet fry tortillas quickly in hot oil; drain; keep warm in covered casserole. Dip tortillas in heated sauce, spoon equal amounts of meat filling into each; roll tightly and place seam side down in a greased 9 × 13-inch baking dish. Sprinkle with remaining cheese. Heat in 350° oven for 10 minutes. Spoon heated sauce over all and serve.

Janie Coulter La Bounty
Kremling, Colorado
Joni Friday

WHITE ENCHILADAS
6 servings.

1 pound ground beef	1 (4-ounce) can green chilies, chopped
1 medium onion, chopped	Salt to taste
1 (10¾-ounce) can cream of chicken soup	12 flour tortillas
1 pint sour cream	½ pound longhorn cheese, grated
¼ cup milk	

In a skillet brown beef and onions; drain. Combine with all ingredients except tortillas and cheese. In a 9 × 13-inch baking dish, alternate layers of tortillas, beef mixture, and grated cheese. Repeat layers, topping with cheese. Bake at 350° for 40 minutes.

Polly Pate
Pam Goldman

BEEF AND BISCUITS
6 servings.

1 pound ground beef	1 cup milk
½ cup chopped onion, divided	2 cups prepared biscuit mix
½ cup chopped green pepper	¼ cup melted butter
Dash black pepper	1 tablespoon olive oil
1 teaspoon salt	1 (8-ounce) can tomato sauce
2 tablespoons flour	½ teaspoon basil

In a skillet brown beef, ¼ cup onion, and green pepper; drain. Add salt and pepper; blend in flour and milk. Cook over medium heat until thick; cool. Prepare biscuit mix according to package directions; roll dough to ½-inch thickness; spread with meat mixture. Roll as for jelly roll. Cut into 1¼-inch slices; place in a greased 9 × 9-inch baking dish; brush tops with melted butter. Bake at 400° 20 to 25 minutes. In sauce pan sauté ¼ cup onion in oil until limp; add tomato sauce and basil; simmer until thick. Serve as sauce over meat.

Judy Gordon

MEXICAN BEEF-CORN CASSEROLE
8 servings.

2 (6-ounce) packages Mexican cornbread mix	1 green pepper, chopped
1 (17-ounce) can cream-style corn, divided	Salt and pepper to taste
1 pound ground beef	1 tablespoon oil
1 onion, chopped	½ pound Cheddar cheese, grated

Prepare cornbread mix according to package directions; add ½ can corn to the mixture. In a skillet sauté meat, onion, and pepper, seasoned to taste; drain well; add remaining corn. Heat oil in an iron skillet; pour in half the cornbread mixture; layer this with meat mixture; top with grated cheese. Spread remaining cornbread mixture over cheese. Bake at 350° 45 minutes to 1 hour.

Billie Snow
Richardson, Texas
Lennie Pickett
Norma Needham

TAMALE PIE
10 to 12 servings.

1 tablespoon oil	2 teaspoons chili powder
1 large onion, chopped	3 cups milk
1 cup chopped green pepper	1 teaspoon salt
2 cloves garlic, minced	6 tablespoons butter
3 pounds lean ground beef	1 cup corn meal
2 (8-ounce) cans tomato sauce	2 cups grated sharp cheese
2 (16-ounce) cans whole kernel corn, drained	4 eggs, beaten
Salt and pepper to taste	1 (8-ounce) can ripe olives, sliced, drained

Coat a large skillet with oil; sauté onion, green pepper, garlic and beef until meat loses its color. Add tomato sauce, corn, chili powder, and salt and pepper to taste; simmer 10 minutes. In a sauce pan heat milk with salt and butter; gradually add cornmeal, stirring constantly. Cook until thick, stirring; remove from heat; stir in cheese and eggs. Add olives to meat mixture; turn into a greased 3-quart casserole. Spoon corn meal mixture around edge. Bake at 425° for 25 to 30 minutes.

Katie Alderson
Forrest City, Arkansas

TACO FROM THE OVEN
6 to 8 servings.

1½ to 2 pounds lean ground beef	½ cup water
1 or 2 cloves garlic, minced	1 (12-ounce) can yellow corn, drained, optional
1 onion, finely chopped	1 (5-ounce) package taco shells, crumbled
1 (.87-ounce) package taco seasoning mix	2½ cups grated mild Cheddar cheese
1 (15-ounce) can tomato sauce	

In a large skillet sauté beef, garlic, and onion until beef loses its color; drain well. Add seasoning mix, sauce, and water; simmer 3 to 5 minutes. Stir in corn. In a lightly-greased 3-quart baking dish, alternate layers of crumbled shells, meat sauce, and cheese, ending with cheese. Bake, uncovered, at 350° for 30 to 40 minutes.

Terita Friday
Fouke, Arkansas

MEXICAN SPAGHETTI SAUCE
6 to 8 servings.

1½ to 1¾ pounds lean ground beef	¼ teaspoon thyme
½ cup chopped onion	¼ teaspoon dry mustard
1½ cups water	¼ teaspoon rosemary
1 (10¾-ounce) can tomato puree	¼ teaspoon mace
1 (8-ounce) can tomato sauce	½ teaspoon salt
1 (8-ounce) can sliced mushrooms	½ teaspoon red pepper
1 (3-ounce) jar sliced green olives	½ teaspoon black pepper
½ cup chopped celery	½ teaspoon chili powder
½ cup chopped bell pepper	4 small bay leaves
	1 cup burgundy, or other full-bodied red wine
	1 pound Cheddar cheese, cubed

In a large, heavy pot sauté beef and onion until lightly browned. Add remaining ingredients except cheese; simmer 2½ to 3 hours, stirring occasionally. Remove bay leaves; stir in cheese; simmer 20 minutes, stirring to incorporate cheese. Serve over hot spaghetti.

Teresa Mallette

SICILIAN SPAGHETTI SAUCE
6 to 8 servings.

1 quart tomato juice, or V-8 juice	1 tablespoon grated Romano cheese
1 bay leaf	½ teaspoon garlic powder
1 (6-ounce) can Italian-style tomato paste	½ teaspoon oregano
	½ teaspoon basil
2 cups pureed canned tomatoes	½ teaspoon rosemary
	½ teaspoon thyme
⅛ teaspoon black pepper	½ teaspoon celery seeds, or celery salt
1 tablespoon brown sugar	
½ cup diced onion	1½ pounds lean ground beef
1 tablespoon grated Parmesan cheese	

In a large, heavy pot simmer juice with bay leaf 15 minutes; add remaining ingredients except beef. Blend; simmer 30 to 45 minutes; adjust seasonings. Cover; simmer, stirring occasionally, for 3 to 4 hours; remove bay leaf. In a skillet sauté beef until it loses color; add to sauce; cook, skimming and discarding grease several times, until meat is fully cooked. If thick sauce is desired, combine 1 tablespoon cornstarch with cold water or tomato juice; stir into sauce before adding meat. Serve over hot spaghetti.

Mrs. John Paul Jones
Bobby Jones

ITALIAN CASSEROLE
4 to 6 servings.

1 (8-ounce) package crescent rolls	1 teaspoon salt
	½ teaspoon seasoned black pepper
1 pound lean ground beef	
1 onion, chopped	½ pound fresh mushrooms, sliced
1 (16-ounce) can tomato sauce with tomato bits	
	2 cups grated Mozzarella cheese
1 tablespoon spaghetti sauce seasoning mix, or oregano to taste	
	Grated Parmesan cheese

Spread out crescent roll dough in bottom of a greased 8 × 12-inch baking dish. In a skillet brown meat well; drain. Add onion, tomato sauce, and seasonings; cover; cook 10 to 15 minutes. Spread meat sauce over dough; layer mushrooms; top with Mozzarella and sprinkle with Parmesan. Bake at 350° until hot, 10 to 15 minutes. Let stand 10 minutes before serving.

Bernice Swint
Texarkana, Arkansas
Gretchyn DeShazo

ORIENTAL MEATBALLS WITH SWEET AND SOUR SAUCE
10 to 12 servings.

2 pounds ground beef	⅓ cup milk
1 pound ground pork	1 cup uncooked oats
1 (8¾-ounce) can crushed pineapple, drained	1½ teaspoons soy sauce
	1 clove garlic, pressed
1 (8-ounce) can water chestnuts, drained, finely chopped	1 teaspoon salt
	¼ teaspoon ginger, optional
	½ teaspoon pepper
2 eggs, beaten	

Combine all ingredients; shape into small balls. In enough oil to cover bottom of a large skillet, fry until brown on all sides. Drain on paper towels. Combine with hot Sweet and Sour sauce; serve with rice.

Sweet and Sour Sauce:

3 tablespoons cornstarch	1½ cups pineapple juice
1½ cups brown sugar	2 tablespoons soy sauce
1 cup vinegar	

In a sauce pan mix cornstarch and brown sugar; add remaining ingredients. Bring to a boil; reduce heat; simmer 2 minutes. Yield: about 3 cups.

Fae Beyette
Netta Patterson

EASY MEATLESS TOMATO SAUCE
Yield: 3½ cups.

1 (16-ounce) can stewed tomatoes	½ teaspoon basil
	½ teaspoon oregano
1 (15-ounce) can tomato sauce	1 clove garlic, pressed

Combine all ingredients in a heavy sauce pan; bring to a boil. Reduce heat; simmer, covered, 10 to 20 minutes. Serve over your favorite pasta.

Gerry Helms

SWEDISH MEAT BALLS
6 to 8 servings.

1½ cups bread crumbs	¼ teaspoon ginger
1 cup light cream	Dash black pepper
½ cup minced onion	Dash nutmeg
4 tablespoons butter, divided	2 tablespoons flour
1½ pounds ground chuck	¾ cup beef broth
1 egg, beaten	¼ cup water
¼ cup chopped parsley	½ teaspoon instant coffee
1½ teaspoons salt	

In a bowl soak crumbs in cream. In heavy skillet lightly sauté onion in 1 tablespoon butter; lift with slotted spoon into large mixing bowl. Add soaked crumbs, beef, egg, parsley, and seasonings; mix thoroughly. Shape into balls. Add remaining butter to skillet; heat and brown balls lightly; remove; set aside. Stir flour into skillet drippings; add remaining ingredients. Heat and stir until thick; return meat balls to gravy, cover and simmer 30 to 45 minutes. Serve over rice or noodles.

Katie Sue Smiley
Davis Thompson

BARBECUED MEATLOAF
6 to 8 servings.

1½ pounds ground beef	¼ cup water
1 cup bread crumbs	3 tablespoons brown sugar
1 onion, minced	3 tablespoons vinegar
1 egg, beaten	2 tablespoons prepared mustard
1½ teaspoons salt	
¼ teaspoon pepper	2 teaspoons Worcestershire sauce
2 (8-ounce) cans tomato sauce, divided	

In mixing bowl combine first 6 ingredients with ½ can tomato sauce; mix well; shape into a loaf. Place in an 8 × 12-inch baking pan. In a sauce pan heat water and sugar until sugar dissolves; add remaining tomato sauce and other ingredients; pour over loaf. Bake at 350° 1 hour, or until done, basting often with pan liquids.

Willie Bowers
Joann Stringfellow

CROCK POT MEATLOAF
6 to 8 servings.

2	pounds ground chuck	1	egg
½	cup chopped green peppers	1	(7/8-ounce) envelope brown gravy mix
½	cup chopped onion	1	cup milk
1½	teaspoons salt	6	small potatoes, scrubbed
1	cup cracker crumbs		

In a large bowl combine all ingredients except potatoes; mix well; shape into a loaf. Place loaf in crock pot; arrange potatoes around loaf. Cover; cook on LOW 8 to 10 hours, or HIGH for 4 to 5 hours.

Frances Roberts

EL PASO BEEF
6 to 8 servings.

1	cup corn meal	2 or 3 teaspoons chili powder	
1	cup cold water	2	cups tomatoes, or 1 cup tomatoes and 1 (10-ounce) can tomatoes with green chilies
3	cups boiling water		
1	pound ground beef, or ½ pound Italian sausage and ½ pound ground beef		
½	cup chopped onion	1	(4-ounce) jar sliced mushrooms, drained
½	cup chopped green pepper	1	(7-ounce) can pitted ripe olives, halved, drained, divided
1	(1.5-ounce) envelope spaghetti sauce mix		
1	teaspoon salt	1	cup grated cheese, divided

In a sauce pan mix corn meal and cold water; stir in boiling water. Cook, over low heat, stirring frequently, until very thick, about 15 minutes. Divide mush into 2 greased 9 × 13-inch baking pans, spreading in an even layer. Place one pan in refrigerator; chill until firm. In a skillet brown meat, onion, and pepper; stir in next 4 ingredients; heat to boiling, stirring constantly. Stir in mushrooms, ½ the olives, and ½ cup cheese. Pour over unchilled corn meal mush. Cut chilled mush into wedges or strips; arrange on top of meat mixture. Top with remaining cheese. Bake at 400 to 425° for 40 minutes, or until bubbly. Garnish with reserved olives.

Charles Nash

GROUND BEEF STROGANOFF CASSEROLE
6 to 8 servings.

¼ cup butter	¼ teaspoon paprika
1 pound ground round	1 (4-ounce) can mushrooms
¼ cup minced onion	1 (10¾-ounce) can cream of mushroom soup
1 garlic clove, minced	1 cup sour cream
2 tablespoons flour	1 (8-ounce) package egg noodles, cooked, drained
1 teaspoon salt	
¼ teaspoon pepper	

In a sauce pan sauté meat, onion, and garlic in butter. Stir in flour, seasonings, and mushrooms; simmer 5 minutes. Stir in soup; simmer 10 minutes; remove from heat. Stir in sour cream; fold in noodles. Pour into a buttered 2-quart casserole; heat at 350° until just heated through; do not allow to bubble or boil.

Irene Romine

WILD HOG CHILI
10 to 12 servings.

2 large, or 3 medium, yellow onions, finely chopped	2 tablespoons sugar
10 cloves garlic, minced	1 tablespoon red pepper flakes
½ cup oil	3 tablespoons paprika
4 pounds coarsely-ground chuck steak	1 (8-ounce) can tomato paste
2 pounds round steak, cubed	2 or 3 (12-ounce) cans beer
2 pounds pork roast, cubed	2 quarts beef bouillon
3 tablespoons seasoned salt	1 jalapeño pepper, seeded, chopped, or 2 tablespoons jalapeño pepper juice, to taste
Black pepper to taste	
8 tablespoons chili powder	
4 tablespoons cumin	3 tablespoons masa harina flour
3 tablespoons oregano	
2 tablespoons MSG	Hot water to make paste

In a skillet, sauté onion and garlic in oil until soft; drain well; set aside. In a large, heavy pot, brown all meats; drain. Add onion mixture and remaining ingredients except jalapeño pepper and flour. Bring to a boil; reduce heat; simmer 1½ hours. Add jalapeño or pepper juice, to taste; simmer 1½ hours longer; skim and discard grease as necessary. Stir occasionally. Make paste with flour and hot water; add 15 minutes before serving to "tighten" chili.

Don Jacks
Littleton, Colorado

GORDITOS
6 to 8 servings.

1 (12-ounce) package tortilla chips	1 (16-ounce) can refried beans
1 pound ground beef, browned	2 (16-ounce) cans chili without beans
1 large onion, chopped	½ pound Cheddar cheese, grated
2 (4-ounce) cans green chilies	

In a greased 9 × 13-inch baking dish, layer ingredients in order listed. Bake at 375° until cheese melts.

Thelma Scott Corley Green
Artesia, New Mexico
Trish Crow

TORTELLINI
4 to 6 servings.

1 tablespoon olive oil	¼ teaspoon red pepper flakes
1 tablespoon minced garlic	1 teaspoon basil
1 cup chopped onion	½ teaspoon oregano
1 pound ground beef	½ teaspoon rosemary
Salt and freshly ground pepper	2 (7-ounce) boxes tortellini with cheese, cooked and drained
3 cups canned tomatoes	
3 tablespoons tomato paste	
½ cup dry red wine	Grated cheese

In large, heavy skillet sauté garlic and onion in oil until wilted; add meat; cook until it loses its color; season to taste. In blender or food processor blend tomatoes and tomato paste; add to meat mixture with wine and remaining seasonings; simmer about 1 hour. To serve, pour meat sauce over hot tortellini; top with grated cheese.

Patti Morris

BEEF IN CASSEROLE
8 servings.

1 pound ground chuck	1 (8-ounce) package thin egg noodles, cooked, drained
1 (16-ounce) can tomatoes	1 cup sour cream
1 (8-ounce) can tomato sauce	1 (3-ounce) package cream cheese, softened
2 teaspoons salt	6 green onions and tops, chopped
2 teaspoons sugar	1 cup grated Cheddar cheese
2 cloves garlic, crushed	
Black pepper to taste	

In a skillet sauté beef until it loses its color; add tomatoes, sauce, garlic, and seasonings; simmer 10 to 15 minutes. In a mixing bowl combine noodles, sour cream, cream cheese and onions. In a greased 2-quart casserole, alternate layers of meat mixture and noodles; top with grated cheese. Bake at 375° for 30 minutes, or until heated through and cheese melts.

Dot Stainton
Doylene Young

LASAGNA
10 to 12 servings.

1½ pounds ground chuck	2 (12-ounce) containers large curd cottage cheese
3 tablespoons parsley flakes, divided	2 eggs, beaten
1 clove garlic, minced	½ teaspoon pepper
1 tablespoon basil	½ cup grated Parmesan cheese
2½ teaspoons salt, divided	1 (10-ounce) package lasagna noodles, cooked, drained
1 (16-ounce) can tomatoes, chopped	1 pound Mozzarella cheese slices
2 (6-ounce) cans tomato paste	

In a heavy sauce pan brown meat; drain. Add 1 tablespoon parsley flakes, garlic, basil, ½ teaspoon salt, tomatoes and tomato paste; simmer, covered, 45 minutes, stirring often. In a mixing bowl combine cottage cheese, eggs, pepper, Parmesan cheese, and remaining salt and parsley flakes. In a greased 9 × 13-inch baking pan layer half the noodles; add ½ cheese mixture, ½ cheese slices, and ½ meat mixture. Repeat layers. Bake at 375° 30 minutes, or until bubbly. Let stand 10 to 15 minutes before serving.

Dottie Lou Buffington
Wanda Titsworth

DON'T-COOK-THE-PASTA MANICOTTI

8 servings.

1 pound lean ground beef	2 cups ricotta cheese, or cottage cheese
½ cup chopped onion	
2 cloves garlic, minced	1 (10-ounce) package frozen chopped spinach, thawed, drained
4 cups tomato juice, divided	
1 (6-ounce) can tomato paste	
2 teaspoons oregano	2 eggs, slightly beaten
1 teaspoon sugar	½ cup grated Parmesan or Romano cheese
1 teaspoon salt	
⅛ teaspoon pepper	1 (8-ounce) package manicotti shells
3 cups shredded Mozzarella cheese, divided	

In a large skillet brown meat with onion and garlic; drain well. Stir in 2 cups tomato juice, tomato paste, sugar and seasonings; simmer while preparing filling. In a large bowl combine 2 cups Mozzarella cheese, ricotta cheese, spinach, eggs, and grated cheese; mix well. Stuff dry pasta shells with cheese mixture; arrange in a greased 9 × 13-inch baking dish. Spoon meat sauce evenly over shells; pour remaining tomato juice on top. Cover with foil; place pan on a baking sheet; bake at 350° 1 hour. Remove from oven; remove foil; top with remaining Mozzarella cheese. Let stand 15 minutes before serving.

Camille Clay
Austin, Texas

UPSIDE DOWN CHILI CORNBREAD

6 to 8 servings.

1 pound ground beef	½ envelope onion soup mix
1 (10¾-ounce) can tomato soup	1 (14-ounce) can pinto beans, drained
½ soup can water	2 to 3 cups cornbread batter
1 tablespoon chili powder	1 cup grated Cheddar cheese

In a 12-inch iron skillet brown meat; drain fat. Add soup, water, seasonings, and beans; simmer 10 to 15 minutes. Mix a cornbread batter; pour over chili; bake at 400 to 425° 25 to 30 minutes, or until cornbread is done. Turn out onto platter; sprinkle with cheese.

Elverna Sykes
Ruthie Karr

BEEF-GREEN BEAN-POTATO CASSEROLE
6 to 8 servings.

1 to 1½ pounds ground beef
1 medium onion, chopped
Salt and pepper to taste
Chili powder to taste, optional
1 (15 to 16-ounce) can whole or French-style green beans, drained
1 (16-ounce) can whole kernel corn, drained, optional
1 (10¾-ounce) can cream of mushroom soup, or 1 (16-ounce) can tomatoes
2 cups mashed potatoes, or 1 (12-ounce) box tater tots with 4 slices American cheese

In a skillet sauté beef and onion until brown; drain; season to taste. Place meat mixture in bottom of a greased 2-quart casserole; add layers of corn and green beans; layer with soup or tomatoes. Make top layer of mashed potatoes, or cheese slices dotted with tater tots. Bake at 350° 30 minutes, or until heated through.

Pat Dempsey
Carole Southworth
Teresa Robinson

HACIENDA BAKE
6 servings.

1 pound ground beef
1 to 2 onions, chopped
1 clove garlic, minced
1 bell pepper, chopped, optional
1 teaspoon chili powder
Salt and pepper to taste
1 (10¾-ounce) can tomato soup, or 1½ cups whole tomatoes, minced
1 cup water, barbecue or enchilada sauce
1 (12-ounce) can whole kernel corn, drained
1 (16-ounce) can ranch-style beans, drained, optional
2 cups cooked noodles or macaroni
2 cups grated cheese, divided

In a large skillet brown beef, onion, garlic, and pepper; drain. Add seasonings and next 4 ingredients; simmer 15 to 20 minutes. Add pasta and 1 cup cheese; turn into a greased 9 × 13-inch baking dish; sprinkle with remaining cheese. Bake at 350° 15 to 20 minutes; let stand 10 minutes before serving.

Vashti Peek
Martie Griffin
Mary E. Lewis

SUPER MEXICAN CASSEROLE
8 servings.

1½ pounds ground chuck
1 large onion, chopped
1 tablespoon chili powder
Salt and pepper to taste
1 (12-ounce) package corn chips, or 10 corn tortillas, torn into bite-size pieces
1 (16-ounce) can ranch-style beans
1 pound Velveeta cheese, sliced
1 (10¾-ounce) can cream of mushroom soup
1 (10-ounce) can tomatoes with green chilies
Grated Parmesan cheese

In a skillet sauté meat and onion until brown; drain; add seasonings. Layer bottom of a greased 9 × 13-inch baking dish with chips or tortilla pieces; spread meat mixture evenly over chips; add a layer of beans; top with cheese slices. Combine soup and tomatoes; pour over cheese. Bake at 350° 25 to 30 minutes; let stand 10 minutes before serving. Sprinkle with Parmesan cheese, if desired.

Dottie Philips
Winthrop, Arkansas
Iona Baker Jones
Carolyn Frachiseur

BEEF AND ZUCCHINI
6 servings.

1 pound ground beef
1 medium onion, finely chopped
1 (16-ounce) can tomatoes, drained, chopped
1 (8-ounce) can tomato sauce, or 1 (6-ounce) can tomato paste
1 green pepper, chopped
1 cup grated Cheddar cheese
2 to 4 cups zucchini, unpeeled, thinly sliced
½ cup chopped ripe olives
¼ cup rice
½ teaspoon salt
¼ teaspoon garlic powder
⅛ teaspoon oregano
Black pepper to taste
Grated Parmesan cheese

In a large skillet sauté meat and onion until lightly browned; drain; add remaining ingredients except Parmesan cheese; simmer, uncovered, 10 minutes. Turn into a greased 2½-quart casserole; top with Parmesan cheese. Bake at 350° for 1 hour.

Suzanne Pate Mize

MEXICAN RED SAUCE
Yield: 1 cup.

1 medium tomato, peeled, cut up	1 to 2 tablespoons fresh minced cilantro, or 1 to 2 teaspoons dried cilantro (fresh parsley may be substituted for fresh cilantro)
1 (4-ounce) jar chili peppers	
1 small onion, chopped	
1 clove garlic	
½ teaspoon salt	
1 tablespoon olive oil	

Combine all ingredients in a blender; process. Pour into a sauce pan; bring to a boil; reduce heat; simmer, stirring, until thick, about 5 minutes.

Sandra K. Taylor

NINFA'S MEXICAN GREEN SAUCE
Yield: about ¾ cup.

1 ripe avocado, mashed	2 scant tablespoons lemon juice
¼ cup sour cream	
¼ cup milk	1 tablespoon minced fresh cilantro or 1 teaspoon dried cilantro leaves (fresh parsley may be substituted for fresh cilantro)
1 teaspoon minced onion	
1 clove garlic, crushed	
¼ teaspoon salt	
½ teaspoon hot pepper sauce, or jalapeño pepper juice	

Combine all ingredients; whisk to blend; chill 1 hour before using. Use with Mexican dishes, or as a dip.

David Smith
Little Rock, Arkansas

Herb equivalents: ½ teaspoon dried or ¼ teaspoon powdered is equivalent to 1 tablespoon fresh herbs.

LAMB STEW

8 servings.

2½ pounds boned lamb shoulder, cubed	¼ cup chopped parsley
¼ cup olive oil	1 teaspoon salt
4 small onions, quartered	⅛ teaspoon black pepper
2 teaspoons ginger	1 (16-ounce) can tomatoes
2 cloves garlic, crushed	1 cup raisins

In a 6-quart Dutch oven brown lamb in hot oil over medium heat; remove pieces as they brown; set aside. To drippings add onion, ginger, and garlic; sauté, stirring, until onion is golden, about 5 minutes. Add next 3 ingredients; mix well. Return lamb to mixture; stir in tomatoes; cover and bring to boiling. Reduce heat; simmer, covered, 1 hour and 15 minutes, stirring occasionally, until meat is tender. In small bowl cover raisins with hot water; let stand. Prior to serving, drain raisins; stir into meat mixture; simmer, covered, 5 minutes. Turn into serving dish, garnish with sautéed blanched almonds, chopped egg and parsley; serve with hot rice.

Ilene Smith

ROLLED ROAST LEG OF LAMB

6 to 8 servings.

3 tablespoons crushed dried peppercorns (1 tablespoon each black, green, and white, mixed), divided	5 cloves garlic, crushed
	½ cup raspberry vinegar
	¼ cup oriental soy sauce
	½ cup dry red wine
1 tablespoon fresh rosemary leaves, or 1½ teaspoons dried rosemary	1 boned leg of lamb, untied, pounded a little after boning
	2 tablespoons mustard
½ cup fresh mint leaves, or 3 or 4 tablespoons dried mint	

In a shallow roasting pan, combine 1 tablespoon mixed peppercorns, rosemary, mint, garlic, vinegar, soy sauce, and wine. Place roast in pan; marinate 8 hours, turning occasionally. Remove lamb; drain; reserve marinade. Roll roast and tie. Spread mustard over meat and sprinkle with remaining peppercorns. Place roast in roasting pan; pour marinade around, *not over,* it. Bake at 350° for 1½ hours, or 18 minutes per pound. Let stand 10 to 15 minutes before cutting.

David Smith
Little Rock, Arkansas

HAM RING WITH CHERRY SAUCE
6 servings.

1	pound ground smoked ham	½	cup milk
1	pound ground fresh pork	¼	cup brown sugar
2	eggs, beaten	1	teaspoon prepared mustard
1½	cups wheat flakes cereal	1	teaspoon cloves

In mixing bowl combine first 5 ingredients; mix well. Turn into a lightly greased 1½-quart ring mold, or 5 × 9-inch loaf pan. Combine remaining ingredients; spread over top. Bake at 350° 1 hour for ring mold, or 1½ hours for loaf. Drain; invert on serving platter. Serve with Cherry Sauce.

Cherry Sauce:

1	(16½-ounce) can red tart cherries, drained, liquid reserved	2	tablespoons cornstarch
		¼	teaspoon cloves
		¼	teaspoon red food coloring
½	cup sugar		

In sauce pan combine sugar, cornstarch, and cloves; gradually stir in cherry liquid. Cook, stirring constantly, until thickened. Add food coloring and cherries.

Polly Crank
Foreman, Arkansas

◇ Marion Crank, Arkansas State Representative, Little River County, 1951-1969.

SWEET AND SOUR PORK ROAST
8 to 10 servings.

1	(4- to 5-lb.) pork roast	1	(16-ounce) can chunk pineapple
	Salt and pepper		
1	tablespoon oil	1	green pepper, cut in 1-inch squares
1	(12-ounce) bottle chili sauce		
1	(12-ounce) jar apricot preserves		

Season roast with salt and pepper; brown in oil in a Dutch oven. Cover; bake at 250° 1 hour. Add chili sauce and preserves; bake 5 hours at 250°. Add pineapple and green pepper; bake 1 hour more.

Elizabeth Wilson Harris
Nelda Smith Wilson
Nashville, Arkansas

GLAZED HAM
10 to 14 servings.

1 (5 to 7 lb.) uncooked ham	1½ teaspoons flour
Whole cloves	½ teaspoon dry mustard
½ cup firmly packed brown sugar	1 tablespoon cider vinegar

Score fat on ham in a diamond design; stud with cloves. Place ham, fat side up, on rack in a shallow roasting pan. Bake, uncovered, about 2½ to 3 hours (allowing 22 to 25 minutes per pound, or until meat thermometer reaches 160°). Combine remaining ingredients; spread glaze over ham during last 30 minutes of baking.

Mrs. Morris Bushnell
Fort Acres, Texas
Margaret Tollett

HAM-SAUSAGE LOAF
6 to 8 servings.

3 cups ground cured ham	½ cup apple cider
2 cups ground sausage	4 tablespoons chili sauce
1 cup fine bread crumbs	1 tablespoon prepared mustard
½ cup finely minced green pepper	1 tablespoon Worcestershire sauce
½ cup finely minced onion	
2 eggs, beaten	2 or 3 bacon slices

In mixing bowl combine all ingredients except bacon thoroughly. Turn into a 5 × 9-inch loaf pan; top with bacon slices. Bake at 350° for 1 hour. For a spicier loaf, use hot sausage meat.

Jeanette Rockefeller
Seattle, Washington
Lucile Brown
Los Angeles, California

PORK IN SWEET AND SOUR SAUCE
6 servings.

1 pound pork tenderloin, cut in 1-inch cubes	1 small green pepper, cut in 1-inch squares
1 tablespoon white wine	½ cup sliced carrots
2 tablespoons soy sauce	1 small onion, quartered
1 teaspoon ginger	½ cup bamboo shoots, drained
½ teaspoon Accent	½ cup pineapple chunks, drained
½ clove garlic, pressed	
2 egg yolks, or 1 egg, beaten	2 tablespoons oil
4 tablespoons cornstarch	¼ teaspoon salt

Combine meat with next 5 ingredients; marinate 2 to 3 hours, or overnight. Combine egg and cornstarch; drain meat; combine with batter; deep fry at 420° until crisp. Drain; set aside; keep warm. In a skillet, sauté green pepper, carrots, and onion until crisp-tender; add bamboo shoots and pineapple; heat through; season with salt. To serve, combine meat, vegetables, and sauce; serve over steamed rice.

Sweet and Sour Sauce:

6 tablespoons sugar	½ cup pineapple juice
2 tablespoons soy sauce	½ cup water
1 tablespoon white wine	2 tablespoons cornstarch
2 tablespoons white vinegar	

Combine first 5 ingredients in a sauce pan; bring to a boil. Mix water and cornstarch; gradually add to hot mixture, stirring constantly. Cook and stir until thickened.

Nelda Smith Wilson
Nashville, Arkansas

SAUSAGE-APPLE BAKE
4 servings.

3 cups mashed sweet potatoes	½ teaspoon cinnamon
1 cup applesauce	¼ teaspoon nutmeg
2 eggs, beaten	1 pound link sausages
½ teaspoon salt	

Combine all ingredients, except sausages, in a shallow 1½-quart baking dish. Cook sausages until well browned; arrange over potato mixture. Bake at 350° about 30 minutes.

Arkansas Egg Council
Arkansas Poultry Federation

HAM ROLLS
6 to 8 servings.

1⅓ pounds ground ham	½ cup brown sugar
⅓ pound ground pork	1 teaspoon prepared mustard
2 eggs, beaten	½ tablespoon vinegar
2 cups cracker crumbs	½ cup water
2 cups milk	

In large bowl combine first 5 ingredients; mix well. Shape into a thick roll; cut in slices 1-inch thick; place cut side down in a greased 9 × 13-inch baking pan. Combine sugar, mustard, vinegar, and water; pour over slices. Bake at 350° for 1 hour, basting occasionally.

Mrs. Clem Moore
Batesville, Arkansas

◇ *Governor J. M. Futrell, 1933-1937.*

PORK CHOP-NOODLE CASSEROLE
6 to 8 servings.

3 or 4 pounds lean pork chops	1 (10¾-ounce) can cream of mushroom soup
1 cup chopped onion	1 pound Velveeta cheese, cubed
½ cup chopped bell pepper	1 (2-ounce) can mushrooms, sliced
½ cup chopped celery	Salt and pepper to taste
¼ cup butter	1 (12-ounce) package macaroni, or noodles, cooked, drained
1 (13-ounce) can evaporated milk	
1 (10¾-ounce) can cream of chicken soup	

In a skillet, fry chops; cool; cut meat in bit-size pieces; set aside. In same skillet, sauté onion, pepper, and celery in butter; set aside. In a large sauce pan, mix and heat soups and milk; add cheese; stir over low heat until cheese melts. Add meat, sautéed vegetables, and mushrooms; season to taste. Add noodles; gently combine; heat through; remove from heat. Cover; let stand for 10 minutes.

Virginia Terral
Poplar Grove, Arkansas

 Governor Thomas J. Terral, 1925-1927.

ORANGE-GLAZED PORK CHOPS

4 servings.

4 large lean pork chops	2 tablespoons orange marmelade
Salt and pepper	
Flour	2 tablespoons brown sugar
1 tablespoon shortening	1 tablespoon vinegar
½ cup orange juice	

Dredge chops in seasoned flour; in a heavy skillet, brown on both sides in shortening. Combine remaining ingredients; pour over chops. Cover; simmer until meat is tender, about 45 minutes. Remove cover for last 10 minutes cooking. To serve, spoon sauce over meat.

Olive Whitmore
Arkadelphia, Arkansas
Faye Mobbs

PAT McGOLDRICK'S ONE-STOP CHOPS

8 servings.

1 teaspoon salt	½ cup water
8 lean pork chops	1 (8-ounce) package egg noodles
1 cup chopped celery	
1 (10¾-ounce) can tomato soup	

Sprinkle salt in a skillet; fry chops lightly on both sides; remove; set aside. Add celery, sauté until tender; stir in soup and water. Place raw noodles in bottom of a greased 9 × 13-inch baking pan; pour most of the sauce over noodles. Arrange chops over noodles; spoon remaining sauce on top. Cover: bake at 350° about 1 hour, or until chops are tender.

Kathy McGoldrick

TASTY PORK TENDERS
4 servings.

3 tablespoons flour	2 to 3 tablespoons oil
1 teaspoon dry mustard	1 cup chicken broth
¼ teaspoon pepper	½ cup white wine
2 pounds pork tenderloin, cut in 1-inch strips	½ cup water
	1 (4-ounce) can mushrooms

Mix dry ingredients; rub into meat. In a skillet, brown meat in oil over high heat; pour in liquids and mushrooms. Reduce heat and simmer, covered, for 30 to 40 minutes, stirring occasionally. Serve over rice.

Cathy Wilson
Nashville, Arkansas

PORK CHOP SKILLET MEAL
4 servings.

1 tablespoon oil	4 tablespoons rice
4 pork chops, 1-inch thick	3 cups chopped stewed tomatoes
4 slices onion, ½-inch thick	1 cup diced celery
4 green pepper rings, ¼-inch thick	1 teaspoon salt

Grease a heavy covered skillet with oil; brown chops well on both sides. On each chop place 1 slice onion and 1 pepper ring; spoon 1 tablespoon rice into rings. Combine remaining ingredients; pour over chops. Cover; cook on high heat until steaming, about 8 minutes; reduce heat and simmer about 1 hour, or until meat is tender.

Emma Phillips
Norma Dell Pell

SWEET AND SOUR WIENERS
4 servings.

1 cup catsup	1 pound wieners, sliced diagonally
½ cup vinegar	
1 cup brown sugar	

Combine all ingredients, mixing well. Cook in crock pot on LOW 4 to 5 hours, or simmer in a heavy skillet, covered, for about 1 hour.

Glenda Campbell
Steve Stallard

PORK CHOP DINNER
4 to 6 servings.

6 pork chops, ¾ inch thick	1 egg, beaten
Prepared mustard	1 cup soft bread crumbs
½ teaspoon salt	¼ cup chopped onion
Dash of pepper	¼ cup chopped green pepper
1 (18-ounce) can cream-style corn	2 tablespoons chopped pimento
1 (12-ounce) can whole kernel corn	

In a skillet, brown pork chops over medium heat; remove; spread lightly with mustard; salt and pepper. Arrange chops in a greased 9 × 13-inch baking pan. Combine remaining ingredients; spoon mixture around chops. Bake, uncovered, at 350° about 1 hour, or until meat is tender.

Allie Patrick
Arkadelphia, Arkansas

BARBECUED PORK CHOPS
6 servings.

3 tablespoons catsup	1 teaspoon salt
3 tablespoons vinegar	1 teaspoon dry mustard
3 tablespoons lemon juice	1 teaspoon chili powder
2 tablespoons Worcestershire sauce	1 teaspoon paprika
4 tablespoons water	½ teaspoon red pepper
2 tablespoons butter	6 lean pork chops, 1-inch thick
3 tablespoons brown sugar	

In a sauce pan, combine and heat all ingredients except pork chops. Dip chops, one at a time, into heated sauce; seal individually in foil. Place on a baking sheet; bake at 500° for 15 minutes; lower temperature to 300° and bake 1 hour and 15 minutes.

Florence Whitmore Bethea
Bearden, Arkansas
Stella Mize

PORK CHOPS AND CREAM GRAVY
4 servings.

4 lean pork chops, ½- to ¾-inch thick	1 tablespoon oil
Salt and pepper to taste	2 tablespoons flour
	1½ cups milk

In a heavy skillet, brown seasoned chops in oil over medium heat; remove with slotted spoon; set aside. Add flour to pan drippings; cook until bubbly, stirring constantly. Gradually add milk; simmer until slightly thickened, stirring constantly. Add chops to gravy; cover and simmer 30 to 45 minutes, or until meat is tender. Stir occasionally.

Kimberly and Myra Hale

GOLDEN HAM CASSEROLE
4 servings.

2 cups cubed potatoes	¼ cup margarine
1 cup diced carrots	3 tablespoons flour
1 cup chopped celery	2 cups milk
3 tablespoons butter	½ cup shredded cheese
2 tablespoons finely chopped green pepper	½ teaspoon salt
	¼ teaspoon black pepper
1 tablespoon finely chopped onion	2 cups cubed cooked ham
	½ cup bread crumbs

Steam first 3 ingredients until crisp-tender; set aside. In sauce pan, sauté green pepper and onion in butter until transparent; set aside. In separate pan melt ¼ cup margarine; stir in flour; cook 1 minute, stirring constantly; gradually add milk. Reduce heat; add cheese, salt, and pepper; cook and stir until thickened. Combine steamed and sautéed vegetables with ham; turn into a greased shallow 2-quart casserole. Pour sauce over mixture; sprinkle with bread crumbs. Bake at 350° for 25 minutes.

Grace Stuart
Mineral Springs, Arkansas

COUNTRY HAM AND RED-EYE GRAVY
4 servings.

1 pound cured ham, in ¼-inch slices	½ cup strong black coffee, or cold water

Fry ham slices in a skillet until light brown; remove; keep warm. Quickly add coffee to pan drippings, stirring constantly; simmer 5 minutes. Serve gravy spooned over ham. Recipe adjusts easily; increase liquid for each pound of ham.

Serena Cusson

ITALIAN SAUSAGE SUPPER
4 to 6 servings.

1 pound bulk pork sausage	1 teaspoon garlic salt
1 cup chopped onion	1 teaspoon salt
1 cup chopped green pepper	1 teaspoon oregano
1 (16-ounce) can tomatoes	1 (8-ounce) package egg noodles
1 cup water	
1 tablespoon sugar	1 cup sour cream

In large skillet sauté meat, onion, and pepper until meat is browned and onion is tender; drain fat. Stir in remaining ingredients except sour cream; cover; simmer 20 minutes or until noodles are tender; add more water if needed. Add sour cream; heat through.

Hilda Sinesh
Powderly, Texas

SAUSAGE-RICE CASSEROLE
8 to 10 servings.

1 cup rice	1 (14½-ounce) can chicken broth
2 cups chopped carrots	
1 large onion, chopped	¼ cup water
1 cup chopped celery	1 pound bulk pork sausage
½ cup chopped green pepper	1 (8-ounce) can sliced mushrooms

Spread rice evenly in a lightly greased 3-quart casserole; spoon vegetables over rice. Combine broth and water; pour over mixture. In a skillet, brown sausage; drain well; spoon over vegetables. Cover; bake at 350° for 30 minutes. Remove from oven; stir well; add mushrooms. Cover; bake an additional 30 minutes.

Gregory Hale
Bryan Clay

SAUSAGE SUPPER DISH
4 to 6 servings.

1 pound Hot Rudy's Sausage	1½ cups buttermilk
1 bell pepper, finely chopped	1 (6 to 8-ounce) package wide noodles
Pinch of salt	
1 onion, finely chopped	Dash chili powder, optional
2 (16-ounce) cans tomatoes	

In large skillet brown sausage; drain fat. Add vegetables and seasonings; simmer 15 to 20 minutes. Add buttermilk and noodles; cook until noodles are tender.

Jeanette C. Rudy
RUDY'S SAUSAGE

RUDY'S SAUSAGE has a processing plant in North Little Rock.

OVEN "BOILED" DINNER
4 servings.

1 pound knockwurst, or smoked sausage	½ teaspoon caraway seed
2 large baking potatoes, scrubbed, quartered	2 apples, quartered, cored
	1 tablespoon flour
4 medium carrots, sliced	2 teaspoons brown mustard
1 head cabbage, quartered	½ teaspoon prepared horseradish
1¼ cups apple juice, divided	

Prick skin of knockwurst, or slash several times, arrange with vegetables in a large shallow roasting pan. Pour 1 cup apple juice over all; sprinkle with caraway seed; cover tightly. Bake at 375° 50 to 60 minutes, or until potatoes are tender. Place apples in small baking dish; cover tightly; place in oven 15 to 20 minutes before main dish is done. With slotted spoon, lift meat, vegetables, and apples from pans; arrange on serving platter. Pour pan juices into a sauce pan; stir flour into ¼ cup apple juice; stir into pan liquid. Bring to a boil; stir until thickened; add mustard and horseradish. Pour sauce over "boiled" dinner.

Janet Sharum

PIZZA

Yield: 1 12-inch pizza

1 clove garlic, minced	3 (6-ounce) cans tomato paste
1 onion, chopped	2 teaspoons sugar
3 tablespoons olive oil	1 bay leaf
3 (15-ounce) cans stewed tomatoes	Salt, pepper, oregano, and sweet basil to taste

In large sauce pan, brown garlic and onion in oil; add tomatoes, tomato paste and seasonings. Simmer 1 hour; remove bay leaf; puree in a blender.

Pizza Dough:

1 package yeast	1 teaspoon salt
1 cup warm water (105-115°)	2 tablespoons salad oil
1 teaspoon sugar	2½ cups flour

Dissolve yeast in warm water; combine with remaining ingredients; beat vigorously about 20 strokes. Cover dough; let rest 5 minutes. Punch down; pat evenly into a 12-inch pizza pan. Spread 1 to 1½ cups sauce evenly over dough. Cover with desired toppings: browned sausages or ground beef, pepperoni, sliced mushrooms, green peppers, or green onions. Top with grated cheese. Bake at 350° about 30 minutes.

Jan Hendrix
Morene Akers

◊ Carl E. Hendrix, Speaker, Arkansas House of Representatives, 1949.

SAUSAGE AND PEPPERS

4 servings.

1 pound Italian sausage, sliced	1 large onion, sliced
2 large green peppers, cut in strips	¼ teaspoon oregano

In a skillet, brown sausage well on all sides; remove; set aside. Add remaining ingredients; sauté until crisp-tender; add sausage and heat through.

Sally Quinn

SPAGHETTI WITH WIENER SAUCE

4 to 6 servings.

⅓ cup chopped onion	1 to 2 teaspoons chili powder
⅓ cup chopped celery	¼ teaspoon salt
1 tablespoon oil	Pinch of pepper
2 (8-ounce) cans tomato sauce	1 (8-ounce) package spaghetti, cooked, drained
1 pound wieners, sliced diagonally	Grated Cheddar cheese

In large skillet, sauté onion and celery in oil until crisp-tender. Add remaining ingredients except spaghetti and cheese; cover; cook over medium heat 30 minutes; stir occasionally. To serve, spoon wieners and sauce over spaghetti; sprinkle with cheese. Serve immediately.

Reuben Maxwell
Grace Crosslin

HOG DOG CASSEROLE

6 servings.

½ cup rice	¾ cup catsup
10 wieners, sliced diagonally	½ cup water
1 (17-ounce) can whole kernel corn, drained, liquid reserved	½ cup diced green pepper
	1 teaspoon chili powder
	½ teaspoon dry mustard
2 tablespoons butter	¼ teaspoon garlic powder
1 cup chopped onion	½ bay leaf

Layer rice in bottom of a greased 2½-quart casserole; add wieners; spread with a layer of corn. In a skillet, sauté onion in butter; add corn liquid and remaining ingredients; mix well and pour over corn layer. Cover; bake at 400° for 30 minutes, or until rice is done.

Cedell Thomas
Saginaw, Michigan
Marsha Higgins

BRAISED VEAL
8 servings.

2 pounds veal stew meat, cut in 1-inch slices	1 teaspoon curry powder
½ cup seasoned flour	Pinch of tarragon
¼ cup butter	10 small onions
1 large onion, diced	1 small turnip, quartered
1 cup hot water	4 carrots, cut in 1-inch slices
1 bay leaf, crumbled	Salt and pepper to taste

Dredge meat in seasoned flour; in a large skillet sauté meat in butter over low heat, stirring to prevent sticking. As the meat browns, add onion. Add hot water, bay leaf, curry powder and tarragon; simmer, covered, 1½ hours. Add vegetables; season to taste; simmer until vegetables and meat are tender, about 30 minutes.

Richelean Counts

VEAL PARMESAN
6 servings.

6 tablespoons butter, melted	1 (16-ounce) can tomato sauce
1 cup corn flake crumbs	1 tablespoon sugar
½ cup grated Parmesan cheese	1 teaspoon oregano
½ teaspoon salt	Dash onion salt
½ teaspoon pepper	4 or 5 slices Mozzarella cheese
3 eggs, beaten	
1 pound veal cutlets, or tenderized round steak	

Coat bottom of a 9 × 13-inch baking dish with butter. Combine corn flakes, cheese, salt and pepper in small bowl; the beaten eggs in a separate bowl. Dip meat pieces in egg, then in crumb mixture; arrange in baking dish. Bake at 400° 20 minutes; turn meat, cook 15 more minutes. In sauce pan bring tomato sauce, sugar and spices to a boil; pour over steak. Top with cheese slices; return to oven until cheese melts.

Eva T. Verducci

LOW-CALORIE VEAL SCALLOPINI
4 servings.

1	tablespoon lemon juice	1	medium zucchini, grated
½	teaspoon salt, divided	1	large yellow squash, grated
½	teaspoon basil	1	teaspoon margarine
¼	teaspoon oregano	½	pound fresh mushrooms, sliced
2	cloves garlic, pressed		
4	medium veal scallops	1	medium onion, sliced

In a small bowl combine lemon juice, ¼ teaspoon salt, basil, oregano, and garlic. Brush veal on both sides with lemon-herb mixture; set aside; reserve remaining lemon-herb mixture. Season squashes with ¼ teaspoon salt; steam, covered, 3 minutes; keep warm.

In a skillet sauté veal in margarine over high heat until brown on one side; turn; add mushrooms and onion; cook 3 minutes. Place zucchini-squash mixture on platter; arrange veal on top. Sauté mushrooms and onion, covered, 1 minute longer; stir in reserved lemon-herb mixture; spoon over veal.

Geraldine Smith Helms

SQUIRREL STEW
6 servings.

3	squirrels, cleaned	1	(12-ounce) can whole kernel corn
2	onions, chopped		
1	green pepper, chopped	½	teaspoon garlic powder
3	medium potatoes, diced		Dash Tabasco sauce
¼	cup diced celery		Salt and pepper to taste
1	(18-ounce) can tomatoes		

In large heavy pot cover squirrels with water; cook until tender. Lift from broth; cool; reserve broth. When cool, bone; return meat to broth. Bring mixture to a boil; add remaining ingredients; reduce heat and simmer until vegetables are tender.

Joe Beyette
DeWayne Houser

SMOTHERED VENISON
4 to 6 servings.

1½ to 2 pounds venison steaks	1 (10¾-ounce) can cream of mushroom soup
Flour	¾ soup can milk
¼ to ½ cup oil	Salt and pepper to taste
½ cup chopped onion	Dash Tabasco sauce

Lightly flour steaks. In large, deep skillet brown meat in oil; drain; set aside. Combine remaining ingredients in skillet; stir well; return meat to pan; cover. Over medium heat, bring to a boil; reduce heat; simmer for 30 minutes. Serve over rice or noodles.

Paddy Dickinson Bell

SKILLET BBQ VENISON
6 to 8 servings.

1 large onion, chopped	1 (10-ounce) can beer
6 tablespoons margarine, divided	1 tablespoon mustard
2 tablespoons Worcestershire sauce	1 jalapeño pepper, finely chopped
2 tablespoons lemon juice	½ teaspoon black pepper
1 tablespoon vinegar	½ teaspoon red pepper
½ cup brown sugar	3 to 3½ pounds venison steak, cubed
1 teaspoon salt	1 cup water

In Dutch oven sauté onion in 2 tablespoons margarine until clear. Add next 10 ingredients; simmer while preparing meat. In a heavy skillet sauté venison in remaining margarine until brown; add water; simmer until tender. Add steaks and skillet liquid to mixture in Dutch oven; simmer, covered, about 30 minutes.

Roy Hickman
Cedar Hill, Texas
Jerry Killian

POULTRY

SOUTHERN FRIED CHICKEN
4 to 6 servings

1 (2½- to 3½-lb.) fryer, cut up	2 teaspoons salt
Salt	½ teaspoon pepper
1½ cups flour	Shortening or vegetable oil

Salt fryer pieces; refrigerate several hours or overnight; rinse. Place flour, salt and pepper in a paper bag; drop in chicken pieces, a few at a time; shake until well coated. Pan fry, covered, in hot shortening or oil (350° to 360°) 20 to 30 minutes, until golden crispy on both sides. Turn often with tongs or slotted spoon; do not pierce meat while frying. Drain well.

Leoti Cox

CHICKEN WITH ARTICHOKES
6 servings.

- 3 large chicken breasts, skinned, boned, and split
- 1 cup flour
- Salt and pepper to taste
- ½ cup olive oil
- 2 onions, chopped
- 1 bell pepper, chopped
- 1 (14-ounce) can artichoke hearts, drained
- 1 (4-ounce) can mushrooms, drained
- 1 cup cream sherry
- 1 (10¾-ounce) can cream of mushroom soup
- Paprika, tarragon, salt and pepper to taste

Dredge chicken pieces in seasoned flour. In a skillet brown chicken in olive oil; drain and place in a greased 9 × 13-inch baking dish. In same pan sauté onions and pepper; spoon over chicken. Combine remaining ingredients; season to taste; pour over chicken. Cover; bake at 350° 1 hour.

Mary E. Steel Allison

 Governor Harris Flanagin, 1862-1864.

BAJA CALIFORNIA CHICKEN
Yield: 8 servings.

- 8 boned chicken breasts
- Seasoning salt and pepper, to taste
- 2 cloves garlic, crushed
- 4 tablespoons olive oil
- 4 tablespoons tarragon vinegar
- ⅔ cup dry sherry

Sprinkle chicken with seasoning salt and pepper. Crush garlic into oil and vinegar in a skillet. Sauté chicken pieces until golden brown, turning frequently. Remove; place in an oiled 9 × 13-inch baking dish. Pour sherry over chicken and place in 350° oven for 10 minutes.

Nancy Reagan
The White House
Washington, D. C.

CALIFORNIA CHICKEN BREASTS
4 to 6 servings.

6 whole chicken breasts	Onion powder, Accent, and seasoning salt, to taste
1 cup mayonnaise	Crushed potato chips
1 (10¾-ounce) can cream of chicken soup	Slivered almonds
2 tablespoons lemon juice	

Cook chicken breasts in seasoned water until tender; cool, skin and bone. Combine mayonnaise, soup, and lemon juice; season to taste with onion powder, Accent, and seasoning salt. Coat chicken breasts thoroughly with sauce; place in a buttered 9 × 13-inch baking dish; cover with remaining sauce; sprinkle with chips and almonds. Bake at 350° until well browned and bubbly, about 30 minutees.

Polly Crank

◇ Marion Crank, Speaker, Arkansas House of Representatives, 1963.

SWEET AND SOUR CHICKEN
4 servings.

2 whole chicken breasts, skinned, boned, cut in 1-inch pieces	1 tablespoon paprika
	1 (20-ounce) can pineapple chunks
½ teaspoon salt	¼ cup soy sauce
1 egg, beaten	¼ cup cider vinegar
¾ cup biscuit mix	1 cup green pepper strips
1 cup cooking oil	½ cup sliced onion
⅔ cup sugar	2 medium tomatoes, cut up
2 tablespoons cornstarch	

Sprinkle chicken with salt, coat with egg, then biscuit mix; fry in hot oil in a small skillet until brown. Remove; drain on paper towels; place in warm oven. In a 10-inch skillet combine sugar, cornstarch, and paprika. Drain pineapple; add water to juice to measure 2 cups; add with soy sauce and vinegar to cornstarch mixture. Cook, stirring constantly, until mixture boils. Boil 1 minute; add green pepper and onion; cover, cook vegetables until crisp-tender, about 5 minutes. Add pineapple and tomatoes; heat through. To serve, arrange chicken on bed of hot rice; pour sauce over chicken; serve immediately.

Betty Bumpers
Charleston, Arkansas

◇ Dale Bumpers, Governor, 1971-1975; U. S. Senator, 1975-1987.

CASSOULET

6 to 8 servings.

1½ pounds chicken, cut up	1 tablespoon thyme
6 sweet Italian sausages, or 1 pound smoked sausage, cut in 1-inch pieces	1 tablespoon salt
	1 bay leaf
	Black pepper to taste
2 tablespoons butter	Tabasco sauce to taste
1 large onion, sliced	2 (15½-ounce) cans white navy beans, drained
1 clove garlic, crushed	
1 green pepper, sliced	¼ cup dry white wine
1 (16-ounce) can tomatoes	

In a large skillet sauté chicken and sausage in butter until well browned; add onion, garlic, and green pepper; sauté lightly. Add tomatoes and seasonings; reduce heat and simmer 30 minutes. Add beans and wine; cook, covered, an additional 30 minutes, or until chicken is tender.

Richard Norton
Benton, Arkansas

CHERRY CHICKEN

4 to 6 servings.

3 whole chicken breasts, halved	¼ cup oil
⅓ cup flour	1 (16-ounce) can pitted dark sweet cherries
1½ teaspoons salt	
1½ teaspoons garlic salt	1 cup Sauterne, or other sweet dessert wine
1½ teaspoons paprika	

Dredge chicken in mixture of flour, salt, garlic salt, and paprika. In a skillet brown chicken in oil. Add cherries, including liquid, and wine; cover, and simmer about 1 hour. Serve over hot rice.

Carolyn Coulter Kueteman
LaMarque, Texas

CHICKEN IN CHILI-TOMATO SAUCE
4 servings.

2	tablespoons butter	1	(28-ounce) can tomatoes
2	tablespoons oil	1	(4-ounce) can green chilies, seeded, chopped
3	pounds chicken pieces		
1	large onion, chopped	1	cup water
2	cloves garlic, crushed	1	cube chicken bouillon, crushed
½	cup chopped fresh parsley, divided		
			Salt and pepper to taste

In a large skillet over medium-high heat, heat butter and oil. Brown chicken, a few pieces at a time, on all sides; remove from pan as browned. Discard all but 2 tablespoons fat in pan; add onion, garlic and ⅓ cup parsley; cook, stirring, until onion is soft. Add tomatoes, including liquid, breaking them with a spoon, chilies, water, and bouillon cube. Simmer rapidly, uncovered, about 15 minutes, or until slightly thickened; season to taste. Return chicken to pan; cover, and simmer until tender, about 45 minutes. Turn into serving dish; garnish with remaining parsley. Serve with hot rice.

JoAnn Todd
Vancouver, British Columbia

CHICKEN DRUMETTES TERIYAKI
4 to 6 servings.

½	cup oil	½	cup soy sauce
½	cup flour	1½	cups water
2	pounds chicken drumettes (meaty side of wings)	½	cup sugar
		1	cup chopped green onions

Mix oil and flour; coat chicken pieces in mixture and arrange in a greased 8 × 12-inch baking dish. In a sauce pan combine remaining ingredients; heat until sugar is dissolved; pour hot mixture over chicken. Bake, uncovered, at 350° for 1 hour, stirring chicken once or twice to brown evenly.

Bess Emerson Torgerson
Aiea, Hawaii

HERBED CHICKEN BREASTS
4 servings.

4 large chicken breasts, boned
Herb Basting Sauce
1½ tablespoons minced parsley

Turn each breast in Herb Basting Sauce to coat well. Tuck edges under, forming a compact shape about 1½ inches thick; place skin side up in a 9-inch-square baking dish. Roast at 425°, basting occasionally with pan drippings, about 15 to 20 minutes, until tender. Remove to warm plates, spoon pan juices over chicken; sprinkle with parsley.

Herb Basting Sauce:

3½ tablespoons melted butter
1 tablespoon finely grated onion
1 large clove garlic, crushed
1 teaspoon crumbled thyme
½ teaspoon salt
½ teaspoon fresh ground pepper
½ teaspoon crumbled rosemary
¼ teaspoon sage
⅛ teaspoon crumbled marjoram
Dash hot pepper sauce

Stir all ingredients together until well blended.

Hillary Rodham Clinton
Little Rock, Arkansas

 Governor Bill Clinton, 1979-1981; 1983-1987.

ITALIAN CHICKEN
4 to 6 servings.

6 boneless chicken breasts, cut in strips
4 eggs, beaten
Italian bread crumbs
½ to ¾ cup butter
1 cup sliced fresh mushrooms
½ cup dry white wine
¼ to ½ cup chicken broth
4 to 6 slices Muenster cheese

Coat chicken strips in eggs; cover; refrigerate 4 hours. In a skillet lightly sauté mushrooms; remove with slotted spoon; set aside. Roll chicken strips in bread crumbs; in same skillet used to cook mushrooms, fry until lightly browned. Place chicken in greased 9 × 13-inch baking dish; cover with mushrooms. Mix wine and broth; pour over chicken; cover with cheese slices; bake, uncovered, 30 minutes at 350°.

Linda Warren

BO PILGRIM'S ITALIAN CHICKEN MEDLEY

6 to 8 servings.

1	Pilgrim's Pride Boneless Chicken, cut into 8 pieces, drained
2	tablespoons olive oil
2	tablespoons butter
1	large onion, thinly sliced, separated into rings
2	cloves garlic, minced
1	large green pepper, cut in thin strips
2	tomatoes, seeded, cut in wedges
8	ounces fresh mushrooms, sliced
1	(6-ounce) can artichoke hearts, drained, cut in quarters
1	cup dry red or white wine
1	bay leaf
⅓	teaspoon sage
1	tablespoon oregano
½	teaspoon basil
1	teaspoon sugar
Salt and pepper to taste	

In a heavy, deep skillet brown chicken in oil and butter, skin side down; remove. Add onion, garlic, and green pepper; sauté until tender. Add tomatoes, mushrooms and artichokes; cook 5 minutes. Add wine and seasonings and blend. Return chicken to skillet; cover and simmer 1 hour, or until chicken is tender.

Bo Pilgrim
Pilgrim Industries of Arkansas
DeQueen, Arkansas

BAKED CHICKEN ITALIAN

6 to 8 servings.

1	(2-to 3-lb.) fryer, cut up
Salt to taste	
½	cup chopped onion
1	tablespoon Italian seasoning
1	tablespoon leaf oregano
½	cup wine vinegar
½	cup water
1	tablespoon Worcestershire sauce
1	tablespoon A-1 Steak sauce
Dash Tabasco sauce	

Salt chicken; place in a greased 9 × 13-inch baking dish; sprinkle with onions, Italian seasoning, and oregano. Combine remaining ingredients; pour over chicken. Cover; bake at 350° 30 minutes. Remove cover; bake an additional 15 to 20 minutes, or until brown.

Fannie Pickett

CURRIED MANGO CHICKEN
4 servings.

3 tablespoons butter	½ cup golden raisins
1 medium onion, sliced, separated into rings	1½ cups chicken broth
	2 teaspoons curry powder
2 large chicken breasts, skinned, boned, halved	1 tablespoon cornstarch
	2 tablespoons water
2 large ripe mangos, peeled	

In a large heavy skillet sauté onion and chicken until golden brown. Remove chicken from pan; arrange alternately with slices of mango in a buttered 1-quart casserole.

Add raisins and broth to the onion in the pan; heat. In small bowl whisk until smooth the curry, cornstarch and water. Stirring, add gradually to skillet mixture. Stir and cook until sauce is smooth and thickened; pour over chicken and mango. (Dish may be refrigerated at this point.) Bake at 375° about 30 minutes, or until chicken is tender. Serve with hot rice.

Annie Quinn Dilday
Vancouver, British Columbia

CHICKEN MARENGO
4 servings.

1 (2½-lb.) fryer, cut up	½ cup dry white wine, or chicken broth
¼ cup vegetable oil	
½ cup chopped onion	1 (3-ounce) can sliced mushrooms, drained, liquid reserved
1 clove garlic, minced	
¼ teaspoon marjoram	
1 teaspoon salt	2 tomatoes, peeled, quartered
⅛ teaspoon pepper	Chopped parsley

In large skillet brown chicken slowly in hot oil. Add onion, garlic and marjoram; cook until onion is soft; season with salt and pepper. Add wine and mushroom liquid; scrape bottom of pan to loosen browned bits. Cover; cook over low heat until chicken is tender, about 35 minutes. Add mushrooms and tomatoes; continue cooking, covered, 5 minutes. Garnish with parsley.

Helen Montgomery

MINTY CHICKEN
6 servings.

1 (2-to 3-lb.) fryer, cut up	1 teaspoon oregano
2 tablespoons lemon juice	1 tablespoon mint leaves, crushed
1 tablespoon salt	
1 teaspoon pepper	¼ teaspoon garlic powder

Place chicken in a greased 9 × 13-inch baking dish; drizzle with lemon juice. Mix spices; sprinkle over chicken. Bake at 350° for 20 minutes; turn, and bake 20 minutes longer, or until tender.

Norma McDonald

PAELLA ESPAÑOLA
10 to 12 servings.

½ cup olive oil	½ teaspoon saffron
2 chicken breasts, boned, cubed	4 cups clam juice
	½ cup frozen green peas
2 pork chops, boned, cubed	Salt, pepper, and Tabasco sauce to taste
½ pound sirloin, cubed	
1 onion, chopped	1 (8½-ounce) can artichoke hearts, drained, sliced
2 bell peppers, chopped	
2 cloves garlic, minced	1 pound fresh shrimp, cooked, shelled
4 tomatoes, peeled, quartered	
2 cups long grain rice	

In a skillet brown chicken, pork and beef in hot oil; remove and set aside. Sauté onion and pepper until tender; add garlic and tomatoes; simmer 5 minutes. In large mixing bowl, combine all ingredients; mix well. Pour into a greased 10 × 13-inch baking pan; bake uncovered at 350° for 30 minutes.

Janie Williams
San Antonio, Texas

PAPRIKA CHICKEN
4 to 6 servings.

3 pounds chicken pieces	4 tablespoons water, divided
2 tablespoons butter	2 tablespoons flour
½ cup chopped onion	½ teaspoon salt
1 teaspoon paprika	Black pepper to taste
2 tablespoons lemon juice	½ cup sour cream

In a large skillet brown chicken and onion in butter; add paprika, lemon juice and 2 tablespoons water; cover; cook over low heat until chicken is tender, 30 to 35 minutes. Remove pan from heat; transfer chicken to platter; keep warm. Skim and discard fat from skillet juices. Mix a smooth paste of flour and remaining 2 tablespoons water; stir into skillet juices; season. Bring to a boil, stirring; reduce heat; stir and cook until thickened. Blend in sour cream; warm. To serve, arrange chicken over bed of hot rice; pour a little sauce over chicken, serving remainder separately.

Janice Strauss
Denver, Colorado

CHICKEN DIVAN
6 to 8 servings.

2 (10-ounce) packages frozen broccoli spears, thawed	1 cup mayonnaise
2 to 3 cups chopped, cooked chicken	1 scant tablespoon lemon juice
2 (10¾-ounce) cans cream of chicken soup	1 cup grated Cheddar cheese
	1 cup buttered bread crumbs

Arrange broccoli stalks in a greased 2-quart casserole; place chicken evenly over broccoli. Combine soup, mayonnaise and lemon juice; pour over chicken. Sprinkle with cheese; top with bread crumbs. Bake at 350° 30 to 40 minutes.

Alta Faubus
Huntsville, Arkansas

 Governor Orville Faubus, 1952-1964.

BAKED CHICKEN PARMESAN
6 servings.

¼ cup butter, melted	½ teaspoon salt
½ cup flour	⅓ cup evaporated milk
¼ cup grated Parmesan cheese	1 fryer, cut up
1 teaspoon oregano	

Coat bottom of a 9 × 13-inch baking pan with butter. In a bowl combine flour, cheese, oregano, and salt. Pour milk into a small bowl. Dip chicken pieces, one at a time, into milk; roll in flour mixture, coating well. Place, skin side down, in pan. Bake at 400° for 20 minutes; turn and bake 20 to 30 minutes longer, or until tender.

Janice Frady

PEANUT CHICKEN WITH MUSTARD SAUCE
6 servings.

8 tablespoons butter, divided	3 tablespoons peanut oil
5 tablespoons Dijon mustard, divided	1 cup sour cream
6 to 8 boneless chicken breasts, pounded thin	¼ cup chopped parsley
1½ cups finely chopped roasted peanuts	¼ teaspoon salt
	¼ teaspoon pepper

In a sauce pan melt 6 tablespoons butter over medium heat; whisk in 3 tablespoons mustard until smooth. Dip breasts into mixture; then coat completely with peanuts.

In a large skillet over medium heat melt remaining butter; stir in oil. Sauté chicken breasts, 3 at a time, 3 minutes on each side, or until done; repeat with remaining breasts; keep warm. In small sauce pan combine sour cream, remaining mustard, parsley, salt and pepper; stir until smooth and heated through. To serve, spoon a portion of sauce onto each plate, top with chicken breast, garnish with parsley.

Donna Steel Matteson
Foreman, Arkansas

◇ Judge James S. Steel, Circuit Judge, 9th Circuit, 1902.

PEANUT CHICKEN ORIENTAL

8 servings.

2 pounds diced, boneless chicken breasts	3 tablespoons flour
¼ cup peanut oil	1 clove garlic, minced
1 (8-ounce) can sliced mushrooms	¼ cup molasses
½ cup chopped roasted peanuts	¼ cup soy sauce
	⅛ teaspoon ginger
	Dash cayenne pepper
½ cup minced green onions	¼ cup dry sherry

In a skillet brown chicken in oil. Add remaining ingredients, except sherry. Cook, stirring, until thickened. Cover and cook over low heat 10 minutes, stirring occasionally. Add sherry; heat through; serve over hot rice.

Charlotte Loftin
Colorado Springs, Colorado

POLYNESIAN CHICKEN

3 to 6 servings.

¼ pound butter, melted	2 tablespoons lime juice
1 envelope onion soup mix	3 whole chicken breasts, boned and split
1 tablespoon cornstarch	
1 (20-ounce) can pineapple chunks, drained, ¾ cup juice reserved	

In a small sauce pan combine butter, soup mix, cornstarch, and juices. Cook until mixture comes to a boil.

Roll chicken breasts; secure with toothpicks. Arrange chicken and pineapple chunks in a greased 2-quart oblong baking dish; pour hot sauce over chicken and fruit. Bake at 350° 45 minutes, or until chicken is tender. Delicious served with fried or wild rice.

Rita Formby
Shreveport, Louisiana
Joanne Todd
Vancouver, British Columbia

POPPY SEED CHICKEN

6 to 8 servings.

1 large fryer, cooked, boned, and chopped	50 Ritz crackers, crushed
2 (10¾-ounce) cans cream of chicken soup	2 tablespoons poppy seeds
	1 stick margarine, melted
1 (8-ounce) package cream cheese	

Arrange chicken evenly in bottom of a greased 9 × 13-inch baking dish. In sauce pan heat soup and cream cheese until mixed; pour over chicken. Mix crackers with poppy seeds; sprinkle over soup mixture. Pour margarine over crumbs. Bake at 350° until bubbly and slightly browned, about 30 minutes. Serve warm. Reheats well.

Keri Rusterholz

RELAXING CHICKEN

6 to 8 servings.

1 (2½-to 3-lb.) chicken, cut up	1 cup margarine, divided
Salt and pepper to taste	¼ cup lemon juice
Flour	¼ cup honey

Dredge chicken pieces in flour seasoned to taste. Melt ½ cup margarine in a 9 × 13-inch baking dish; place chicken in dish, turning to coat in the butter. Bake at 400°, skin side down in a single layer, 30 minutes. In a sauce pan melt ½ cup margarine; blend well with lemon juice and honey. Turn chicken; pour honey-lemon sauce over pieces; continue baking, basting often, until done, about 15 to 20 minutes.

Christine Brewer

CHICKEN ROSALIE
12 servings.

12 chicken breasts, boned, skinned	½ cup white wine
½ pound margarine	1 teaspoon poultry seasoning
12 slices ham	1 teaspoon thyme
1 cup sliced fresh mushrooms	¼ teaspoon sage
1 (10¾-ounce) can cream of mushroom soup	1 teaspoon paprika
1 (10¾-ounce) can cream of chicken soup	1 teaspoon Tabasco sauce
	¼ cup minced fresh parsley

In a skillet sauté chicken breasts lightly in margarine, a few at a time. Place each on a ham slice in 2 greased 9 × 13-inch pans. In same skillet sauté mushrooms; add remaining ingredients; mix well and spoon over chicken and ham. Sprinkle with parsley; cover and bake at 275° for 2½ hours.

Hope J. Norman
Alexandria, Louisiana

RUSSIAN CHICKEN BREASTS
6 servings.

6 chicken breasts, skinned	1 envelope onion soup mix
1 (8-ounce) bottle Russian salad dressing	1 (8-ounce) can water chestnuts, drained, sliced
1 (10-ounce) jar apricot preserves	

Place chicken in a greased 9 × 13-inch baking dish. Blend salad dressing, preserves, and soup mix; pour over chicken; cover, and bake at 350° 45 minutes. Remove cover; continue baking 20 minutes. Sprinkle water chestnuts over chicken 5 minutes before cooking time is completed. Serve over cooked rice.

Mrs. Howard Young
Texarkana, Texas
Nancy Jenkins

SCALLOPED CHICKEN WITH VEGETABLES
6 to 8 servings.

1½ tablespoons butter	2 cups milk
⅓ cup slivered almonds	2 cups sliced, cooked potatoes
1 envelope onion and mushroom soup mix	2 cups diced, cooked chicken
2 tablespoons flour	2 cups sliced, cooked carrots

In a sauce pan sauté almonds in butter until golden. Stir in soup mix, flour and milk; bring to a boil; reduce heat, and simmer, stirring, until slightly thickened, about 5 minutes. In a greased 1½-quart casserole layer 1 cup potatoes, 1 cup chicken and 1 cup carrots; cover with half the sauce. Repeat layers; top with remaining sauce. Bake at 350° until hot, about 30 minutes.

Betty Willich
Oklahoma City, Oklahoma

COUNTRY CAPTAIN CHICKEN
6 servings.

1½ pounds chicken pieces	¼ cup diced green pepper
¼ teaspoon salt	1 clove garlic, minced
⅛ teaspoon pepper	1¼ teaspoons curry powder
2 teaspoons flour	1½ cups drained tomatoes
2 tablespoons oil	2 tablespoons raisins
½ cup diced onion	¼ cup chicken broth
¼ cup diced carrots	

Sprinkle chicken with salt, pepper, and flour. In a large skillet, brown chicken on all sides in oil; remove; set aside. In same skillet sauté onion, carrots, pepper and garlic until tender but not brown. Add curry powder, tomatoes and raisins; bring to a boil. Return chicken to pan; pour in broth. Reduce heat; cover and simmer 30 minutes. Remove cover; simmer 5 to 10 minutes longer, or until chicken is tender.

Alice Parks

OVEN-FRIED SESAME CHICKEN

2 to 4 servings.

2 whole chicken breasts, or 1 small fryer, cut up	½ cup corn oil
1 teaspoon ginger	2 to 4 teaspoons sesame seeds
Salt and pepper to taste	

Rub chicken with ginger; sprinkle with salt and pepper; brush with oil. Place, skin side down, in a 9-inch square baking pan. Bake at 400° for 30 minutes; turn, sprinkle with sesame seeds and cook 15 minutes longer.

Mrs. Roy F. Golden
Arkadelphia, Arkansas

CHICKEN SAN JOSÉ

6 to 8 servings.

3 pounds chicken pieces	½ cup ripe tomatoes, peeled, seeded, quartered
1½ teaspoons paprika	
⅛ teaspoon cayenne pepper	2 cups hot chicken broth
1 cup brown rice	2 tablespoons chopped parsley
1 cup sliced onion	¼ cup sliced ripe olives
1 cup sliced celery	

Place chicken, skin side up, in a greased 9 × 13-inch baking pan; sprinkle with paprika and cayenne. Brown 20 minutes at 425°; remove from oven; lift out chicken with slotted spoon; set aside; add rice and next 4 ingredients to baking pan and stir well; arrange chicken over rice mixture. Cover; bake at 350° for 50 minutes, or until rice and chicken are tender and liquid is absorbed. Sprinkle with parsley and olives.

Myra Coulter Clay

SHERRIED CHICKEN

6 servings.

3 tablespoons butter	1 (8-ounce) can button mushrooms, drained, ⅓ cup liquid reserved
Seasoned salt to taste	
6 chicken breast halves	
⅓ cup sherry	1 (¾-ounce) package chicken gravy mix
	8 ounces sour cream

Melt butter in a large ovenproof skillet. Lightly salt chicken; brown in the butter. Add sherry and liquid from mushrooms; cover bake at 375° 1 hour, or until tender. Remove from oven; lift chicken from pan; cover; keep warm.

Add gravy mix to skillet liquid; stir over medium heat until thickened; reduce heat; fold in sour cream; add mushrooms. To serve, place chicken on bed of hot rice; pour sauce over chicken.

Josephine Matlock Futrell
Shreveport, Louisiana

◇ *Governor J. M. Futrell, 1933-1937.*

BREAST OF CHICKEN SUPREME

12 servings.

12 chicken breasts, boned, skinned	1 pound fresh mushrooms, sliced
1 cup flour	1 pint cream, or half and half
1 teaspoon salt	1 cup sauterne, or other sweet dessert wine
¼ teaspoon pepper	
½ pound butter	1 tablespoon cornstarch
	12 slices cooked ham

Dredge chicken with flour, salt and pepper. In a skillet brown chicken in butter, about 20 minutes. Add mushrooms; simmer, covered, until chicken is tender. Remove chicken and mushrooms to heated platter. Deglaze pan with cream. Mix wine and cornstarch; add to cream and simmer, stirring constantly, until thick and smooth. To serve, place a chicken breast with some of the mushrooms on a slice of heated ham. Spoon cream sauce over top.

Jennifer Mays
Little Rock, Arkansas

CHICKEN LOAF WITH LEMON SAUCE
6 to 8 servings.

1 (2½ to 3-lb.) chicken, cooked, boned, diced	2 cups bread crumbs
½ stick margarine	1 cup cooked rice
¼ cup chopped onion	2 cups chicken stock
½ cup chopped celery	3 eggs, beaten
¼ cup chopped bell pepper	Salt, pepper, Tabasco sauce to taste
¼ cup chopped pimentos	

Sauté onion, celery and pepper in margarine. In large bowl combine sautéed vegetables with remaining ingredients; blend well; season to taste. Pour into a greased 5 × 9-inch loaf pan. Set into a pan of hot water; bake at 325° for 1 hour, or until set. Unmold, slice, serve with Lemon Sauce.

Lemon Sauce:

¼ pound butter, melted	2 egg yolks, beaten
1 (8-ounce) can sliced mushrooms, drained	3 tablespoons lemon juice
¼ cup heavy cream	Salt, pepper, Tabasco sauce to taste
2 cups chicken stock	Fresh parsley, chopped
¼ cup flour	

Combine all ingredients; cook over low heat, stirring constantly, until thickened. Add parsley just before serving. Yield: 2½ cups.

Janie Williams
Old Paraclifta House
Mildred Brown

CHICKEN A LA KING
4 to 6 servings.

2 tablespoons butter	1 cup fresh or frozen English peas, cooked
3 tablespoons flour	
2 cups chicken broth	1 cup sliced mushrooms
3 cups cubed, cooked chicken	3 eggs, hard-boiled, sliced

In sauce pan heat butter and flour until bubbling; add broth; stirring constantly, cook until slightly thickened. Add next 3 ingredients; heat through; gently fold in eggs. Serve piping hot on toast; garnish with pimentos.

Sibbie Thornton Bullard

HOT CHICKEN LOAF WITH MUSHROOM SAUCE
12 servings.

1	(4-to 6-lb.) hen	1	tablespoon paprika
2	ribs celery with leaves	1	tablespoon salt
1	onion, quartered	1	(3-ounce) can chopped pimentos
2	bay leaves		
Whole pepper corns		1	cup chopped celery
1	tablespoon salt	1	large onion, chopped
2	tablespoons flour	1	clove garlic, minced
2	tablespoons melted butter	6	hard-boiled eggs, finely chopped
2	eggs, beaten		
1	cup milk	1	cup rich chicken stock
1	tablespoon chopped parsley	Buttered cracker crumbs	
1	cup cooked rice	1	cup chopped pecans
1	tablespoon pepper		

Boil hen with next 5 ingredients; drain; strain stock and reserve. When chicken is cool, debone; cut into bite-size pieces. In sauce pan brown flour in butter; add eggs and milk; cook over low heat, stirring, until sauce is thick. In large bowl combine chicken with sauce and remaining ingredients except crumbs and nuts. Turn into a buttered 9 × 13-inch baking pan. Sprinkle top with crumbs and nuts. Bake at 350° 45 minutes, or until firm. Cut in squares and serve with Mushroom Sauce.

Mushroom Sauce:

2	tablespoons butter	1	(10¾-ounce) can cream of mushroom soup
2	tablespoons flour		
1	onion, finely chopped	Half and half	
Salt and pepper to taste		1	(3-ounce) can chopped mushrooms, drained
¼	teaspoon Beau Monde		

In sauce pan brown flour in melted butter. Add onions, seasonings, soup and enough thin cream to make a thin sauce. Add mushrooms. Yield: 1½ cups.

RED APPLE INN
Heber Springs, Arkansas

EASY BAKE CHICKEN
4 to 6 servings.

8 boneless chicken breasts
½ cup mayonnaise
1 cup Italian seasoned bread crumbs

Brush chicken breasts with mayonnaise, coating thoroughly. Roll in bread crumbs. Place on a cookie sheet; bake at 350° 35 to 40 minutes, until brown and crispy.

Juanita Karr

CHICKEN IN WINE SAUCE
6 servings.

1 fryer, cut up, skinned
Salt to taste
½ stick margarine
3 tablespoons lemon juice
¼ to ½ cup sherry
1 (13-ounce) can evaporated milk

In large skillet brown lightly-salted chicken in margarine. Drizzle lemon juice over chicken; cover and cook over low heat 10 to 15 minutes. Remove cover; pour sherry over chicken; continue to cook an additional 10 to 15 minutes. (At this point, you can remove from heat and hold chicken until serving time.) At serving, pour milk in and heat; allow to bubble slightly. Serve over hot rice.

Edna Faye Purtell Dixon
Albuquerque, New Mexico

OVEN BARBECUED CHICKEN
6 to 8 servings.

1 (3-to 3½-lb.) chicken, cut up
1 teaspoon Accent
½ cup melted margarine
¼ cup lemon juice
2 tablespoons chopped parsley
2 tablespoons tomato paste
1 tablespoon grated onion
2 teaspoons salt
¼ teaspoon paprika
Dash garlic salt

Sprinkle chicken with Accent. Blend remaining ingredients for sauce. Dip chicken pieces in sauce; arrange in a greased 9 × 13-inch baking dish. Bake, uncovered, at 400° 40 to 60 minutes, or until tender. Baste occasionally with remaining sauce.

Ann Elizabeth Turner Wardlaw
Paso Robles, California

CHICKEN SURPRISE

6 to 8 servings.

1 whole boneless chicken	½ cup chopped onion
Salt and pepper to taste	½ cup chopped green pepper
½ teaspoon poultry seasoning	1 (6-ounce) package long grain
¼ teaspoon oregano	and wild rice
¼ teaspoon rosemary	2⅓ cups water
½ cup margarine	

Wash out chicken cavity; rub cavity with seasonings.

In a sauce pan sauté green pepper and onion in butter; add rice and stir until golden. Add water and package seasonings; simmer, covered, until water is absorbed.

Stuff chicken with rice mixture; skewer closed. Place on smoker, or unlit side of grill; cook with lid closed. Cooking time: Smoker: (Minimum 5 lbs. charcoal, 4 quarts liquid) Allow 1 hour per pound. Grill: 1½ to 2 hours, turning every 30 minutes. Remove when done; slice crosswise to serve.

Margot Henderson

SATURDAY CHICKEN

6 servings.

1 (2-to 3-lb.) fryer, cut up	1 (10¾-ounce) can cream of
Salt to taste	mushroom soup
¼ teaspoon garlic salt	1 cup cream
1 tablespoon paprika	¼ cup chopped parsley

Place chicken in a greased 9 × 13-inch baking dish. Sprinkle lightly with salt and garlic salt; season with paprika. Mix soup and cream; pour over chicken. Sprinkle with parsley. Bake, uncovered, at 350°, 45 to 50 minutes, or until tender.

Jackie Hale
Tulsa, Oklahoma
Floy Clinton Lane
Grannis, Arkansas

CHICKEN SWEET'N HOT
8 servings.

8	(5-ounce) boneless chicken breasts	1	clove garlic, minced
¼	pound butter	1	tablespoon Dijon mustard
¼	cup Worcestershire sauce	½	cup orange juice
½	cup red currant or raspberry jelly	1	teaspoon ginger
		3	dashes Tabasco sauce

Place chicken in a 9 × 13-inch dish. In a sauce pan combine remaining ingredients. Heat, stirring, until jelly is melted and sauce is smooth; cool. Pour sauce over chicken; cover, and marinate in refrigerator 12 to 24 hours.

Place chicken on grill; broil, basting with sauce. Breasts will require 5 to 6 minutes cooking time per side.

Jane Norwood

NANCY'S CHICKEN STUFF
6 to 8 servings.

1	(5-lb.) hen	3	tablespoons oil
1	onion, halved	1	(2-ounce) jar pimentos
2	ribs celery with leaves	1	(8-ounce) can mushrooms
1	cup chopped celery	1	(12-ounce) package noodles
1	medium onion, chopped	1	pound sharp Cheddar cheese, sliced
1	small green pepper, chopped		

Place hen in large kettle with water to cover, plus the halved onion, and celery ribs; season to taste; cook until tender. Remove chicken, cool, debone, cut into bite-size pieces. Strain stock; reserve. In large skillet brown chopped vegetables in oil until tender; add pimentos, mushrooms and chicken; cook over low heat 20 minutes, stirring often. Cook noodles in chicken stock until almost done; drain, reserving 1½ cups liquid. Combine noodles and chicken-vegetable mixture; pour into a greased 2-quart casserole, or 9 × 13-inch dish. If mixture appears too dry, add some of reserved liquid. Cover with sliced cheese. Bake at 350° 30 minutes, or until cheese melts.

Nancy Hall Bailey

◇ Nancy J. Hall, State Treasurer, 1962-1978
C. G. "Crip" Hall, Arkansas Secretary of State, 1937-1961.

COUNTY FAIR SPECIAL
6 servings.

1 cup rice	¼ (10-ounce) can rotel tomatoes and chilies, chopped
4½ cups chicken broth, divided	
1 (10¾-ounce) can creamy chicken mushroom soup	2 cups cooked, boned chicken, in medium pieces
2 tablespoons chopped pimentos	1½ cups grated American cheese, divided
2 tablespoons chopped onion	
2 tablespoons chopped bell pepper	2 cups slightly crushed regular fritos
2 tablespoons taco seasoning	

Cook rice in 2½ cups broth until liquid is absorbed; rice will not be quite done. Mix with soup, vegetables, seasoning, tomatoes, and 1½ cups broth. Layer half of mixture in a greased 9 × 13-inch baking dish. Top with chicken, 1 cup cheese, and remaining rice mixture. If casserole seems dry, pour last ½ cup broth over top. Bake, uncovered, at 375 degrees for 25 to 30 minutes until casserole is bubbly in the center. Remove from oven; sprinkle a 3-inch ring of fritos around out edge of casserole. Sprinkle remaining cheese in center of ring; return to oven to melt cheese.

Sarah Roach
Arkansas County MISS FLUFFY RICE 1984
DeWitt, Arkansas

CHICKEN RICE CASSEROLE
4 servings.

1 (6-ounce) box long grain and wild rice	2 cups cooked chicken, diced
2 cups chicken broth	1 (10¾-ounce) can cream of mushroom soup
1 cup chopped celery	¾ cup mayonnaise
4 tablespoons chopped onions	1 cup crushed corn flakes
2 tablespoons butter	3 tablespoons melted butter

Cook rice with package seasonings in chicken broth. Sauté celery and onions in butter. Combine with rice, chicken, soup and mayonnaise; pour into a greased 1½-quart baking dish. Combine corn flakes and melted butter; sprinkle over top of mixture. Bake at 325° 45 minutes.

Cordelia Baker
Bonnie Moore

CHICKEN AND WILD RICE CASSEROLE
8 to 10 servings.

2 (3-lb.) fryers, cut up	4 tablespoons butter
3 cups water	2 (6-ounce) packages long grain and wild rice
1 cup dry sherry	
1½ teaspoons salt	1 cup sour cream
½ teaspoon curry powder	1 (10¾-ounce) can cream of mushroom soup
1 medium onion, sliced	
½ cup diced celery	1 (8-ounce) package dried apricots, diced
1 pound fresh mushrooms, sliced	
	¼ cup slivered almonds

Simmer chickens with water, sherry, seasonings, onion, and celery for 1 hour, or until done. Strain broth; refrigerate chicken in broth at once, without cooling. Bone cooled chicken and cut into bite-size pieces; set aside. Measure chicken broth; cook rice, according to package directions, using broth for liquid. Combine chicken and rice with remaining ingredients; turn into a greased 3½ to 4-quart casserole. Bake covered at 350° 1 hour. Freezes well; thaw thoroughly before heating.

Judy Stewman

SCALLOPED CHICKEN AND RICE
6 to 8 servings.

1 (2-to 4-lb.) chicken, cooked, boned, cut in bite-size pieces	3 eggs, beaten
	½ cup bell pepper, finely diced
	½ cup chopped pimentos
2 cups cooked rice	1 (10¾-ounce) can cream of mushroom soup
3 cups chicken broth	
2 cups bread crumbs	

Combine all ingredients except soup. Turn into a buttered 8 × 12-inch baking dish; spread soup over top of mixture. Bake, covered, at 325° for 45 minutes.

Snowie Brown

HUNTINGTON CHICKEN

8 to 10 servings.

1 (4-to 5-lb.) hen, boiled, boned, cut up, broth reserved	1 (2-ounce) can pimentos, drained
1 (12-ounce) package noodles	½ cup grated Cheddar cheese
1 stick margarine	1 (10¾-ounce) can cream of mushroom soup
½ cup chopped onion	1 (8-ounce) can water chestnuts, drained, sliced
3 cups chopped celery	
1 bell pepper, chopped	Salt and pepper to taste

Cook noodles in chicken broth; drain and toss with margarine. In a sauce pan simmer onion, celery and pepper in small amount of water until tender; drain. Combine chicken, noodles, vegetables, and remaining ingredients, mixing well. Pour into a greased 3-quart casserole; bake at 350° for 30 minutes.

W. H. McClellan
Little Rock, Arkansas

◇ *John L. McClellan, U. S. Senator, 1943-1977.*

CHICKEN CASSEROLE FOR A CROWD

16 servings.

3 cups cooked chicken, diced	1 (10¾ ounce) can cream of mushroom soup
1 cup chopped celery, sautéed	1 (10¾ ounce) can cream of chicken soup
3 cups cooked rice	
½ pound Velveeta cheese, cubed	½ cup milk
2 (15½-ounce) cans Chinese noodles	1 cup chicken broth
	6 hard-boiled eggs, sliced
1½ cups mayonnaise	1 cup crushed potato chips, or buttered bread crumbs

In large bowl combine first 5 ingredients. In separate bowl combine mayonnaise, soups and liquids; blend with chicken mixture; fold in eggs. Pour into a greased 3-quart casserole. Bake 45 minutes at 350°; remove, cover top with crumbs. Bake 15 minutes more, or until brown.

Myrtle Sims

CHICKEN SPECTACULAR
10 to 12 servings.

3 to 4 cups diced, cooked chicken	1 (16-ounce) can green beans, drained
1 (6-ounce) package long grain and wild rice, cooked with package seasonings	1 cup sliced water chestnuts
	1 cup mayonnaise
1 (10¾-ounce) can cream of celery soup	1 (4-ounce) can sliced mushrooms, drained
1 (2-ounce) jar chopped pimentos, drained	Salt and pepper to taste

In a large bowl combine all ingredients. Turn into 1 buttered 3-quart casserole, or 2 1½-quart dishes. Bake at 350° for 30 to 45 minutes.

Jean Rea
Dallas, Texas

CRUNCHY CHICKEN CASSEROLE
6 servings.

2 cups cooked chicken, cubed	1 tablespoon lemon juice
1 (10¾-ounce) can cream of mushroom soup	1 teaspoon grated onion
	1 (3½-ounce) can sliced mushrooms, drained
¾ cup mayonnaise	
½ cup diced celery	½ cup slivered almonds, toasted
½ cup diced green pepper	
1 cup cooked rice, cooked in chicken broth	1 cup crushed corn flakes
	2 tablespoons butter, diced

In a large bowl combine all ingredients except corn flakes and butter. Turn into a greased 2-quart casserole. Sprinkle with corn flakes; dot with butter. Bake at 350° for 30 minutes.

Mrs. Lewis A. McClain
Arkadelphia, Arkansas

PARTY CHICKEN CASSEROLE
15 servings.

2 (2½-lb) fryers, or 1 (5-lb.) hen	1 4-ounce) can sliced mushrooms, drained
2 cups wine	4 tablespoons butter
1½ teaspoons salt	1 (10¾-ounce) can cream of mushroom soup
4 to 6 cups water	
2 (8-ounce) packages white and wild rice with herbs	1 cup sour cream
	1 cup half and half
3 ribs celery, chopped	

In large pot simmer chickens in wine, salt and water to cover until tender. Remove chicken; bone and cut into bite-size pieces. Reserve broth; cook rice in 5 cups broth 25 minutes or until nearly dry. In skillet sauté celery, onion and mushrooms in butter until tender. Combine chicken, rice, sautéed vegetables, and remaining ingredients; mix gently. Turn into a buttered 3-quart casserole; bake at 350° for 30 to 40 minutes.

Becky Tackett Steel
Nashville, Arkansas

◇ George Edwin Steel, Prosecuting Attorney (9th Circuit) 1945-1948.

QUICK CHICKEN-RICE BAKE
6 to 8 servings.

1 cup rice	1½ cans water
1 (10¾-ounce) can cream of celery soup	½ teaspoon salt
	1 (2½-to 3-lb.) fryer
1 (10¾-ounce) can cream of chicken soup	¼ margarine, melted

Pour rice evenly over bottom of greased 9 × 13-inch baking dish. Mix soups, water and salt; pour over rice. Coat chicken pieces with melted margarine; arrange in dish. Bake covered at 250° for 2½ hours.

Kathryn Hale
Avis Lofton

KING RANCH CASSEROLE
6 servings.

1 cup diced onion	1 clove garlic, minced
¼ pound fresh mushrooms, sliced	1 tablespoon chili powder
	1 cup chicken broth
¼ cup margarine	1 (8-ounce) package soft tortillas
1 (10¾-ounce) can cream of mushroom soup	2 cups diced cooked chicken
1 (10¾-ounce) can cream of chicken soup	1 pound Cheddar cheese, grated
1 (10-ounce) can rotel tomatoes	

In medium sauce pan sauté onion and mushrooms in margarine; add soups, tomatoes, garlic and chili powder; blend. Soften tortillas in chicken broth for 10 minutes. Line a greased 9 × 13-inch baking dish with tortillas. Fill remainder of dish with alternate layers of chicken, sauce, and cheese, ending with cheese. Bake at 350° 30 minutes.

Shirley Mears
Alleene, Arkansas
Imogene Leverett
Vivian F. Fears

CHICKEN SQUARES
4 servings.

1 (3-ounce) package cream cheese, softened	1 tablespoon dried chives
	1 tablespoon chopped pimentos
2 tablespoons melted butter	
2 cups diced, cooked chicken	1 (8-ounce) can crescent dinner rolls
½ teaspoon salt	
⅛ teaspoon pepper	¼ cup crushed seasoned croutons
2 tablespoons milk	

Combine first 8 ingredients, blending well. Separate rolls into 4 rectangles on an ungreased cookie sheet, sealing perforations. Spoon ½ cup chicken mixture into center of each rectangle; fold and seal. Brush tops with butter and sprinkle with croutons. Bake at 350° for 20 to 25 minutes. These freeze well; when reheating, tent with foil to keep from over-browning.

Dolores Burchette Mottesheard
Jonesville, North Carolina

HOT CHICKEN TURNOVERS
Makes 16 large turnovers.

1½ cups chopped, cooked chicken	¼ cup sour cream
1½ cups shredded Cheddar cheese	½ teaspoon salt
1 (2¼-ounce) can deviled ham	2 (10-ounce) can refrigerated biscuits
⅓ cup chopped onion	1 egg, beaten
	Sesame seeds

Combine first 6 ingredients; mix well. Separate biscuits; on a lightly-floured board, roll out each to a 5-inch circle. Place circles on large, lightly-oiled cookie sheets; place about 2 tablespoons of the chicken mixture in the middle of each. Moisten edge of biscuit with water; fold each circle in half to form a semicircle; seal edges by pressing with a fork. Brush top side with beaten egg; sprinkle with sesame seeds. Bake at 425° about 15 minutes, or until golden brown. Serve warm.

Donna Friday

BAKED CHICKEN BREASTS WITH STUFFING
6 to 8 servings.

8 boneless chicken breasts	¼ can water
4 ounces Swiss cheese, grated	2 cups Pepperidge Farm stuffing mix
1 (10¾-ounce) can cream of chicken soup	1 stick butter

Place chicken in a greased 9 × 13-inch baking dish; cover with cheese. Dilute soup with water; pour over chicken. Cover evenly with dry stuffing mix; dot with butter. Bake, covered, at 350° 30 minutes; remove cover, bake 30 minutes longer.

June Slayton Tollett

PEACHY KEEN CHICKEN
4 to 6 servings.

4 whole boneless chicken breasts, halved	1 (4-ounce) package almonds or pecan pieces, divided
1 (8-ounce) package Pepperidge Farm poultry stuffing	1 tablespoon cornstarch
	½ cup water
	½ teaspoon cinnamon
1 onion, chopped, sautéed in ½ cup margarine	¼ teaspoon white pepper
	1½ teaspoons soy sauce
1 (16-ounce) can sliced peaches, drained, juice reserved	Fruit juice, or white wine
	Salt to taste

Prepare stuffing as directed, adding sautéed onion, 5 finely diced peach slices, and half the nuts. Place 1 heaping tablespoon of the stuffing mix on each breast half; roll up and secure with toothpick. Place seam side down in greased 9 × 13-inch baking dish; cover with foil; bake 30 minutes at 350°. In sauce pan, add fruit juice or wine to reserved peach juice to make 1 cup. Combine spices and cornstarch in ½ cup water; stir into juice with soy sauce; heat until thickened and transparent; season to taste. Remove chicken from oven; drain and add pan juice to sauce; add peach slices; stir and pour over chicken. Top with remaining nuts. Bake, uncovered, 30 minutes longer, basting during last 15 minutes.

Margot Henderson

CHICKEN CASSEROLE WITH CORNBREAD STUFFING
8 servings.

1 (14- to 16-ounce) package cornbread stuffing mix	2 (10½-ounce) cans chicken broth, or same amount reserved stock
1 (2½- to 3-lb.) chicken, cooked, boned, and cubed	1 stick margarine, melted
2 (10¾-ounce) cans cream of mushroom or cream of chicken soup	

Place half-package dry stuffing mix in bottom of greased 3-quart casserole. Combine chicken, soup, broth, and margarine; pour over mix. Spread remaining stuffing over chicken mixture. Bake at 350° for 45 minutes.

Sherry Bolin

BISCUIT NUGGET CHICKEN
4 to 6 servings.

2 cups cubed, cooked chicken or turkey, or 2 (5-ounce) cans boned chicken	1 (4-ounce) can mushroom pieces, drained
1 teaspoon paprika, divided	1 (10-ounce) can refrigerated biscuits
½ teaspoon dillweed	¼ cup grated Parmesan cheese
¼ teaspoon salt	1 tablespoon instant minced onion, or ¼ cup chopped onion
1 cup milk	
1 (10¾-ounce) can cream of chicken, or cream of mushroom, soup	1 teaspoon parsley flakes, or 1 tablespoon fresh chopped parsley

In a sauce pan combine chicken, ½ teaspoon paprika, dillweed, salt, milk, soup and mushrooms; heat until hot and bubbly. Pour into an ungreased 9-inch square baking dish.

Separate biscuits; cut each biscuit into 4 pieces. In a plastic bag combine ½ teaspoon paprika, cheese, onion, and parsley; shake biscuit pieces, 3 or 4 at a time, in mixture until coated. Arrange over hot chicken mixture; sprinkle remaining cheese-herb mixture over top. Bake at 375° 15 to 18 minutes, or until a deep golden brown.

Nina Cassady
Nashville, Arkansas

◇ Neely Cassady, State Senator, 20th District, 1981-1985.

CHICKEN CURRY
4 servings.

4 chicken breasts	1 (10¾-ounce) can cream of chicken soup
Salt to taste	
⅓ cup mayonnaise	1½ teaspoons curry powder
⅓ cup chopped celery	

Place chicken in a greased 9-inch square baking pan; salt to taste; bake at 350° 30 minutes. Combine mayonnaise, celery, soup and curry powder; pour over chicken; cover and bake 40 minutes longer. Serve over hot rice.

Grace Stuart
Mineral Springs, Arkansas

CHICKEN NORMANDY
6 to 8 servings.

1	(8-ounce) package seasoned bread stuffing
1	stick margarine, melted
1	cup water
2½ to 3	cups diced, cooked chicken
½	cup chopped onion
¼	cup chopped chives, or green onion tops
½	cup chopped celery
½	cup mayonnaise
¾	teaspoon salt
1	(10¾-ounce) can cream of mushroom soup
	Grated Cheddar or Parmesan cheese

In mixing bowl lightly combine first 3 ingredients; place half the mixture in bottom of a buttered 8 × 12-inch baking dish. In a separate bowl combine chicken, vegetables, mayonnaise, and salt, blending well. Spread mixture over stuffing in casserole; top with remaining bread mixture. Cover; refrigerate overnight. Take out 1 hour before baking; spread soup over top. Bake, uncovered, at 325° for 40 minutes. Sprinkle with cheese; return to oven for 10 minutes.

Flo Tilley

For a light, spicy flavor similar to but milder than curry powder try Garam Masala (Indian Seasoning): Blend ¼ cup toasted coriander seed, 2 tablespoons toasted cumin seed, ¼ cup black peppercorns, 1 tablespoon whole cloves, 2 tablespoons cardamon seeds, 1 stick cinnamon, broken, and ½ teaspoon ground nutmeg. Keep in air tight bottle.

For a homemade Country Mustard, combine ½ cup each sifted flour, dry mustard, and sugar; ⅛ teaspoon salt; blend and stir until smooth with ¾ cup Heinz cider vinegar. Must be aged a few days; keeps indefinitely in refrigerator.

FRIED CHICKEN WITH ONION GRAVY
8 servings.

1 (2½-to 3-lb.) chicken, cut up	2 cups thinly sliced onions
1 cup plus 2 tablespoons flour, divided	2 cups water
	1 tablespoon white vinegar
2½ teaspoons salt	Salt and pepper to taste
¼ teaspoon black pepper	1 cup cream
1½ cups shortening	

Dredge chicken in 1 cup seasoned flour. In a large skillet fry chicken in shortening over medium heat (350°), covered, turning to brown; cook 10 to 15 minutes, or until tender. Transfer to paper towel-lined dish; keep warm in oven. Pour off all but 2 tablespoons fat from pan; add onions and sprinkle with 2 tablespoons flour. Cook, stirring, until onions are golden brown. While stirring, add water; bring to a boil; stir in vinegar; season to taste. In small pan, bring cream to a boil; add to gravy; adjust seasoning. Serve chicken with side dish of hot gravy.

Bettie Frazier

JIM'S FAVORITE CHICKEN PIE
6 servings.

1 cup flour	1¾ cups chicken broth
½ teaspoon salt	⅔ cup milk or cream
⅓ cup shortening	2 cups chopped, cooked chicken
2 tablespoons cold water	
6 tablespoons butter	¼ cup pimentos, diced
6 tablespoons flour	1 hard-boiled egg, sliced, optional
½ teaspoon salt	
¼ teaspoon pepper	1 to 2 cups cooked peas and carrots, drained, optional
¼ teaspoon poultry seasoning, optional	

For pastry, mix first 4 ingredients; blending well. On a floured board, roll out ½-inch thick; cut into triangles. Bake on a cookie sheet at 475° for 10 minutes, or until barely done, not brown. For filling, combine butter, flour, and seasonings in a large, heavy sauce pan. Cook, stirring, over low heat until smooth; gradually add broth and milk; cook, stirring, 2 minutes. Add chicken and pimentos; cook about 10 minutes, or until mixture thickens. Fold in egg and vegetables, if desired. Place a layer of crust in a greased 1½ quart casserole; add chicken mixture; top with layer of crust triangles. Bake at 350° for 15 minutes, or until crust is brown.

Orlon Smith Coulter
Kremmling, Colorado
Gladys Cowling

CURRIED CHICKEN
8 to 10 servings.

1	(2½-to 3-lb.) chicken, cut up, skinned	1	teaspoon garlic salt
1	large onion, chopped	½	teaspoon turmeric
1	stick butter	½	teaspoon cloves or 5 whole cloves
1	(6-ounce) can tomato paste	1	medium bell pepper, chopped
1	(8-ounce) container plain yogurt	1	cup chopped celery
1	teaspoon salt	1	cup water
1	teaspoon ginger	1	(4-ounce) can mushrooms
½	teaspoon red pepper		

In large pot sauté onion in butter until golden brown; add chicken; cover and cook 15 minutes. In mixing bowl combine remaining ingredients, blending well. Pour over chicken; stir well; cover and cook over medium to low heat, stirring occasionally, until chicken is tender and gravy is to the desired thickness. Serve over hot rice with choice of condiments.

Carla Kamruddin

LOW CALORIE CHICKEN CACCIATORE
4 servings.

¾	cup sliced fresh mushrooms	½	teaspoon pepper
1	(8-ounce) can tomatoes	2	whole chicken breasts, skinned, boned, and halved
½	cup chopped green pepper	¼	teaspoon paprika
½	cup chopped onion	2	teaspoons cornstarch
1	clove garlic, pressed	2	tablespoons cold water
½	teaspoon oregano		

In medium skillet combine all but the last 3 ingredients. Bring to a boil; reduce heat; cover and simmer for 25 minutes, or until chicken is tender. Remove chicken to warm platter; sprinkle with paprika. Combine cornstarch and water; stir into skillet mixture; cook, stirring, until thickened. Spoon over chicken. Serve over hot rice.

Stella Gallaher
Ashdown, Arkansas

CHICKEN CACCIATORE
6 to 8 servings.

¼ cup flour	½ green pepper, chopped
1 teaspoon salt	1 (8-ounce) can sliced mushrooms
¼ teaspoon pepper	
3 to 3½ pounds boneless chicken breasts	1 clove garlic, crushed
	1 cup water
¼ cup oil	1 teaspoon Italian seasoning
1 (14-ounce) can whole tomatoes	½ teaspoon oregano
	½ teaspoon basil
1 (16-ounce) can tomato sauce	1 (8-ounce) package fettucine, cooked and drained
1 (12-ounce) can tomato paste	
1 onion, chopped	

Dredge chicken in flour, salt and pepper; in large, deep skillet, brown in oil. Combine remaining ingredients, breaking up tomatoes; pour over chicken; cover and simmer 45 minutes, or until chicken is tender. Thicken sauce, if desired. Serve chicken and sauce over hot fettucine.

Alison Correll Hargis
Little Rock, Arkansas

EASY CHICKEN TETRAZZINI
6 to 8 servings.

1 cup chopped onion	1 (10¾-ounce) can cream of chicken soup
1 cup chopped celery	
2 tablespoons butter	1 cup shredded Cheddar cheese
2 to 3 cups diced, cooked chicken	
	1 (2-ounce) jar pimentos, drained
1 (10¾-ounce) can cream of mushroom soup	
	Salt, pepper, and garlic salt to taste

In large skillet sauté onion and celery in butter until tender. Add remaining ingredients; season to taste with salt, pepper and garlic salt; simmer 30 minutes. Serve over hot rice or noodles.

Martha Tanner

PARTY CHICKEN TETRAZZINI
12 servings.

1 (5-to 6-lb.) hen, cooked, boned, broth reserved	1 (3-ounce) package slivered almonds, toasted
¼ pound butter	3 tablespoons finely minced onion
8 tablespoons flour	
1 cup heavy cream	3 tablespoons minced bell pepper
¾ pound Cheddar cheese, cubed	
	3 tablespoons minced celery
1 (16-ounce) can black olives, sliced	Salt and pepper to taste
	8 ounces thin noodles, cooked, drained
1 (4-ounce) can sliced mushrooms, drained	

Cut chicken into bite-size pieces; set aside. In large sauce pan, heat butter; blend in flour; stirring constantly, gradually add 4 cups chicken broth, then cream. Cook over low heat, stirring, until thickened; add cheese, and stir until melted. Combine sauce with chicken and all other ingredients; pour into a buttered 3-quart casserole; bake at 350° until bubbly and heated through. Dish may be prepared ahead of time; also freezes well.

Becky Tackett Steel

◇ *Boyd Tackett, U. S. Congressman 1949-1953.*

CHICKEN-SPAGHETTI CASSEROLE
4 to 6 servings.

2 cups diced, cooked chicken	1 (8-ounce) package thin spaghetti, cooked and drained
2 cups chicken broth	
½ cup diced celery	
¼ cup chopped bell pepper	1 cup grated cheese
1 (14½-ounce) can tomatoes	Salt and pepper to taste
1 (10¾-ounce) can mushroom soup	

In large sauce pan simmer celery, onion and bell pepper in chicken broth until tender. Add tomatoes and soup; season to taste; bring to a boil. Remove from heat; fold in chicken and spaghetti; pour into a greased 9 × 13-inch baked dish; top with cheese. Bake at 400° until cheese melts.

Margaret Locke Hill

CHICKEN SPAGHETTI
8 servings.

1 (3-to 4-lb.) chicken	1 (4-ounce) can pimentos, drained, chopped
1 large onion, chopped	1 pound Velveeta cheese, cubed
1 green pepper, chopped	
1 cup chopped celery	
2 tablespoons butter	1 (12-ounce) package spaghetti, cooked and drained
1 (10¾-ounce) can tomato soup	
1 (10¾-ounce) can mushroom soup	

Place chicken in large pot; cover with salted water; bring to a boil; cover; reduce heat and simmer until tender, about 1 hour. Remove chicken; cool; bone; cut into bite-size pieces; set aside. Reserve 2 cups stock. In large sauce pan sauté vegetables in butter until tender; add reserved broth, soups, pimentos, cheese and chicken. Blend and heat until cheese melts. Serve over hot spaghetti.

Sue Conatser Ward
Avery, Texas
Dianne Cowden
Elaine Harshbarger

CREPES WITH CHICKEN, CHEESE, JALAPEÑO FILLING
12 to 16 servings.

24 to 36 crepes*	4 jalapeño peppers, seeded, finely chopped
6-pound hen, or 2 fryers, or equivalent in chicken breasts	½ cup heavy cream
	1 pint whipping cream
1 pound Swiss cheese, grated, divided	Chopped pimentos, for color, optional

Stew or steam chicken; remove meat from bones (discard skin and all fat); cut into cubes or strips. Combine chicken, all but ¼ cup of the cheese, peppers, and heavy cream. Place a spoonful of chicken mixture down center of each crepe; roll up; place seam side down in a large shallow casserole. When casserole is filled, sprinkle crepes with reserved cheese; pour whipping cream over all. Cover and bake at 400° for 30 to 40 minutes, removing cover last 5 minutes.
*See Index for recipe.

Harriet Aldridge
Food Editor, ARKANSAS GAZETTE
Little Rock, Arkansas

STIR-FRY CHICKEN
4 to 6 servings.

2 whole boneless chicken breasts	¼ pound mushrooms, sliced
3 tablespoons cornstarch	2 cups fresh bean sprouts
4 tablespoons soy sauce	1 (8-ounce) can water chestnuts, drained, sliced
1 stalk fresh broccoli	2 tablespoons peanut oil
1 small onion, thinly sliced, separated into rings	1 cup chicken broth

Cut chicken into thin slices. In small bowl combine cornstarch and soy sauce; stir in chicken; stir to coat; marinate 15 minutes. Cut off broccoli flowerets; thinly pare stalks; slice inner stalk into thin slices. Heat oil in wok or deep skillet over high heat. Add chicken; stir fry until browned; remove; set aside. Add broccoli and onion; stir fry 2 minutes; add mushrooms, bean sprouts, water chestnuts and chicken. Stir in broth; cover and cook gently 5 minutes or until vegetables are crisp-tender. Serve over hot rice.

Casey Correll-Wray

BREAST OF TURKEY WITH APPLE RAISIN SAUCE
8 to 10 servings.

1 (2¾- to 3½-lb.) Butterball boneless turkey breast	¼ teaspoon cinnamon
1 cup apple juice	⅛ teaspoon salt
1 tablespoon cornstarch	1 apple, peeled, sliced
1 teaspoon brown sugar	¼ cup raisins

Thaw and roast turkey according to directions. Combine remaining ingredients in a sauce pan. Bring to a boil, stirring constantly. Reduce heat; simmer 5 minutes. Makes 1½ cups sauce. Serve over sliced turkey.

SWIFT AND COMPANY
Huntsville, Arkansas

Swift's toll free Butterball Turkey Talk-Line, open November and December each year, is 1-800-323-4848.

TURKETTI
4 to 6 servings.

1¼ cups spaghetti, broken into 2-inch pieces	1 (10¾-ounce) can cream of chicken or mushroom soup
2 cups cooked turkey, cubed	½ can water
¼ cup pimentos, drained	½ teaspoon salt
¼ cup chopped green pepper	⅛ teaspoon pepper
1 small onion, chopped	½ pound Cheddar cheese, grated, divided

In large bowl combine all ingredients except ½ cup cheese. Turn into a greased 2-quart casserole; top with reserved cheese. Bake at 350° for 45 minutes. Great dish for left-over turkey.

Ruth Renaud

TURKEY-RICE CASSEROLE
4 to 6 servings.

1 onion	1 (10¾-ounce) can cream of mushroom soup
4 ribs celery	
1 bell pepper	1 (5-ounce) can boned turkey, or 1 cup leftover turkey
½ dozen fresh, large mushrooms	
2 tablespoons butter	1 tablespoon Cavender's Greek Seasoning
1 cup cooked rice	
	½ teaspoon salt
	½ cup shredded Swiss cheese

In food processor with steel blade, chop onion, celery, bell pepper and mushrooms. Sauté in butter. Combine thoroughly with rice, soup, turkey, and seasonings. Pour into a greased 1½-quart casserole; top with cheese. Bake 40 minutes at 325°.

S-C SEASONING COMPANY, INC.
Harrison, Arkansas

Cement mixer with specially-made stainless steel tub mixes spices for Cavender's Greek Seasoning.

CHEDDAR TURKEY CASSEROLE
4 to 6 servings.

1	cup cooked rice	1	(10¾-ounce) can cheese soup
2	tablespoons minced onion	1	cup milk
3	tablespoons butter	1	cup finely crushed, round cheese crackers
5	ounces frozen green peas, thawed	2	tablespoons butter, melted
2	cups diced, cooked turkey		

Sauté onion in butter; combine with rice; spread into a greased 6 × 10-inch baking dish. Sprinkle with peas. Combine turkey, soup, and milk; pour evenly over rice and peas. Combine crumbs and melted butter; sprinkle over top. Bake at 350° for 35 minutes, or until heated through.

Andee Southworth

JACK'S FAVORITE CURRY
6 to 8 servings.

¾	cup chopped onion	1 to 2 teaspoons curry powder, or to taste
¾	cup chopped celery	Salt, pepper, Tabasco sauce to taste
½	cup chopped bell pepper	6 to 8 cups diced smoked turkey
1	stick margarine	
½	cup flour	
3	cups hot chicken stock	
1	(10¾-ounce) can mushroom soup	

Sauté vegetables in margarine; add flour, mixing well. Blend in hot chicken stock until smooth. Add soup, seasonings, and turkey; blend and heat thoroughly. Serve over rice with choice of condiments—currants, chopped green onions, ripe olives, cashew nuts, coconut chips, grated cheese, crumbled bacon, chopped eggs, and chutney.

Jack T. Williams
San Antonio, Texas

CHICKEN DIP'N SAUCES

HONEY:

2 cups honey	1½ cups sour cream
½ cup Dijon mustard	1 tablespoon lemon juice
1 tablespoon cinnamon	½ teaspoon nutmeg
½ teaspoon curry powder	

Combine all ingredients, mixing well. Yield: 4 cups.

PLUM:

1 (10-ounce) jar red plum jelly	1 teaspoon lemon juice
1 tablespoon prepared horseradish	1 tablespoon prepared mustard
¼ teaspoon soy sauce	

Combine all ingredients, mixing well. Yield: 1½ cups.

MUSTARD:

¼ cup boiling water	2 tablespoons oil
¼ cup dry mustard	½ teaspoon salt

Stir boiling water into mixture of mustard, oil and salt, mixing well; cool before serving. Yield: ½ cup.

TYSON FOODS
Springdale, Arkansas

CHICKEN FRITTERS

6 servings.

½ cup flour	1 egg, beaten
1 teaspoon baking powder	1 teaspoon sugar
2 cups chopped, cooked chicken	½ teaspoon salt
	¼ teaspoon pepper
1 tablespoon melted butter	½ cup chopped celery

Sift flour and baking powder into mixing bowl. Add remaining ingredients, mixing well. Drop batter mixture by teaspoonfuls into hot deep fat; fry until golden brown; drain. Excellent for leftover chicken.

Carol Craun

MORNAY SAUCE
Yield: about 3 cups.

3 tablespoons butter	Dash cayenne pepper
4 tablespoons flour	½ cup cream
2½ cups milk	2 egg yolks, well beaten
½ teaspoon salt	¼ cup shredded Swiss,
⅛ teaspoon pepper	Gruyere, or Gouda cheese

In heavy sauce pan, over low heat melt butter; add flour; cook 1 minute, stirring constantly. Gradually add milk; cook over medium heat, stirring constantly, until thickened; add seasonings. Stir cream into egg yolks; stir some of hot mixture into yolk mixture; add to hot mixture, stirring constantly. Cook 2 or 3 minutes over medium heat, until thickened. Add cheese; stir until melted. Excellent sauce for poached eggs, chicken, or seafood.

Jeanne Marshall

GRILLED DOVE OR DUCK
6 servings.

6 whole duck breasts, or 12 doves, cleaned	½ cup olive oil
½ cup soy sauce	Butter
	Bacon strips

Marinate duck breasts in a mixture of soy sauce and oil 6 hours, turning frequently. Doves do not need to be marinated; pierce breasts several times; rub with butter and season with salt and pepper. Wrap each breast or dove in a bacon strip; secure with toothpick. Place in a foil cup; place on grill. Cook duck over medium heat 30 to 40 minutes; dove at medium-low heat 20 to 30 minutes, basting frequently.

Paddy Dickinson Bell

ROAST WILD DUCK
6 to 8 servings.

4 ducks, dressed	1 clove garlic, minced, optional
Salt and pepper	
1 large onion, chopped	1 stick margarine, melted
2 tablespoons butter	2 cups consomme
2 large apples, chopped	1 cup apple juice
2 ribs celery, chopped	1 cup dry red wine, optional

Rub ducks with salt and pepper inside and out. Sauté onion in butter until limp. Stuff cavities of ducks with onion, apples, celery, and garlic; place breast side down in a Dutch oven. Pour margarine and liquids over ducks; ducks should be covered; add water if needed. Roast, uncovered, at 325° for 3 to 4 hours, basting often. Turn breast side up; roast until brown, basting often, about 30 minutes. Serve garnished with candied sweet potatoes.

Ruby Lantrip Martin
Humphrey, Arkansas

Arkansas, Rice and Duck Capitol of the World

WILD DUCK GUMBO
10 to 12 servings.

2 to 3 ducks, dressed	1 (10-ounce) package frozen okra, optional
1 teaspoon salt	
1 teaspoon pepper	½ cup flour
1 large onion, chopped	½ cup oil
1 cup chopped celery	¼ cup chopped green onions and tops
1 bell pepper, chopped	
1 or 2 cloves garlic, minced	¼ cup chopped parsley
4 tablespoons margarine	File, optional

In a Dutch oven boil ducks with salt and pepper in water to cover until tender; drain, reserving stock; cool, and bone. Return meat to pan with 2 quarts stock, adding water to total measure. In a heavy skillet sauté vegetables and garlic in margarine until limp; add to duck mixture with okra; simmer, uncovered, 30 minutes. In same skillet make a roux by heating oil, adding flour, and stirring; cook over low heat to a rich dark brown. Add roux to duck mixture; simmer 10 minutes; adjust seasoning. When ready to serve, add green onions, parsley, and file. Serve over plain or wild rice.

Ruby Wilson
Humphrey, Arkansas

FRIED QUAIL
6 servings.

12 quail, cleaned	Flour
Salt and pepper	1 to 2 cups peanut oil

Sprinkle birds inside and out with salt and pepper to taste; dredge in flour. In large skillet heat oil over medium heat (350°); add quail; cook 10 to 12 minutes on each side, or until done. Drain on paper towels.

Joe O. Wray

BAKED PHEASANTS
4 servings.

2 pheasants, quartered	1 cup chopped celery with leaves
Salt, pepper, and seasoned salt	
Flour	1 pint cream
3 tablespoons butter	1 cup dry sherry
½ pound sliced, fresh mushrooms	2½ teaspoons salt
	1 teaspoon pepper
1 small onion, chopped	

Dredge pheasant pieces in seasoned flour; brown in butter; set aside. In same pan sauté mushrooms, onion, and celery until limp. Place birds in a Dutch oven; pour sautéed mixture over birds; cover; bake at 350° 1½ hours. Combine remaining ingredients; pour over meat; cover and bake until birds are tender, about 30 minutes.

Blanche Scott
Nashville, Arkansas

SEAFOOD

FISHERMAN'S CATCH
6 to 8 servings

Fish (bass, crappie, perch, catfish), cleaned and dressed, 8 whole small fish or 3 to 4 pounds fillets, approximately ½ pound per person

2 cups cornmeal
Salt and pepper
Shortening or vegetable oil

Heat shortening or oil in skillet (375°). Sprinkle fish with salt and pepper; place cornmeal in a paper bag; drop in fish, 1 at a time, shaking until coated. Pan fry until fish is crisp and golden on underside; gently turn with a spatula and cook until fish browns and flakes easily with a fork. Drain on paper towels and lift to heated platter. Serve immediately.

Suzanne Allison Wray

CRISPY CATFISH FRY WITH TARTAR SAUCE
6 servings.

¼ cup evaporated milk
1½ teaspoons salt
Pepper to taste

½ cup flour
¼ cup cornmeal
2 pounds fresh catfish

In a small bowl mix milk, salt and pepper. In a separate bowl combine flour and cornmeal. Dip fish into milk, then roll in flour mixture. Fry in deep, hot oil for 4 to 5 minutes, or until fish is brown and flakes easily. Drain on paper towel. Serve with Tartar Sauce.

Tartar Sauce:

1 (10¾-ounce) can cream of onion soup
⅓ cup mayonnaise

¼ cup finely chopped dill pickle
2 tablespoons chopped pimentos, optional

Combine all ingredients, blending well; chill. Yield: 2 cups.

Eula Crowley Hughes
Paragould, Arkansas

◇ *Benjamin Crowley, first settler of Crowley's Ridge, 1821.*

BAKED FISH
4 to 6 servings.

2 pounds fresh fish fillets
2 tablespoons lemon juice
2 tablespoons prepared mustard

½ to 1 teaspoon Worcestershire sauce
1½ cups sour cream

Place fish in a greased 9 × 13-inch baking pan. Mix lemon juice, mustard and Worcestershire sauce; pour over fish. Smooth sour cream over fish. Bake at 350° until golden brown and fish flakes easily.

Jan Taggart
Moss Point, Mississippi

CRAB MUFFINS

6 servings.

6 English muffins, split, toasted and buttered	1 tablespoon lemon juice
1 cup shredded Colby cheese, divided	2 tablespoons mayonnaise
	1 teaspoon soy sauce
½ pound frozen or canned crab meat, drained	2 tablespoons chopped green onions
¼ cup chopped water chestnuts	1 teaspoon seasoned sauce
	¼ teaspoon hot pepper sauce
½ cup sour cream	

Combine ½ cup cheese with all other ingredients. Divide mixtures evenly onto 6 muffin halves. Sprinkle with remaining cheese. Broil until bubbly. Serve hot and open-faced with remaining muffin halves.

Cherry Hood McAfee
Longview, Texas

CRAB MEAT AU GRATIN

4 to 6 servings.

⅓ cup chopped green onions	2 egg yolks, well beaten
½ cup finely chopped celery	¼ cup grated American cheese
½ cup margarine	¼ teaspoon salt
6 tablespoons flour	Dash pepper
1 (5⅓-ounce) can evaporated milk	3 cups white lump crab meat
	Grated Cheddar cheese

In a heavy skillet sauté onion and celery in margarine; gradually stir in flour. Combine milk and yolks; gradually add to hot mixture. Add American cheese; stir over low heat until cheese melts. Add seasonings and gently fold in crab meat. Pour into a buttered 1½-quart casserole. Sprinkle with Cheddar cheese. Bake, uncovered, at 350° until hot and bubbly and top is medium brown.

Jan Taggart
Moss Point, Mississippi

FILLETED FISH A LA MICROWAVE
4 servings.

4 flounder, bass, or trout fillets	2 teaspoons fresh lemon juice
¼ cup melted margarine	½ teaspoon garlic powder, or fresh minced garlic
1 tablespoon Worcestershire sauce	½ teaspoon salt
¼ cup chopped green onion tops	¼ teaspoon cayenne pepper, or ½ teaspoon Tabasco sauce
	½ teaspoon ginger

Dry fish on paper towels; place in a glass microwave dish. In a 2-cup glass measure, combine other ingredients; cook on HIGH 1 minute; pour over fish. Cover dish with waxed paper; cook on HIGH 5 to 6 minutes, until fish is white and flaky. Turn dish once during cooking time. Serve hot.

Nate Coulter
Little Rock, Arkansas

◇ Nathan G. Coulter, Arkansas State Senator, 1962-1963.

SALMON LOAF
6 servings.

2 (16-ounce) cans salmon	½ cup chopped onion
4 eggs, beaten	¼ cup melted butter
1½ cups milk	2 teaspoons lemon juice
3 cups coarse cracker crumbs	Salt and pepper to taste
½ cup chopped celery	

Drain and flake salmon, reserving liquid. Combine liquid and remaining ingredients; stir in salmon. Turn into a greased 5 × 9-inch loaf pan. Bake at 350° for 1 hour.

Lenora Wood

SOLE AU GRATIN
6 servings.

2 cups long grain rice	1 (10-ounce) package frozen green peas, cooked, drained
6 sole fillets	
½ cup water	2 tablespoons flour
¼ cup lemon juice	¼ cup water
½ teaspoon salt	4 to 6 slices Muenster cheese

Cook rice according to package directions; drain; set aside. Fold sole fillets in half crosswise to form triangular pieces; place in large skillet with water, lemon juice and salt. Cover and poach 5 minutes. Combine rice and peas in a 9 × 13-inch baking dish. Lift poached fillets with slotted spoon; arrange over rice mixture. Measure fish broth; add or reduce to make 1½ cups; return to skillet; bring to a boil. Mix flour with ¼ cup water; stir into broth. Cook stirring until thickened; spoon over fillets. Top with cheese slices. Place in 350° oven until cheese melts.

Mrs. Fred Campbell

SALMON CROQUETTES
6 servings.

1 (15½-ounce) can red or pink salmon	Salt, pepper, and onion salt to taste
2 eggs, beaten	1 cup flour, cornmeal, or cracker crumbs
1 cup toasted bread crumbs	
½ cup shredded Cheddar cheese	

Drain salmon; remove skin and bones; flake. Add next 4 ingredients, blending well. Shape mixture into croquettes; coat with flour, cornmeal, or cracker crumbs. Pan fry in hot oil until golden brown.

Elsa Cowling

SALMON LOAF WITH SAUCE VERTE
6 to 8 servings.

2 (15½-ounce) cans red or pink salmon	¼ cup lemon juice
Milk	½ teaspoon salt
¼ cup finely chopped onion	½ teaspoon pepper
¼ cup chopped parsley	½ teaspoon thyme
2 cups cracker crumbs	4 eggs, beaten lightly
	¼ cup melted butter

Drain salmon, reserving liquid; flake. To reserved liquid add enough milk to make 1 cup. In mixing bowl combine all ingredients, mixing well. Turn into a greased 5 × 9-inch loaf pan; bake at 350° for 1 hour. Let stand 5 minutes; unmold onto serving dish. Serve with Sauce Verte.

Sauce Verte:

1 cup mayonnaise	2 tablespoons chopped chives, or parsley
1 cup sour cream	
1 teaspoon dry mustard	½ teaspoon salt
2 cucumbers, seeded, chopped	1 teaspoon dillweed, optional

Combine all ingredients; chill before serving. Yield: 2½ cups.

Mrs. Sidney McMath
Little Rock, Arkansas

◇ *Sidney McMath, Governor, 1949-1953.*

SHRIMP VICTORIA
4 servings.

1 pound raw shrimp, shelled	1 tablespoon flour
1 small onion, finely chopped	¼ teaspoon salt
¼ cup butter	Dash cayenne pepper
1 (6-ounce) can whole mushrooms	1 cup sour cream
	¼ cup white wine

In a skillet sauté shrimp and onion in butter for 5 to 10 minutes, or until shrimp are almost tender; add mushrooms; simmer 5 minutes. In a bowl combine flour, salt and pepper; stir in sour cream and wine; pour over shrimp; cook gently for 10 minutes; do not boil. Serve over rice.

Linda Ridlon

CASHEW STUFFED SHRIMP WITH LEMON SAUCE

4 servings.

- 12 fresh jumbo shrimp, shelled
- 22 soda crackers, unsalted tops, finely rolled (about ¾ cup crumbs)
- ½ cup dry roasted unsalted cashews, coarsely chopped
- ¼ cup grated Parmesan cheese
- 3 tablespoons margarine, melted
- 2 tablespoons dry sherry
- 1½ teaspoons paprika
- ¼ cup water

Butterfly shrimp by splitting almost completely through center. Lay cut-side up in a 9-inch square baking dish. Mix together crumbs, cashews, cheese, margarine, and sherry. Mound 1 tablespoon mixture on top of each shrimp. Sprinkle with paprika. Pour water into bottom of dish. Bake at 350° for 20 minutes, or until shrimp are tender. Transfer to serving platter; drizzle with Lemon Sauce.

Lemon Sauce:

- ¼ cup margarine
- 3 tablespoons lemon juice
- 1½ teaspoons white vinegar
- ¼ teaspoon Worcestershire sauce

In sauce pan combine all ingredients; heat until butter melts. Whisk until blended.

Jennifer Mays
Little Rock, Arkansas

BAKED TUNA WITH BISCUITS
6 to 8 servings.

3 tablespoons melted margarine	1 medium onion, chopped
6 tablespoons flour	1 small green pepper, chopped
3 cups milk	½ cup shredded Cheddar cheese
Salt and pepper to taste	1 (10-count) can buttermilk biscuits
2 (7-ounce) cans tuna, drained, flaked	

Combine margarine and flour; cook over low heat until bubbly. Gradually add milk; cook, stirring constantly, until smooth and thick; season to taste. Combine sauce with tuna, onion and pepper. Spoon into a lightly greased 2-quart casserole; top with cheese. Arrange biscuits on top; bake at 375° for 40 minutes.

Dot Latimer Tyndall
Nashville, Arkansas

SHRIMP STIR-FRY WITH VEGETABLES
6 to 8 servings.

2 cups coarsely shredded Chinese cabbage	4 to 5 tablespoons peanut oil, divided
1 onion, thinly sliced, separated into rings	¼ cup water
3 ribs celery, diagonally sliced	5 tablespoons soy sauce
1 cup sliced green pepper	1 tablespoon cornstarch
1 medium zucchini, unpeeled, thinly sliced	¼ teaspoon ginger
1 cup sliced fresh mushrooms	2 pounds shrimp, cooked, shelled
½ cup sliced water chestnuts	2 cups pork, cooked, cubed, optional
1 (6-ounce) package frozen Chinese pea pods, thawed, drained	

Heat wok or large skillet to high heat (375°) for 2 or 3 minutes; add 3 tablespoons oil and heat 1 minute. Add all vegetables but pea pods; stir-fry 5 minutes. Add 1 or 2 tablespoons oil, as needed; add pea pods; lower heat (325°); cover and cook 2 to 3 minutes, or until vegetables are crisp-tender. Combine water, soy sauce, cornstarch, and ginger; stir well. Add mixture with shrimp (and pork) to vegetables. Reduce heat; simmer, stirring constantly, until thickened. Serve over hot plain or fried rice or thin noodles, with additional soy sauce, if desired.

Wayne Clay

BARBECUED SHRIMP
4 servings.

2	cloves garlic, minced	3	tablespoons chopped parsley
½	cup peanut oil	½	cup chili sauce
¼	cup soy sauce	2	pounds fresh shrimp, shelled
1	tablespoon lemon juice		

In a mixing bowl combine all ingredients except shrimp; mix well. Pour marinade over shrimp; cover; refrigerate 24 hours. Remove shrimp from marinade; place on broiling rack. Broil for 7 to 8 minutes. Serve hot or cold.

Vicki Masten

SHRIMP PAELLA
6 to 8 servings.

Pinch saffron
3 cups hot chicken broth
4 tablespoons olive oil, divided
1 large onion, finely diced
1 clove garlic, minced

Salt to taste
½ pound green peas
2½ pounds fresh shrimp, shelled
2 tomatoes, skinned, seeded
1 cup rice

Dissolve saffron powder in hot broth; if using saffron beads, steep in the hot liquid at least 15 minutes. In a large, deep skillet sauté onion and garlic in 3 tablespoons oil until onion is just transparent. Add to chicken-saffron broth; simmer 10 minutes. Add salt and peas; bring to a boil. Add shrimp and tomatoes; simmer. In another pan heat 1 tablespoon oil; add rice and stir until grains are well-coated; pour into first mixture; stir once and let boil 10 minutes. Reduce heat; cover pan; simmer 20 minutes. Serve garnished with pimento strips. Other seafoods, as well as boned chicken, may be used in addition to the shrimp.

Janie Dickinson

SHRIMP PUFFS
4 servings.

2 cups bread flour, sifted	1 egg, beaten
3 teaspoons baking powder	1 cup milk
⅓ teaspoon salt	½ pound cooked shrimp, shelled, chopped
Dash nutmeg	
Dash thyme	

Combine sifted flour, baking powder, salt and seasonings; sift a second time into mixing bowl. Combine egg and milk; stir into dry ingredients; beat until smooth; add shrimp. When ready to serve, drop mixture by tablespoonfuls into hot, deep fat (360 to 375°); fry until delicately browned and well puffed. Serve at once with a tartar sauce.

Glennie Dickinson Klug
Little Rock, Arkansas

MICKEY'S SHRIMP CREOLE
4 to 6 servings.

⅓ cup shortening	1 (8-ounce) can tomato sauce
¼ cup flour	1½ teaspoons salt
½ cup chopped onion	2 bay leaves
2 green onions, chopped	½ teaspoon crushed thyme
½ cup chopped bell pepper	⅛ teaspoon cayenne pepper
½ cup sliced celery	3 thin-cut lemon slices
¼ cup minced parsley	1 pound cooked shrimp, shelled
4 cloves garlic, chopped	
1 cup water	

Heat shortening in heavy pan; blend in flour; cook very slowly, stirring constantly, until roux is brown. In separate pan sauté onions and bell pepper; add with remaining ingredients except shrimp to roux; cook over low heat 30 to 45 minutes, stirring often. Remove bay leaves; add shrimp; simmer 10 to 15 minutes. Serve over hot rice.

Evelyn Wilkerson

SHRIMP CURRY
4 to 6 servings.

4 large onions, chopped	1 (6-ounce) package frozen grated coconut
3 cloves garlic, minced	¾ teaspoon ginger
4 tablespoons butter	1 tablespoon sugar
3 cups water	1½ tablespoons curry powder
3 large tomatoes, peeled, chopped	1½ tablespoons flour
2 apples, pared, chopped	1½ teaspoons salt
1 cup chopped celery	¼ teaspoon pepper
	1½ pounds fresh shrimp, shelled

In a Dutch oven sauté onion and garlic in butter until lightly browned. Add water; bring to a boil. Add tomatoes, apples, celery and coconut. In separate bowl blend ginger, sugar, curry, flour, salt and pepper; add cold water to make a paste; add to boiling mixture. Reduce heat; simmer until vegetables are tender, about 30 minutes. Add shrimp; cook 5 minutes. Serve over hot rice.

Mrs. Roy F. Golden
Arkadelphia, Arkansas

BASIC TEMPURA
Yield: 1½ cups batter

1 cup ice water	½ teaspoon sugar
1 egg, slightly beaten	½ teaspoon salt
2 tablespoons oil	1 cup flour

Combine all ingredients, blending well; do not beat. If not using immediately, keep cold until ready for use. Dip well-chilled shrimp or other seafood, and vegetables (broccoli, squash, mushrooms, cauliflower, onions, eggplant, pea pods) into batter, a few at a time. Fry in deep, hot oil (375°) until golden brown. Serve immediately with sauce for dipping.

Laura Eva Turner Maurer
Houston, Texas

CATFISH BATTER
Yield: 1½ cups batter.

1 (6-ounce) package pancake mix
1 (10-ounce) can beer

Combine ingredients, mixing well. Dip fish in batter; fry in deep, hot fat until golden brown and flake easily.

Roscoe Ellis

SHRIMP COCKTAIL SAUCE
Yield: 1½ cups

1½ cups catsup
1 tablespoon Worcestershire sauce
2 tablespoons prepared horseradish
1 tablespoon lemon juice
1½ teaspoons sugar
Dash of liquid hot pepper sauce
Salt and pepper to taste

Combine all ingredients; chill.

Vernard R. Kerlin

A substitute for Chinese Five Spices: Blend 1 tablespoon each of ground cloves and cinnamon, 1 teaspoon black pepper, and ½ teaspoon each ground fennel and regular anise.

SALADS AND DRESSINGS

WILTED LETTUCE SALAD
4 to 6 servings

Fresh garden lettuce and other spring greens (young mustard greens, spinach, dandelion greens), about 1 quart
6 slices bacon, cooked, crumbled
2 or 3 green onions, sliced
3 hard-boiled eggs, sliced
¼ cup bacon drippings
¼ cup vinegar
2 teaspoons sugar
Salt and pepper

Tear greens into bite-size pieces, removing any large stems. Place in large salad bowl with bacon, onions, and eggs; toss lightly. Combine remaining ingredients; heat to boiling; pour over greens, tossing lightly. Serve immediately.

Laverne Corbell

◇ *Joseph A. Corbell, Sevier County delegate to the Arkansas Constitutional Convention of 1868, which drafted the present Arkansas Constitution.*

SUMMER MEAL-IN-A-DISH
8 to 10 servings.

3 zucchini (1-lb.), cut in 1-inch slices
3 summer squash (1-lb.), each cut lengthwise into 6 pieces
½ pound fresh green beans
6 medium carrots (¾-lb.), cut in ¼-inch slices
1 cauliflower, broken into flowerets
3 egg yolks
7 cloves garlic, pressed
1 tablespoon prepared mustard
1 tablespoon lemon juice
Dash of white pepper
1¼ cups salad oil
1 tablespoon warm water
1 tablespoon capers, drained
8 to 12 green onions
3 tomatoes, sliced
1 pound medium-size shrimp, cooked, shelled, chilled
2 (6½-ounce) cans tuna, drained, chilled

Cook each of the first 5 listed vegetables separately in boiling salted water until crisp-tender; drain and chill. In small bowl, combine yolks, garlic, mustard, lemon juice and pepper; with mixer beat at medium speed until thick and lemon-colored; add oil, 1 tablespoon at a time, beating constantly, until thick. Add water, beating until smooth; add capers, cover tightly; chill. To serve, cover large serving platter with salad greens; arrange cooked vegetables, tomato slices, chunks of tuna, and shrimp on top of greens. Garnish with green onions. Serve with side bowl of sauce.

Joy Knight
Cedar Hill, Texas

24-HOUR VEGETABLE SALAD
6 to 8 servings.

6 cups (1 head) lettuce, torn
Salt, pepper and sugar to taste
1 (10-ounce) package frozen green peas, thawed, drained
2 cups thinly sliced celery
1 (8-ounce) can water chestnuts, drained, sliced
½ pound bacon, cooked, crumbled
4 ounces grated Swiss cheese
1 cup mayonnaise
¾ cup sour cream
1 (0.4-ounce) package Hidden Valley Ranch dressing mix
¼ cup sliced green onions with tops
Paprika

Place 3 cups lettuce in bottom of a large bowl; sprinkle with salt, pepper and sugar. Layer, in order, peas, celery, water chestnuts, remaining lettuce, bacon, and cheese. Combine mayonnaise, sour cream and dressing mix. Spread mixture over top of cheese layer, spreading to edge of bowl. Cover; chill 24 hours. Garnish with onions and paprika.

Mary Ann Toler

CREAMY CABBAGE AND APPLE SLAW
6 to 8 servings.

6 cups finely shredded green cabbage	3 tablespoons lemon juice
½ cup finely shredded onion	½ cup mayonnaise
1 green or red pepper, seeded, cut into thin strips	½ cup sour cream
	1 tablespoon honey
1 large red apple, cored, diced	2 teaspoons prepared mustard
¼ cup raisins	1 teaspoon salt
	Dash of pepper

In a large salad bowl, combine cabbage, onion, and pepper strips. Toss apple and raisins with lemon juice; add to cabbage mixture. In separate bowl, whisk together remaining ingredients. Pour over cabbage; toss until evenly coated; chill.

Edna Freeman
Arkadelphia, Arkansas

AVOCADO SALAD
6 to 8 servings.

½ cup olive oil	1 large avocado, chopped
¼ cup white wine vinegar	1 medium onion, chopped
¼ teaspoon ground pepper	1 large tomato, chopped
2 tablespoons lemon juice	1 small head iceberg lettuce, torn in bite-size pieces
1 teaspoon salt	

Combine first 5 ingredients in a a jar; cover and shake vigorously. Combine avocado, onion, and tomato; add dressing; chill and marinate at least 30 minutes. Using slotted spoon, spoon salad onto a bed of lettuce.

Sandra Dunn
Patti Chaney

SPINACH SALAD WITH MUSTARD DRESSING
4 to 6 servings.

1 large bunch spinach, washed, stemmed	½ cup chopped walnuts
1 large red apple, cored, coarsely chopped	¼ cup sliced celery

Tear spinach into bite-size pieces; sprinkle with apples, walnuts, and celery. Toss lightly with desired amount of dressing.

Mustard Dressing:

4 eggs, beaten	2 teaspoons Morton *Nature's Seasons* seasoning
½ cup sugar	2 cups whipping cream, divided
¼ cup dry mustard	⅔ cup white vinegar

In sauce pan thoroughly blend eggs, sugar, dry mustard and seasoning. Slowly stir in 1 cup cream and vinegar. Cook over medium heat until thickened. Remove from heat and whisk in remaining cream.

Denise Henderson
Birmingham, Alabama

POTATO SALAD
12 servings.

8 medium potatoes, boiled, peeled, and diced	1½ teaspoons salt
1 small stalk celery, diced	¼ teaspoon pepper
2 hard-boiled eggs, sliced	¼ teaspoon dry mustard
1 onion, diced	½ cup cider vinegar
4 slices bacon, diced	½ cup water
1 cup sugar	2 eggs, beaten

In large bowl lightly toss together potatoes, celery, sliced eggs and onion. In a heavy skillet fry bacon until browned. In a small bowl whisk sugar and seasonings with water and vinegar; add to beaten eggs, mixing well. Pour this mixture into skillet with bacon drippings and bacon; cook, stirring until mixture thickens. Pour over potato mixture and toss lightly. Chill several hours before serving.

Jane Latimer

IDAHO POTATO SALAD

6 servings.

4 medium potatoes, baked	⅓ cup chopped onion, or as desired
1 tablespoon lemon juice	
¾ cup mayonnaise	3 tablespoons milk
¼ teaspoon dried dillweed	¼ teaspoon pepper
1½ teaspoons salt	2 tablespoons parsley, optional
½ cup chopped celery	

When potatoes are cool, peel and cube. Combine remaining ingredients; pour over potatoes. Mix well and chill several hours.

Kathleen McDaniel
Longview, Texas

BROCCOLI RICE SALAD

8 to 10 servings.

3 stalks broccoli	1 small head cauliflower
Endive, leaf lettuce, romaine, or other salad greens	3 cups cooked rice

Rinse broccoli; with sharp knife, cut off flowerets; pare stalks thinly and slice inner stalk into thin slices. Separate cauliflower into small flowerets; slice thinly. Separate and wash salad greens; pull leaf sections from stalks and stems in bite-size pieces. Combine all ingredients; chill. Serve with dressing.

Blender Dressing:

1 cup vinegar	2 bell peppers, chopped
2 cups oil	1 tablespoon salt
1 cup catsup	1 teaspoon black pepper
1 cup sugar	1 teaspoon garlic powder
1 onion, chopped	

Combine all dressing ingredients in blender; process until smooth. Refrigerate. Yield: 1 quart.

Geraldine Desmond
Ida M. Coulter Stone

CONFETTI COTTAGE CHEESE SALAD
6 servings.

1 (16-ounce) container cottage cheese	½ cup finely chopped onion
1 avocado, diced	1 (4-ounce) can green chilies, diced, drained
1 medium tomato, diced, drained	

Combine all ingredients; toss lightly; refrigerate at least 2 hours before serving. Keeps well.

Mary E. Lawler

GREEN AND WHITE VEGETABLE SALAD
6 to 8 servings.

1 bunch fresh broccoli, chopped	¾ cup salad dressing, or mayonnaise
1 medium head cauliflower, broken into flowerets	¼ cup heavy cream
1½ cups finely chopped celery	2 tablespoons sugar
6 green onions, finely chopped	1 teaspoon salt
	¼ teaspoon pepper

Place all vegetables in a large bowl. Combine remaining ingredients, mixing well; pour over vegetables. Toss lightly; cover and chill 3 hours.

Viola Thornton Thomason
Broken Bow, Oklahoma
Renee Franklin

TOSSED SALAD SUPREME

8 to 10 servings.

1 cup mayonnaise	1 head cauliflower, broken into flowerets
1 (8-ounce) carton sour cream	2 hard-boiled eggs, coarsely chopped
½ teaspoon dried parsley flakes	10 ripe olives, sliced
½ teaspoon dried dillweed	1 small onion, chopped
½ teaspoon onion salt	1 (2-ounce) jar pimentos, drained
½ teaspoon Beau Monde seasoning	
1 bunch fresh broccoli, cut into bite-size pieces	

Combine mayonnaise, sour cream, and seasonings; mix well; set aside. In large bowl combine remaining ingredients. Spoon dressing mixture over vegetables; toss gently to coat. Cover and refrigerate 8 to 10 hours, or overnight, before serving.

Jan Robinson
Wickes, Arkansas
Laura Jones

COLD CAULIFLOWER FRENCH-STYLE

6 to 8 servings.

4 cups cauliflowerets	1 tablespoon cream
⅔ cup mayonnaise	1 teaspoon lemon juice
3 tablespoons sour cream	Salt to taste
2 tablespoons Dijon mustard	

Cook cauliflower in boiling salted water 5 to 6 minutes; do not overcook. Drain and cool slightly. Combine remaining ingredients, mixing well. Toss with cauliflower and chill. To serve, spoon into lettuce cups; garnish with pimento strips and parsley.

Ann Coulter
Raleigh, North Carolina

SLICED TOMATOES VINAIGRETTE
6 servings.

¼ cup wine vinegar
¼ cup olive or salad oil
⅛ teaspoon salt
1 garlic clove, pressed
¼ to ½ teaspoon Dijon mustard, optional
Fresh ground pepper to taste

4 ripe tomatoes, sliced
2 or 3 hard-boiled eggs, sliced
1 cup sliced fresh mushrooms
1 tablespoon chopped fresh parsley
2 tablespoons chopped green onions

Combine vinegar and oil with seasonings; mix well. Arrange tomato slices on serving dish; top with egg slices and mushrooms; sprinkle with parsley and onions. Spoon vinaigrette over all; cover, and let stand 30 minutes before serving.

Martha Gilliam
Elkhart, Kansas

 Gilliam-Norwood House

GERMAN COLE SLAW
8 to 10 servings.

2 quarts shredded cabbage
2 large green peppers, chopped
1 large red pepper, chopped, or 1 (2-ounce) jar pimentos
1 large onion, chopped

2 cups vinegar
2½ cups sugar
1 teaspoon celery seed
1½ teaspoons salt
½ teaspoon turmeric
½ teaspoon mustard seed

Combine cabbage, peppers, and onion in a large bowl. In a sauce pan combine remaining ingredients; heat to boiling; pour hot over vegetables. Cover; chill overnight. This may be frozen.

Imogene Stoker
Joyce Sherman
Emma Lee Mickle

MACARONI SALAD
6 to 8 servings.

1 pound macaroni, cooked in salted water, drained	1 onion, chopped
1 cup diced celery	4 carrots, shredded
1 cup diced green pepper	¾ cup grated cheese

In a large bowl combine all salad ingredients; toss with dressing; cover and chill.

Dressing #1:

1 (14-ounce) can sweetened condensed milk	2 cups mayonnaise
½ cup vinegar	Salt and pepper to taste

Mix all ingredients thoroughly; chill.

Don Stephens
Bonnie Hogg

Dressing #2:

1½ cups sugar	½ teaspoon salt
¼ cup flour	Pepper to taste
½ cup vinegar	1 cup salad dressing
¼ cup water	¼ cup prepared mustard

In a sauce pan combine first 6 ingredients; cook until mixture thickens; remove from heat and add salad dressing and mustard. Stir into salad; chill overnight.

Ollie Mae Parker Zachry
Hooks, Texas

MARINATED VEGETABLES
8 servings.

1 (16-ounce) can green peas
1 (16-ounce) can seasoned green beans
1 (16-ounce) can Chinese vegetables
1 (8-ounce) can water chestnuts, sliced
6 to 8 green onions, chopped
1 cup sugar
⅔ cup wine or tarragon vinegar

Drain all vegetables. Mix vinegar and sugar well; pour over vegetables. Cover; refrigerate; allow to marinate at least 24 hours. (Chopped cauliflower, green pepper, or pimentos may be added.)

Aileen Arnett
Arkadelphia, Arkansas
Carol Honea

SALAD RING
8 servings.

3 envelopes unflavored gelatin
2 cups cold water, divided
½ cup sugar
1 teaspoon salt
⅓ cup vinegar
2 tablespoons lemon juice
1 cup salad dressing
1½ cups finely shredded cabbage
1½ cups chopped celery
1 cup grated carrot
½ cup diced green pepper
2 pimentos, diced

In medium sauce pan sprinkle gelatin over 1½ cups water; place over low heat; stir constantly until gelatin dissolves. Remove from heat; stir in sugar, salt and remaining ½-cup water. In a separate bowl, mix vinegar and lemon juice; whisk in salad dressing thoroughly; add to gelatin mixture. Chill until mixture mounds slightly when dropped from a spoon; stir in vegetables. Turn into a 6-cup mold; chill until firm. To serve, unmold onto large serving platter; arrange salad greens, Swiss cheese slices, and cold cuts around mold.

Katherine S. Conner
Newport, Arkansas

CUCUMBER RING SUPREME
8 servings.

1	tablespoon unflavored gelatin	1	(8-ounce) package cream cheese, cubed and softened
2	tablespoons sugar	6	medium cucumbers
¾	teaspoon salt	3	tablespoons finely chopped onion
⅔	cup water		
2	tablespoons lemon juice	¼	cup chopped parsley

In a sauce pan mix gelatin, sugar, salt and water; stir over low heat until gelatin and sugar are dissolved. Stir in lemon juice; remove from heat. With rotary beater, gradually beat hot gelatin mixture into cream cheese until smooth. Peel cucumbers, scrape out seeds, and grind in food processor, or finely shred. Measure 2 cups drained cucumber; add with remaining ingredients to cream cheese mixture. Pour into a 6-cup mold; chill until firm.

Betty Willich
Oklahoma City, Oklahoma

RICE-A-RONI SALAD
6 servings.

1	(6-ounce) package Chicken Rice-a-Roni	¼	teaspoon curry powder
2	(3-ounce) jars artichoke hearts, drained, liquid reserved, sliced	½	bell pepper, chopped
		3	green onions, chopped
½	cup mayonnaise	8	green pimento-stuffed olives, sliced

Prepare rice according to package directions; cool. Combine artichoke liquid with mayonnaise and curry powder. Reserve a few artichoke pieces for garnish; combine remainder with rice, vegetables, and dressing. Turn into salad bowl; garnish with olive slices and artichoke pieces. Cover; refrigerate at least 6 hours before serving.

Miriam Martin
Sacramento, California

COKE SALAD
12 servings.

- 1 (16-ounce) can dark sweet cherries
- 1 (20-ounce) can chunk pineapple
- 2 (3-ounce) packages cherry gelatin
- 2 (6½-ounce) bottles Coke
- 1 cup chopped nuts
- 1 (8-ounce) package cream cheese, softened

Drain juice from fruits into a sauce pan; add gelatin, and heat, stirring, until gelatin dissolves; cool. Combine fruits and remaining ingredients; mix well, and fold into gelatin. Pour into a 9 × 13-inch dish; chill until firm.

Delta Norwood

◇ Hal Norwood, Attorney General, 1909-1913, 1929-1934.

SUNSHINE SALAD
10 to 12 servings.

- 1 (3-ounce) package orange gelatin
- 1 (3-ounce) package lemon gelatin
- 2 cups boiling water
- 1½ cups cold water
- 1 (20-ounce) can crushed pineapple, drained, 1 cup juice reserved
- 1 (10-ounce) package miniature marshmallows
- 5 medium bananas, sliced thin
- 1 egg, beaten
- 2 tablespoons butter
- 2 tablespoons flour
- ¼ cup sugar
- ½ pint whipping cream, whipped
- 1 cup grated Cheddar cheese

Combine gelatins and boiling water; stir until dissolved; add cold water. Pour into a 9 × 13-inch dish; chill until firm. Layer pineapple, bananas, and marshmallows on top of chilled gelatin. In top of double boiler, combine reserved pineapple juice with next 4 ingredients; cook, stirring constantly, until thickened; cool and fold in whipped cream. Spread topping over marshmallow layer; sprinkle with grated cheese. Chill thoroughly before serving.

Ruth Renaud
Theresa McGaha

APRICOT SALAD
8 servings.

2 (3-ounce) packages apricot gelatin	2 tablespoons butter
2 cups boiling water	1 egg, beaten
2 cups cold water	½ cup sugar
2 bananas, diced	2 tablespoons flour
1 cup miniature marshmallows	1 (3-ounce) package cream cheese
1 (15½-ounce) can crushed pineapple, drained, ½ cup juice reserved	1 (8-ounce) container whipped topping

Dissolve gelatin in boiling water; add cold water; pour into 9 × 13-inch pan; chill until thickened. Add bananas, marshmallows, and pineapple. Chill until firm. In sauce pan combine reserved pineapple juice with next 4 ingredients; cook over medium heat until thickened; remove from heat; add cream cheese. Mix until blended; chill. Fold whipped topping into chilled cooked mixture; spread over firm gelatin. Chill.

Avis Graves
Daisy Cabean

PRETZEL SALAD
12 servings.

2 to 3 cups crushed pretzels	1 (6-ounce) package strawberry gelatin
1½ cups margarine, melted	2 cups pineapple juice
4 (3-ounce) packages cream cheese, softened	1 (10-ounce) package frozen strawberries
1¼ cups sugar	
1 (8-ounce) container whipped topping	

Spread pretzels in bottom of a 9 × 13-inch baking pan; pour margarine over pretzels; bake 10 minutes at 400°; cool. Beat cream cheese and sugar until smooth; spread over warm pretzels. Spread whipped topping over cheese mixture; chill. Heat juice; add gelatin; stir until dissolved; add frozen berries; chill until partially set. Pour over cheese mixture; chill until firm.

Corine Hooker
Paula Hooker

STRAWBERRY CROWN SALAD
8 to 10 servings.

½ cup butter	½ cup cold water
¼ cup firmly packed brown sugar	2 cups strawberries
	1 teaspoon lemon juice
1 cup sifted flour	¾ cup sugar
½ cup chopped pecans or walnuts	Few drops red food coloring
	1 cup whipping cream, whipped
1 envelope unflavored gelatin	

With hands, mix butter, brown sugar, flour and nuts; spread in an 11 × 13-inch baking pan. Bake at 400° 15 minutes, stirring occasionally. Remove from oven; break mixture into crumbs with spoon; cool. Soften gelatin in cold water. Place berries in a sauce pan, reserving a few whole berries for garnish. Mash remainder; add lemon juice and sugar; bring to a boil, stirring occasionally. Remove from heat; add gelatin; stir until dissolved; add food coloring.

Arrange several of uncooked berries on bottom of a 1½-quart mold. Spoon a thin layer of clear syrup of the cooked mixture on bottom of mold; chill until set. Chill remaining berry mixture until partially set; fold in whipped cream. Fill mold in alternate layers of berry and crumb mixtures, starting with the berry mixture and ending with crumb mixture. Chill until set; unmold onto serving tray; garnish with whole berries and dollops of whipped cream.

Cleo Hopson

BLUEBERRY SALAD
8 to 10 servings.

1 (6-ounce) package raspberry gelatin	8 ounces cream cheese, softened
2 cups boiling water	½ cup sugar
1 (16-ounce) can blueberries	½ cup sour cream
1 (8-ounce) can crushed pineapple	Nuts, optional

Dissolve gelatin in boiling water; cool. Add undrained fruits; pour into a 9 × 13-inch dish; chill until set. Combine cream cheese, sugar, and sour cream. Spread over congealed gelatin. Sprinkle with nuts. Chill until firm.

Nelda Koger Nichols
Jonesboro, Arkansas

MIMI'S WALDORF SALAD
6 servings.

2 large red apples, cored, diced	½ cup seedless grapes, halved
½ cup diced celery	1 banana, sliced
1 (15¼-ounce) can pineapple chunks, drained	½ cup raisins
½ cup chopped walnuts or pecans	½ cup miniature marshmallows
	¼ to ½ cup mayonnaise
	Dash of salt

Combine all ingredients, using amount of mayonnaise desired; toss lightly. Chill. Serve on crisp lettuce.

June Knight Allison

Cranberry-Waldorf Variation: Add 1 to 2 cups ground fresh cranberries; 1 cup whipping cream, whipped may be used instead of mayonnaise.

Lucille Stafford
Alleene, Arkansas

CRANBERRY RING
10 servings.

1 (3-ounce) package cherry gelatin	1 cup ground fresh cranberries
1 cup hot water	1 orange and rind, finely ground
¾ cup sugar	1 cup crushed pineapple, drained
1 tablespoon lemon juice	1 cup chopped celery
1 tablespoon unflavored gelatin	½ cup chopped pecans
1 cup pineapple juice	

Dissolve cherry gelatin in hot water; add sugar and lemon juice; set aside. Soften unflavored gelatin in pineapple juice; in top of double boiler, heat to dissolve thoroughly; add to cherry gelatin mixture; chill until partially set. Fold in remaining ingredients; pour into an 8-cup ring mold; chill until firm. Serve on platter of lettuce leaves; spoon chicken or turkey salad into center, or cut and serve on individual plates with a dollop of mayonnaise. (Grape halves may be used instead of celery.)

Opal Cantlon Knod
Doris Sturdevant

CRANBERRY CASSEROLE
6 to 8 servings.

3 cups chopped apples, unpeeled	1 stick butter, melted
2 cups fresh whole cranberries	½ cup brown sugar
1¼ cups sugar	⅓ cup flour
¼ cup water	1½ cups uncooked oatmeal
	1 cup chopped pecans

In a 9 × 13-inch baking dish, layer apples and cranberries. Spread sugar over fruit; drizzle water over sugar. Combine remaining ingredients, mixing well. Spread evenly over fruit. Bake at 350° 1 to 1¼ hours.

Ann Coulter
Cary, North Carolina

HOT FRUIT SALAD
8 to 10 servings.

1 (20-ounce) can chunk pineapple, drained	1 (16-ounce) can pitted dark sweet cherries, drained
1 (29-ounce) can sliced peaches, drained	4 bananas, sliced thin
1 (30-ounce) can apricot halves, drained	1 cup sugar
	3 tablespoons curry powder
	½ stick butter, melted
	Maraschino cherries, optional

Combine fruits, sugar and curry in a large bowl; toss lightly. Pour into a 9 × 13-inch baking dish; garnish with maraschino cherries. Pour butter over fruit. Bake 30 minutes at 350°.

Ruth Hinton Pilger
Mountain Home, Arkansas

FROZEN FRUIT SALAD
12 servings.

- 11 ounces cream cheese, softened
- 1 (16-ounce) can fruit cocktail, drained, juice reserved
- 1 (10-ounce) package frozen strawberries, thawed, drained, juice reserved
- ½ cup sugar
- ½ pint heavy cream
- 2 bananas, sliced
- 1 cup miniature marshmallows
- Red and green Maraschino cherries, optional

In a large mixing bowl, beat cream cheese until fluffy. Add ½ cup each of the reserved fruit juices, sugar, and cream; beat slowly until well blended. Fold in fruits and marshmallows. Pour into a 9 × 13-inch pan; freeze. Thaw 15 minutes before serving.

Dr. T. S. Hedgecock
Hamburg, Arkansas

FROZEN BANANA-STRAWBERRY SALAD
8 to 12 servings.

- 2 cups miniature marshmallows
- 1 (20-ounce) can crushed pineapple
- ½ cup whipping cream, whipped
- 4 bananas, sliced
- 1 cup fresh or canned, diced peaches
- 1 cup sliced strawberries
- ½ cup salad dressing

In a sauce pan heat marshmallows and pineapple, stirring, until marshmallows are melted; cool until slightly thickened. Fold in remaining ingredients. Pour into a ring mold or a 7 × 11-inch pan. Freeze.

Molly Wilson
Lois Smith

TURKEY FRUIT SALAD WITH PINEAPPLE DRESSING
6 servings.

1 (20-ounce) can chunk pineapple, drained, juice reserved	1 orange, sectioned
	1 apple, cored, chopped
1 avocado, sliced	1 pound cooked turkey breast, cut into thin strips

Combine all ingredients in mixing bowl; toss lightly; cover; chill. To serve, spoon into lettuce cups; serve with Pineapple Dressing.

Pineapple Dressing:

2 tablespoons sugar	1 (8-ounce) container low-fat plain yogurt
2 teaspoons cornstarch	
Reserved pineapple juice	1 teaspoon poppy seeds
2 tablespoons lemon juice	

In a sauce pan combine sugar, cornstarch, and fruit juices; cook over medium heat until thickened, stirring constantly. Cool. Stir in yogurt and poppy seeds; chill thoroughly. Yield: 1½ cups.

Jean Tollett

CHINESE SALAD
6 servings.

4 chicken breasts	2 tablespoons sesame seeds
Salt to taste	6 tablespoons vinegar
1 small piece ginger root	6 tablespoons sugar
1 head lettuce, torn	¼ cup oil
4 green onions, chopped	Salt and pepper to taste
½ cup slivered almonds	

Boil chicken with salt and ginger root until tender; cool, debone, and shred. Combine chicken with vegetables, nuts and sesame seeds; cover and chill. When ready to serve, mix vinegar, sugar, oil and seasonings; blend thoroughly. Pour over salad; toss until coated.

Jo Titsworth
Pearland, Texas

CHICKEN SALAD WITH HONEY MUSTARD VINAIGRETTE
6 to 8 servings.

1 tablespoon olive oil	3 ribs celery, sliced
1 clove garlic	1 small red onion, thinly sliced, separated into rings
2½ pounds boneless chicken, skinned, cut into thin strips	4 ounces Edam cheese, cut into thin strips
2 cups cooked rice	
1 medium green pepper, chopped	

In skillet, sauté garlic in olive oil 1 minute. Add chicken; stir-fry 3 to 4 minutes; drain and reserve.

In a bowl combine chicken with remaining ingredients; toss lightly. Serve chilled in lettuce-lined bowls with Honey Mustard vinaigrette.

Honey Mustard Vinaigrette:

½ cup olive oil	1 tablespoon Dijon mustard
⅓ cup white wine vinegar	½ teaspoon dry mustard
2 tablespoons honey	

Combine all ingredients in a covered jar; shake to blend. Yield: about ¾ cup.

Denise Henderson
Brimingham, Alabama
Ann Henderson

SPICY PEACH SALAD
4 servings.

1 (3-ounce) package peach gelatin	1 cup boiling water
¼ cup sugar	2 tablespoons vinegar
¼ teaspoon cinnamon	¾ cup reserved peach juice
⅛ teaspoon cloves	1 cup chopped peaches, drained

In a bowl mix gelatin, sugar, and spices; add boiling water; stir until gelatin dissolves. Add vinegar and peach juice; chill until slightly thickened. Add peaches; pour ino a 3-cup mold; chill until firm.

Lorita McGaha Conger
Irving, Texas

CHICKEN MAYONNAISE

12 servings.

2 envelopes unflavored gelatin	1 cup sliced almonds
1 cup cold water	4 hard-boiled eggs, chopped
1 cup hot chicken stock	2 cups green peas, drained
2 cups mayonnaise	1 cup chow chow
3 to 4 cups cooked, diced chicken	Salt and cayenne pepper to taste
1 cup chopped celery	

In a large bowl dissolve gelatin in cold water. Add chicken stock and mayonnaise; stir until thoroughly blended. Add remaining ingredients; pour into a lightly-oiled 9 × 13-inch pan, or large ring mold. Chill until firm. Serve on lettuce leaves.

Ann Coulter
Cary, North Carolina
Mrs. Carl E. Hendrix, Sr.

◇ Carl E. Hendrix, Sr., Arkansas State Representative, 1945-1951.

HOT CHICKEN SALAD DELUXE

4 to 6 servings.

½ cup sliced almonds	2 teaspoons grated onion
1 tablespoon melted margarine	½ cup mayonnaise
2 cups diced cooked chicken	½ cup undiluted cream of mushroom soup
1 cup diced celery	½ cup shredded Cheddar cheese
½ teaspoon salt	½ cup crushed potato chips
½ teaspoon Accent	

Sauté almonds in margarine; drain. Combine all ingredients except potato chips. Spoon into a lightly greased 1-quart casserole. Sprinkle with potato chips. Bake at 425° for 20 minutes.

Alexa Dillard
Little Rock, Arkansas

CHICKEN SALAD
10 servings.

1	pint salad dressing or mayonnaise	½	cup diced green peppers
2	tablespoons prepared mustard	½	cup stuffed olives, sliced
2	tablespoons grated onion	1	(8-ounce) can pineapple tidbits, drained
5	cups chopped cooked chicken	1	(11-ounce) can mandarin oranges, drained
1	cup chopped celery	1	(15½-ounce) can Chinese noodles, optional

Combine first 3 ingredients, blending well; refrigerate in tightly covered container. Combine chicken, vegetables, olives, and fruits; add dressing as necessary to combine. Chill. Add noodles, if desired, just before serving.

Elizabeth Cooper Laws
Texarkana, Arkansas

CHICKEN POTATO SALAD
8 to 12 servings.

1	(2½ to 3-lb.) chicken, boiled with poultry seasoning, celery, and onion, skinned, boned	½	large bell pepper, finely chopped
		1	cup bread and butter pickles, finely chopped
6	medium red potatoes, boiled, cooled, peeled	2	ribs celery, finely chopped
		1	teaspoon seasoning salt
1	medium onion, finely chopped	1 to 1½ cups mayonnaise	
		Salt and pepper to taste	

Dice chicken and potatoes; add remaining ingredients; toss lightly. Cover and refrigerate overnight. Serve garnished with bell pepper rings and pimento strips.

Dean Norwood

TUNA MACARONI SALAD
6 to 8 servings.

1 (16-ounce) package shell macaroni, cooked and drained	1 bunch green onions with tops, chopped
2 (6½-ounce) cans tuna, drained, flaked	1 small onion, chopped
3 carrots, shredded	4 ribs celery with leaves, chopped
	¾ cup chili sauce, optional
	1¾ cup mayonnaise

Mix all ingredients thoroughly; cover and chill overnight. Serve on lettuce leaves.

Udean Coulter
DeBerry, Texas

◊ T. G. T. Steel, Circuit Judge, 8th District, 1873.

CRAB LOUIS
6 servings.

1½ cups crab meat, flaked	1 teaspoon finely chopped green pepper
⅓ cup mayonnaise	⅛ teaspoon onion juice
1 teaspoon chili sauce	2 large tomatoes, sliced
1 teaspoon prepared horseradish, optional	1 medium avocado, sliced
¼ cup finely cut celery	2 tablespoons black caviar, optional

Combine first 7 ingredients, mixing well. To serve, place one slice each, tomato and avocado, on lettuce cup; heap salad mixture on top. Serve with French Dressing. (Use sprinkles of caviar as garnish, if desired).

French Dressing:

⅔ cup salad oil	Pinch dry mustard
⅓ cup vinegar	Pinch black pepper
¾ teaspoon salt	1 teaspoon paprika
4 teaspoons sugar, or to taste	½ teaspoon onion juice

Beat all ingredients together thoroughly; cover tightly; chill. Shake well before serving. Yield: 1 cup.

Anne E. Brookes

POPPY SEED DRESSING
2½ cups.

1 cup sugar or honey	1¼ teaspoons dry mustard
1¼ teaspoons salt	1⅓ cups oil
½ cup vinegar	1½ tablespoons poppy seeds
1 tablespoon onion juice	

Combine first 6 ingredients in a blender; on low speed, process 30 seconds. Stir in poppy seeds; chill thoroughly. Stir well before using. Makes a savory dressing for fruit salads.

Jane Sevier
Mrs. John Sevier
Arkadelphia, Arkansas

◇ *Ambrose Sevier, Delegate, Arkansas Territory, 1827-1836; U.S. Senator, 1836-1849.*

LE FRENCH SALAD DRESSING
1½ cups.

1 cup mayonnaise	1 tablespoon milk
3 tablespoons lemon juice	2 teaspoons sugar
2 tablespoons chopped parsley	½ teaspoon dried tarragon
1 tablespoon paprika	½ teaspoon dry mustard

Combine all ingredients; mix well. Refrigerate.

Dr. Robert L. Smith, Jr.
Little Rock, Arkansas

ITALIAN DRESSING
1½ cups.

1 teaspoon salt	1 tablespoon lemon juice
½ teaspoon white pepper	1 cup salad oil
¼ teaspoon cayenne pepper	3 cloves garlic, minced
¼ teaspoon dry mustard	Dash hot pepper sauce
3 tablespoons salad vinegar	

Combine all ingredients in a jar; cover; shake until well blended. Refrigerate.

Jean Smith
Little Rock, Arkansas

GUACAMOLE DRESSING

2 cups.

- 1 medium avocado, mashed
- 1 small onion, grated
- 2 teaspoons sugar
- 1 tablespoon lemon juice
- 1 teaspoon Worcestershire sauce
- Dash Tabasco sauce
- 1/8 teaspoon garlic powder
- 1/8 teaspoon Accent
- 1 cup mayonnaise
- Few drops green food coloring

Combine avocado and onion. Add sugar, lemon juice, and seasonings; stir, blending thoroughly. Add mayonnaise and food coloring; mix until smooth. Chill.

Dr. Robert L. Smith, Jr.
Little Rock, Arkansas

THOUSAND ISLAND DRESSING

about 2 cups.

- 1 cup mayonnaise
- 1/3 cup chili sauce
- 1/4 cup pickle relish
- 1/4 teaspoon onion powder
- 1 teaspoon Worcestershire sauce
- Few drops Tabasco sauce
- 1/2 teaspoon lemon juice
- 1/2 teaspoon sugar
- 1/4 teaspoon pepper
- 1 hard-boiled egg, finely chopped

Combine all ingredients, blending well. Refrigerate.

Janice Dilday Strauss

COLE SLAW DRESSING

1½ cups.

- 1/4 cup apple cider vinegar
- 1 (5⅓-ounce) can evaporated milk
- 1 teaspoon salt
- 1/4 teaspoon celery seeds
- 1/8 teaspoon pepper
- 1/2 cup mayonnaise

In medium bowl, stir vinegar with milk; let set 5 to 10 minutes. Add remaining ingredients; chill.

Grace Reeder Coulter
Nashville, Arkansas

BLEU CHEESE DRESSING
2 cups.

4 ounces bleu cheese	¼ cup buttermilk
1 cup mayonnaise	1 tablespoon white vinegar
¼ cup sour cream	1 teaspoon garlic powder

Crumble bleu cheese in a mixing bowl; add mayonnaise and blend. Add sour cream; blend thoroughly again. Add remaining ingredients, mixing well. Refrigerate.

Francis Stafford Hedgecock
Hamburg, Arkansas
Laura Eva Turner Maurer
Houston, Texas

PRIZE-WINNING HOMEMADE MAYONNAISE
2½ cups.

1 egg	2 dashes each, cayenne pepper, paprika, and coarse black pepper
1 teaspoon dry mustard	
1 teaspoon salt	
1 teaspoon sugar	2 tablespoons fresh lemon juice
⅛ teaspoon white pepper	
	2 cups salad oil

Place all ingredients except oil in a food processor. Process, quickly adding oil in a thin stream. Processing should take less than a minute. Refrigerate in tightly covered container.

Carrie Remmell Dickinson
Little Rock, Arkansas

◇ *Isaac Cates, in 1807, one of the first three men granted residence in Hot Springs by the Caddo Indians.*

Always soften gelatin first in cold liquid, then dissolve in hot. Don't boil gelatin; boiling reduces its jelling power.

BEA'S SALAD DRESSING
1 quart.

3 tablespoons salt	3 cups oil
1 tablespoon black pepper	1 cup vinegar
1 tablespoon paprika	¼ cup tarragon vinegar
1½ teaspoons sugar	10 drops Tabasco sauce
1½ teaspoons dry mustard	⅔ cup catsup

Mix dry ingredients well with a small measure of the oil. Add remaining oil, then the other ingredients; mix well. Store in quart jar in the refrigerator. (This faintly resembles the slightly sweet, reddish commercial "French" dressing.)

Harriet Aldridge
Food Editor, ARKANSAS GAZETTE

BANANA NUT DRESSING
6 servings.

½ cup mayonnaise	1 tablespoon lemon juice
1 banana, mashed	1 cup chopped pecans
3 tablespoons whipping cream	

Blend first 4 ingredients until smooth; add nuts and mix well. Mixture may be stored in refrigerator for several days. This is good for fruit salads.

Marian Matlock
Arkadelphia, Arkansas

Cooking: Fresh pineapple contains an enzyme, bromelin, which breaks down egg white, gelatin, the "set" of jams and jellies, and the structure of baked goods. To deactivate bromelin, bring small pieces of fresh pineapple to a boil, then simmer 15 minutes. Cool and use in place of canned pineapple. It is not advisable to use fresh pineapple rings in place of canned pineapple.

Yields: 1 medium-size pineapple (about 6½ inches long and 4 to 4½ pounds) gives you:
12 slices
5 to 5½ cups chunks or cubes
5 cups crushed
16 spears

VEGETABLES

POKE SALLET
4 to 6 servings

3 to 4 pounds poke greens	12 green onions, chopped
4 thick slices bacon	3 eggs, beaten
1 teaspoon salt	

Select tender young greens; remove stems; wash thoroughly in at least 3 rinse waters. Parboil 5 minutes in water to cover; drain. Place greens in fresh water; cook until tender; drain and squeeze water from greens. Fry bacon until crisp; drain; set aside. Add greens, onions, and salt to pan drippings; heat through. Pour eggs into mixture and scramble; top with crumbled bacon.

Blanche Bourns Shelton

ARTICHOKES AND MUSHROOMS
4 to 6 servings.

- 3 tablespoons butter
- 1 cup chopped green onions with tops
- 12 ounces fresh mushrooms, sliced
- 1 (14-ounce) can artichoke hearts, drained, quartered
- 1 (16-ounce) can tomatoes, drained, chopped
- 1 teaspoon dried basil
- 1 tablespoon sugar
- Salt and pepper

Sauté onions in butter until limp; add mushrooms; cook until onions are tender. Stir in remaining ingredients; heat through.

Donna Coulter

ASPARAGUS CASSEROLE
6 servings.

- ½ pound hoop cheese, grated
- 1 cup cracker crumbs
- 1 (15-ounce) can green asparagus tips, drained, liquid reserved
- 1 (10¾-ounce) can cream of mushroom or celery soup
- ½ cup melted butter
- ½ cup chopped blanched almonds

Combine cheese and crumbs; spread half the mixture on bottom of a greased 8 × 8-inch baking dish. Arrange asparagus tips on crumb mixture. Mix butter and liquid from asparagus with soup; pour over asparagus. Sprinkle remaining crumbs and almonds evenly over top. Bake 20 minutes at 350°.

Alice Mayo
Arkadelphia, Arkansas

OLD HICKORY BARBECUED BEANS
6 to 8 servings.

1 pound ground beef	½ (18-ounce) bottle regular OLD HICKORY BARBECUE SAUCE
½ small onion, chopped	
¼ teaspoon garlic salt	
¼ teaspoon chili powder	½ (32-ounce) bottle catsup
Salt and pepper to taste	3 tablespoons brown sugar
2 (16-ounce) cans pork and beans	

In heavy skillet cook beef, onion, and spices until browned. Add beans, Old Hickory, and catsup; stir over low heat until combined. Reduce heat; add brown sugar; simmer about 15 minutes, or until thoroughly heated.

OLD HICKORY Sauce Company, Inc.
El Dorado, Arkansas

OLD HICKORY, an Arkansas product, manufactured in El Dorado since 1944.

RED BEANS AND RICE
6 to 8 servings.

1 pound red kidney beans	1 teaspoon coarsely-ground black pepper
1 ham bone, plus leftover ham, cut up	
2 cups chopped red onion	3 quarts water
2 to 3 cloves garlic, minced	1 tablespoon salt
2 cups chopped celery with leaves	1 pod dried red pepper or 1 teaspoon cayenne pepper
	1 pound smoked sausage, sliced, sautéed and drained

In large Dutch oven bring all ingredients except sausage to a boil; reduce heat and simmer 4 to 5 hours or until beans are soft and liquid is thick. Stir in sausage for the last 30 minutes of cooking. Adjust seasonings. Serve over hot rice.

Hope J. Norman
Alexandria, Louisiana

SPICY BEANS AND CORNBREAD CASSEROLE
8 to 10 servings.

2 cups dried pinto beans	1 teaspoon cumin
3 quarts water	1 teaspoon basil
½ cup cream cheese	Salt and cayenne pepper to taste
1¾ cups plain yogurt, divided	
½ cup grated cheese	1½ cups yellow cornmeal
1½ cups chopped onion	½ cup flour
2 to 4 cloves, garlic, minced	½ teaspoon salt
2 tablespoons oil	1½ teaspoons baking powder
1 medium zucchini, diced	¼ cup milk
2 tomatoes, chopped	1 large egg

Cover beans with water; soak overnight; drain. In large pot cook beans in water until tender. Cut cream and grated cheeses and 1 cup yogurt into warm beans. Sauté onion and garlic in oil until tender; mix into bean mixture; transfer to a greased deep 3-quart casserole. Sauté zucchini, tomatoes, and spices; season to taste; spread on top of beans. Combine next 4 dry ingredients. Beat together remaining yogurt, milk, and egg; stir into dry mixture until well mixed. Spread batter over the zucchini-tomato layer. Bake, uncovered, 40 minutes at 375°; serve warm.

Nancy Coulter Cahn
Boulder, Colorado

"BEATS-ALL" BEETS
4 servings.

⅓ cup sugar	1 tart apple, peeled, cored, and diced
⅓ cup cider vinegar	
2 teaspoons cornstarch	2 tablespoons grated orange peel
1 teaspoon cinnamon or ginger	
2½ cups diced, cooked beets	2 tablespoons butter
	Sour cream
	Minced fresh parsley

Combine sugar, vinegar, cornstarch, and spice in a saucepan; blend until smooth; cook, stirring until sauce thickens. Add beets, apple, orange peel, and butter; simmer 10 minutes. Serve garnished with dollop of sour cream sprinkled with fresh parsley.

Alta Purtell Cure

BROCCOLI CASSEROLE FOR A CROWD
15 servings.

4	(10-ounce) packages chopped broccoli, cooked, drained
½	cup chopped onion
1	cup chopped celery
6	tablespoons butter, divided
1	(10¾-ounce) can cream of mushroom soup
1	(8-ounce) can water chestnuts, drained, sliced
1	(4-ounce) can mushrooms, chopped
1	(4-ounce) can chopped pimentos, drained
½	cup chopped almonds
1	(5-ounce) package garlic cheese
1	cup bread crumbs
Salt to taste	

Place broccoli in a greased 9 × 13-inch baking dish. Sauté onion and celery in 3 tablespoons butter; add remaining ingredients, except crumbs and butter. Mix until cheese melts. Pour over broccoli. Sprinkle with bread crumbs; drizzle remaining butter over top. Bake at 350° until bubbly. This freezes well; thaw before baking.

Lois Carruth
Daina Johnson

SWEET AND SOUR RED CABBAGE
6 to 8 servings.

1	large head red cabbage
1	large onion, chopped
4	tablespoons oil
2	tart apples, pared, cored, thinly sliced
1	tablespoon salt
½	teaspoon pepper
2	tablespoons grenadine or maraschino cherry syrup
¼	cup cider vinegar

Trim cabbage; quarter, core and shred thin. In a large skillet, sauté onion in oil until limp; add remaining ingredients except vinegar. Heat slowly to boiling; reduce heat; cover and simmer until cabbage is tender, about 25 minutes. Remove from heat; drizzle vinegar over cabbage; toss to mix; serve.

Midge Williams

CABBAGE ROLLS
6 to 8 servings.

1 large head cabbage	Sage or poultry seasoning, to taste
1 pound ground beef	2 (8-ounce) cans tomato sauce
1 teaspoon salt	2 tablespoons brown sugar
½ teaspoon pepper	¼ cup sugar
½ cup rice	½ cup water
1 small onion, chopped	
1 egg, beaten	

Cut around stem of cabbage; loosen leaves by running water over them. Place head in boiling water; let stand until wilted. Remove from water; spread leaves apart to cool slightly; separate leaves.

Combine next 7 ingredients. Place about ⅓ cup of meat mixture in center of each leaf. Fold sides of leaf over meat to wrap completely. Place rolls seam side down in Dutch oven; there may be 2 or 3 layers. Combine remaining ingredients; pour over rolls. Bring to a boil; reduce heat; simmer, covered, for 1 hour. Add more water, if needed. Canned tomatoes or tomato juice may be substituted for tomato sauce.

Audrey Boyd
Mt. Holly, Arkansas

CARROTS FLAMBE
8 servings.

2 pounds carrots, sliced	1 teaspoon orange rind
2 tablespoons butter	½ teaspoon lemon juice
¼ cup sugar	¼ teaspoon ginger
3 tablespoons orange juice	

Steam carrots in small amount of salt water until crisp-tender; set aside. In separate pan combine remaining ingredients; drain carrots; add to mixture. Simmer until glazed.

Mrs. Harry Gillespie

LO-CAL CARROTS
6 servings.

4 cups sliced carrots
1 cup water
1 (15-ounce) can unsweetened pineapple tidbits, undrained
2 tablespoons cornstarch
½ teaspoon ginger

In a small saucepan cook carrots in water until crisp-tender; carrots may be steamed. Combine pineapple, cornstarch, and ginger in a small bowl; mix well; add to carrots. Cook over low heat, stirring constantly, until mixture thickens. (60 calories per serving.)

Betty Coulter Henderson
Hot Springs, Arkansas

CREAMY CAULIFLOWER
6 to 8 servings.

1 medium cauliflower
Salt and pepper to taste
1 (16-ounce) can cream of mushroom soup
¼ cup milk
½ cup shredded Cheddar cheese
1 cup Bisquick baking mix
¼ cup firm butter

Break cauliflower into flowerets. Cook 2 minutes in boiling salted water; drain. Place in ungreased 1½-quart casserole. Beat soup and milk until smooth; pour over cauliflower. Sprinkle with cheese. With fork combine Bisquick and butter until crumbly; sprinkle evenly over top of casserole. Bake at 350° until crumbs are light brown, about 20 minutes.

Sue Van Bebber

BRAISED CUCUMBERS
4 to 6 servings.

4 cucumbers	⅛ teaspoon pepper
3 tablespoons butter	Minced parsley or chives
½ cup consomme	

Cut cucumbers in half lengthwise; scoop out seeds. Cut halves into thirds, crosswise. Sauté pieces in butter 2 or 3 minutes; add consomme and pepper. Cover; simmer over low heat until crisp-tender, about 5 minutes. Sprinkle with parsley or chives.

Mrs. C. J. Alexander
Texarkana, Texas

CORN FRITTERS
6 to 8 servings.

1 cup flour	¼ cup milk
1 teaspoon salt	1 tablespoon oil
1 teaspoon baking powder	1½ cups cooked whole kernel corn
2 eggs	

Combine flour, salt, and baking powder; set aside. Beat eggs with milk; add oil and corn. Stir into flour mixture until just moistened. In skillet, in a small amount of heated oil, spoon batter by tablespoonfuls, a few at a time. Fry on one side until golden brown; turn, and cook until centers are done; drain.

Charlotte Chadburn

FRIED CORN
4 to 6 servings.

6 to 8 ears fresh corn	Salt and pepper to taste
2 tablespoons butter, or bacon drippings	⅓ cup milk, or cream
	1 teaspoon sugar

Cut kernels from cob without cutting too deep; then, using dull side of knife, scrape milk from cob into kernels. In heavy skillet heat butter; add corn and fry over medium heat, stirring constantly, 5 minutes. Add cream and seasonings; simmer, stirring frequently, 12 to 15 minutes, or until corn is tender.

Linda McWhorter
Twyla McWhorter

CORN PUDDING
6 to 8 servings.

1 (17-ounce) can cream-style corn	2 cups milk
¼ cup flour	2 eggs, well beaten
3 tablespoons sugar	2 tablespoons margarine, melted
1 teaspoon salt	

Combine corn, flour, sugar and salt, blending well. In separate bowl, combine remaining ingredients; stir into corn mixture. Pour into a lightly greased 1½-quart casserole. Bake 1 hour at 350°; stir twice during baking. Pudding should be rather firm.

Ada Gillian Thomas

PEPPER CORN
Serves 6-8.

1 green pepper	2 cups milk
½ cup chopped onion	2 (16-ounce) cans whole kernel corn, drained
¼ cup butter	
¼ cup flour	1 cup herb-seasoned stuffing croutons
2 teaspoons salt	
½ teaspoon dry mustard	2 eggs, slightly beaten

Cut 2 rings of green pepper for garnish. Chop remaining pepper; sauté with onion in butter for 5 minutes. Add flour, salt, mustard, and milk; blend well. Cook over medium heat until thick and smooth. Remove from heat; stir in corn, croutons and beaten eggs. Pour into greased 2-quart casserole; top with pepper rings; bake at 350° 30 minutes.

Ruby Graves
Broken Bow, Oklahoma
Lou Gray

SCALLOPED CORN
6 to 8 servings.

- 1 (17-ounce) can whole kernel corn, drained
- 1 (17-ounce) cream-style corn
- 2 eggs, beaten
- 1 (2-ounce) jar chopped pimentos, drained
- 2 tablespoons chopped green pepper
- 4 ounces grated Cheddar cheese
- 2 tablespoons flour
- 2 tablespoons sugar
- 1 teaspoon salt

Combine all ingredients; pour into a greased 2-quart casserole. Bake 45 minutes at 325° to 350°, or until set.

Janice Walker
Clinton, Iowa

HOMINY CASSEROLE
6 to 8 servings.

- 1 medium onion, chopped
- 1 stick margarine
- 2 (12- to 14-ounce) cans hominy, drained (yellow, white, or with peppers)
- 1 (10¾-ounce) can cream of chicken or cream of mushroom soup
- 2 jalapeño peppers, finely chopped
- ¾ cup grated cheese
- Salt and pepper to taste
- 1 cup corn chips, optional

Sauté onion in margarine; combine with remaining ingredients in a greased 1½-quart casserole; bake 30 minutes at 350°. If using corn chips, stir in after 20 minutes. (1 (8-ounce) jar jalapeño cheese spread may be substituted for peppers and grated cheese.)

Inez Taylor
Marty Brown

FRIED EGGPLANT
6 servings.

1 large eggplant	½ teaspoon salt
1½ cups flour, divided	¾ cup milk
¼ cup oil	1 egg, beaten

Peel eggplant; cut in 1-inch squares; soak in cold water 1 hour; drain thoroughly. In paper bag with 1 cup flour shake pieces to coat. Combine last 4 ingredients with ½ cup flour, mixing well. Dip floured eggplant in batter; fry in deep, hot oil until golden brown; drain.

Nancy Sullivan

EGGPLANT FRITTERS
6 to 8 fritters.

1 medium eggplant, peeled and chopped	1½ cups coarse cracker crumbs
1 medium onion, finely chopped	2 eggs, beaten
	½ teaspoon basil
	½ cup margarine

Cook eggplant in salted water until tender; drain; cool and mash. Add other ingredients except margarine, mixing well. Melt margarine in skillet; spoon mixture by heaping tablespoons into skillet; cook until golden, turning once. Drain well; serve warm.

Catherine Montgomery

FRANKE'S SCALLOPED EGGPLANT
6 to 8 servings.

1 large or 2 small eggplants	2 cups cornbread crumbs
½ teaspoon salt	Milk
2 cups tomatoes, well drained	Grated cheese
½ cup finely chopped onion	¼ cup chopped green pepper, optional
2 eggs, well beaten	

Peel eggplant, cube and cook until tender in salted water. Drain thoroughly; mash; season to taste. Mash tomatoes; mix with eggplant, onion, eggs and cornbread crumbs. Pour into a greased 1½ to 2-quart casserole. Add enough milk to cover well; top with grated cheese. Bake at 375° for 30 minutes.

Gertrude Remmel Butler
Little Rock, Arkansas

 Governor John E. Martineau, 1927-1928

GOLDEN EGGPLANT CASSEROLE
6 servings.

2½ cups eggplant, peeled and cubed	2 tablespoons chopped pimentos
18 saltine crackers, crushed	1 tablespoon butter, melted
½ cup shredded sharp cheese	½ teaspoon salt
¼ cup chopped celery	⅛ teaspoon pepper
	1 cup evaporated milk

Cook eggplant in boiling salted water 10 minutes; drain well. Combine with remaining ingredients; pour into a greased 1-quart casserole. Bake 45 minutes at 350°.

June Slayton Tollett
Rebecca Harper

GREEN BEAN CASSEROLE
10 to 12 servings.

5 (17-ounce) cans whole green beans	⅛ teaspoon Tabasco sauce
¼ pound dry salt meat	2 teaspoons soy sauce
1 medium onion, chopped	1 teaspoon salt
1 stick butter	¾ pound Cheddar cheese, grated
¼ cup flour	1 (8-ounce) jar sliced mushrooms, drained
2 cups warm milk	1 (8-ounce) can water chestnuts, sliced, drained
1 cup whipping cream	¼ cup slivered almonds

In a large sauce pan combine green beans with liquid, salt meat, and onion; bring to a boil; reduce heat and simmer 40 to 45 minutes. Remove from heat; let stand until onions are clear. In separate pan melt butter; stir in flour; cook over low heat 2 minutes, stirring often. Gradually add milk, then cream, Tabasco, soy and salt; stir constantly until sauce is smooth and thickens. Add cheese, stirring until melted. Drain beans, removing salt meat; mix with mushrooms and cheese sauce. Pour into a greased 9 × 13-inch baking dish; top with water chestnuts and sprinkle with almonds. Heat for 20 to 25 minutes at 325 to 350°, just until bubbly. Do not overheat; sauce will boil and separate.

Mona Moore

ORIGINAL GREEN BEAN CASSEROLE
6 to 8 servings.

2 (16-ounce) cans cut green beans, drained	⅛ teaspoon black pepper
¾ cup milk	1 (2½-ounce) can French fried onion rings (divided)
1 (10¾-ounce) can cream of mushroom soup	

Combine beans, milk, soup and pepper with half the onion rings. Pour into a greased 1½-quart casserole. Bake, uncovered, 30 minutes at 350°. Top with remaining onion rings and bake 5 minutes.

Fannie & Fletcher T. "Demp" Willoughby
Casper, Wyoming

HOPPIN' JOHN
6 to 8 servings.

2	cups dried black-eyed peas	2	teaspoons salt
2	quarts water	2	teaspoons bacon drippings
½	pound ham	¼	teaspoon pepper
1	cup chopped onion	4	cups cooked rice
1	cup chopped celery	¼	teaspoon cayenne pepper

Sort peas; wash thoroughly. Place in large Dutch oven with water; bring to a boil; boil 2 minutes; cover and let stand for 1 hour. Add next 6 ingredients; bring to a boil; reduce heat; cover; simmer 1 hour. Stir in rice and cayenne. Heat thoroughly.

Serena Cusson

JUST PEACHY LIMAS
6 servings.

2	(10-ounce) packages frozen lima beans	2	teaspoons cornstarch
¼	cup sliced green onions	⅓	cup toasted, slivered almonds
1	tablespoon margarine	4 to 6	slices fried bacon, crumbled
⅔	cup peach or apricot preserves		

Cook beans according to package directions; drain. In small sauce pan sauté onions in butter until tender, about 3 munutes. Stir together preserves and cornstarch; add to onions and cook over medium heat until bubbly. Add preserve mixture, almonds, and bacon to beans. Heat through. Serve hot.

MICROWAVE INSTRUCTIONS: Place beans in 1½-quart casserole, cover, cook at HIGH 10 minutes or until tender; drain. Place onions and butter in 4-cup glass measure, cover, cook at HIGH 2 minutes; add preserves and cornstarch. Cook, uncovered, at HIGH 2 minutes or until bubbly, stirring once. Combine all ingredients and heat through.

*Denise Henderson
Home Economist
SOUTHERN LIVING*

MAY'S OKRA CASSEROLE
4 to 6 servings.

Flour
Salt and pepper to taste
1 pound fresh okra, sliced
½ cup bacon drippings
1 large onion, diced
1 (12-ounce) can whole kernel corn, drained
1 (8-ounce) can tomato sauce
1½ cups grated cheese

Combine flour, salt and pepper; coat okra heavily with this mixture. Fry okra in bacon drippings until partially done; add onion and fry until okra is brown; drain well. Place okra in bottom of a greased 1-quart casserole; cover with a layer of corn. Pour tomato sauce evenly over top and sprinkle with cheese. Bake at 350° until bubbly and cheese is melted.

May Smith
Winthrop, Arkansas

OKRA AND TOMATOES
4 to 6 servings.

4 cups fresh sliced okra
1 onion, chopped
1 green pepper, chopped
2 tablespoons bacon drippings
3 tomatoes, peeled, quartered
1 teaspoon sugar
¾ teaspoon salt
¼ teaspoon black pepper

In a 9-inch skillet sauté onion and green pepper in bacon drippings until tender; add remaining ingredients, cover and simmer until okra is tender, about 10 minutes.

Frankie Elkins

SPANISH ONION CUSTARD

6 servings.

2 cups thinly sliced sweet Spanish onions	¼ teaspoon paprika
⅓ cup margarine	¼ teaspoon celery salt
¼ cup flour	1½ cups milk
1 teaspoon salt	3 eggs, beaten
	⅔ cup soft bread crumbs

Sauté onions in butter until tender. Blend in flour and seasonings. Add milk gradually; cook, stirring constantly, until thick; remove from heat. Combine eggs and bread crumbs; fold into onion mixture. Pour into buttered 2-quart baking dish; place dish in pan of hot water; bake 45 minutes at 350°. Serve with Creamy Mushroom Sauce.

Creamy Mushroom Sauce:

8 ounces fresh mushrooms, sliced	¾ teaspoon dry mustard
	¼ teaspoon salt
1 teaspoon butter	Dash of white pepper
1 egg, beaten	½ pound sharp cheese, shredded
1 cup milk	

In small skillet sauté mushrooms in butter until tender. In top of double boiler, combine egg, milk, and seasonings. Cook and stir until slightly thick; stir in cheese and blend until melted. Add mushrooms; heat thoroughly. Yield: 2 cups.

Bulah Miles
Los Angeles, California

ONION PATTIES

6 servings.

2½ cups chopped onions	½ cup dry milk powder
¾ cup flour	1 tablespoon cornmeal
2 tablespoons baking powder	Cold milk
½ teaspoon salt	

In a bowl, combine all ingredients except cold milk; mix well. Add enough milk to form a thick batter. Drop by spoonfuls into hot oil; fry until brown; drain.

Mrs. Ruel Crow
Agnes Nix
Mrs. Earl E. Burt

PURPLE HULL PEAS

4 to 6 servings.

1½ quarts fresh or frozen purple hull peas	1 teaspoon sugar
1½ quarts water	1 teaspoon salt
	3 tablespoons bacon drippings

In large heavy sauce pan, bring water to a boil; add peas and seasonings. Continue to boil gently 1 hour, adding additional hot water if necessary.

Bess Dowdle

CHEESE POTATOES

8 to 10 servings.

10 medium potatoes	1 tablespoon dry parsley
1 (4-ounce) can pimentos, drained	1 teaspoon salt
1 large onion, chopped	1 stick butter, melted
½ green pepper, chopped	½ cup milk
½ pound Velveeta cheese, cubed	2 tablespoons flour

Boil unpeeled potatoes; peel and cut in small pieces. Place in greased 2-quart casserole. Combine next 7 ingredients; pour over potatoes. Mix flour and milk; pour over top. Bake 30 minutes at 350°.

Edna Walden Bernard
Foreman, Arkansas

COUNTRY POTATOES

6 to 8 servings.

6 medium potatoes, peeled and quartered	1 cup sour cream
½ cup butter	1½ cups grated sharp Cheddar cheese
¾ cup chopped green onions, with tops	Salt and pepper to taste

Cook potatoes in water; drain and mash, leaving them a little lumpy. Mix in remaining ingredients, except cheese. Pour into buttered 1½-quart casserole. Top with cheese and bake 20 to 30 minutes at 325°.

Margie Crossley Austin
Kansas City, Missouri
Murl Powell

POTATO CASSEROLE
6 to 8 servings.

8 medium red potatoes	1 small onion, finely diced
1 bay leaf	2 cups grated Cheddar cheese, divided
1 cup cream of chicken soup	
1½ cups sour cream	Crushed potato chips
¼ cup melted margarine	

Peel and boil whole potatoes in water with bay leaf until barely done; drain and cool. In medium mixing bowl grate potatoes; add soup, sour cream, margarine, onion, and 1 cup cheese. Pour into a greased 9 × 9-inch baking pan. Bake 30 minutes at 350°. Remove; sprinkle with potato chips to cover, then with remaining cheese. Bake until cheese melts; cut in squares, and serve hot.

Elizabeth Scoggin
Nashville, Arkansas

QUARTER-BAKED POTATOES
4 servings.

3 or 4 scrubbed potatoes	½ teaspoon garlic powder
½ cup oil	½ teaspoon salt
2 teaspoons grated Parmesan cheese	¼ teaspoon pepper

Quarter potatoes; do not peel. Place in a greased 8 × 8-inch baking dish. Mix remaining ingredients; brush potatoes with mixture. Bake covered 30 minutes at 375°; remove cover and continue baking 15 minutes, until done and golden brown.

Irma Walters

SPEEDY SPINACH
8 servings.

2 (10-ounce) packages frozen chopped spinach	1 pint sour cream
1 (⅜-ounce) package onion soup mix	Salt and pepper to taste
	6 slices Swiss cheese

Place frozen spinach in a large sauce pan over very low heat (add no water). Cover and watch carefully until spinach is thawed and cooked, 10 to 15 minutes. Remove from heat; stir in soup mix, sour cream and seasonings. Pour into a greased 1½-quart casserole; top with cheese slices. Bake 30 minutes at 300°.

Mrs. Lewis A. McClain
Arkadelphia, Arkansas

SPINACH SQUARES
6 to 8 servings.

2 (10-ounce) packages frozen chopped spinach, thawed, drained	4 eggs, beaten
3 tablespoons butter	¼ cup dry bread crumbs
1 small onion, chopped	¼ cup grated Parmesan cheese, divided
¼ pound mushrooms, chopped	⅛ teaspoon basil
1 (10¾-ounce) can mushroom or cream of chicken soup	⅛ teaspoon oregano

Sauté onion and mushrooms in butter. Add spinach, soup, eggs, bread crumbs, seasonings, and ½ the cheese to onion mixture. Pour into a greased 8 × 8-inch baking dish; sprinkle remaining cheese on top. Bake 35 to 40 minutes at 325° uncovered. Can be served warm or cold.

Judy Nelsen

SQUASH-CARROT CASSEROLE
6 to 8 servings.

2 pounds squash, sliced	1 cup shredded carrots
¼ cup chopped onion	½ cup melted butter
1 (10¾-ounce) can cream of chicken soup	1 (8-ounce) herb-seasoned stuffing mix
1 cup sour cream	

Cook squash and onion until tender; drain. Mix sour cream, soup and carrots; fold in squash mixture and butter. Sread half the stuffing mix in bottom of a greased 9 × 13-inch baking dish. Spoon vegetables over mix; sprinkle remaining mix on top. Bake 25 minutes at 350°.

Delia Koger Puckett
Karen Coker

STIR-FRY SQUASH
4 servings.

2 yellow squash, sliced	1 bell pepper, thinly sliced
1 zucchini, sliced	2 tablespoons butter
1 small onion, thinly sliced, separated into rings	1 tomato, cut in eighths
	Grated cheese

In large skillet, heat butter and stir fry vegetables, except tomato, until crisp-tender. Add tomato and cheese; cook only until cheese melts.

Carolyn Smith
Vera Curtis

YELLOW SQUASH CASSEROLE
8 to 10 servings.

6 to 8 cups sliced yellow squash	2 eggs, beaten
½ cup margarine, or bacon drippings	Salt and pepper to taste
¾ cup chopped onion	½ teaspoon Tabasco sauce
15 Ritz crackers, crumbled	1 cup grated sharp cheese
	1½ cups Ritz cracker crumbs
	½ cup melted margarine

Cook squash until tender; drain. Sauté onion in margarine or bacon drippings. Combine squash, onion, crackers, eggs, seasonings to taste, and cheese. Pour into a greased 2-quart casserole; top with buttered cracker crumbs. Bake 35 minutes at 350°.

Corene Horne
Letha Staggs
Nora Staggs

STUFFED SUMMER SQUASH

5 servings.

5 small, whole Patty Pan squash	¼ cup butter
½ cup chopped green pepper	1 teaspoon salt
½ cup chopped celery	Pepper to taste
2 cups fresh corn, cut from cob	¼ cup cream

Place whole squash in large sauce pan; cover with boiling water; cover and cook rapidly about 15 minutes, or until tender. Meanwhile sauté green pepper, celery and corn in the butter until celery is soft. Drain squash; split crosswise; scoop out centers. Combine squash centers with sautéed vegetables and seasonings. Heap mixture into squash shells. Set shells in baking pan; pour a little cream over the filling in each. Cover; bake 10 minutes at 350°. Serve hot.

Frances Brookes

SQUASH FRITTERS

6 servings.

1 cup flour	1 egg, beaten
½ cup milk	3 tablespoons chopped hot chili or jalapeño pepper
¼ cup oil	
1 teaspoon sugar	1 onion, finely chopped
1 teaspoon salt	3 cups shredded fresh squash

Combine flour, milk and oil, stirring until smooth; add remaining ingredients. Drop by tablespoonfuls into hot deep oil. Fry to golden brown; drain.

Louise Lacefield

SPICY SWEET POTATO CASSEROLE
8 servings.

3 cups mashed sweet potatoes	1 teaspoon cinnamon
1 cup sugar	1 cup melted butter, divided
¼ cup milk or orange juice	1 cup coconut, optional
2 eggs, beaten	1 cup nuts
1 teaspoon salt	1 cup brown sugar
1 teaspoon vanilla or nutmeg	1 cup self-rising flour

Combine first 7 ingredients with ½ cup melted butter; add coconut if desired. Pour into a greased 8 × 11-inch baking pan. Combine remaining butter with nuts, brown sugar, and flour. Spread over potato mixture. Bake 35 minutes at 350°.

Mrs. Willie Gibson
Mrs. John Paul Jones

SWEET POTATO CASSEROLE
6 to 8 servings.

5 medium sweet potatoes, sliced, cooked, drained	1 cup brown sugar
	8 marshmallows
3 tablespoons flour	½ pint whipping cream
2 teaspoons salt	

Place sweet potatoes in a greased 9 × 9-inch baking pan. Combine flour, salt and brown sugar; sprinkle over potatoes. Dot with marshmallows. Pour cream evenly over top; bake 30 to 45 minutes at 350°, or until marshmallows are melted and lightly browned.

Lucy Owens

◇*Lena Owens, first Home Demonstration Agent, Sevier County, 1916*

GERMAN SAUERKRAUT
4 to 6 servings.

1 pound fresh pork, cubed, or 1 pound smoked sausage, sliced	1 (32-ounce) jar sauerkraut
	2 tablespoons brown sugar
	¼ teaspoon black pepper
2 cups water	3 fresh apples, peeled, sliced
1 teaspoon salt	

Boil pork in salt-seasoned water until tender; if using sausage, omit salt; simmer 30 minutes. Add remaining ingredients; cook over low heat 45 minutes. Add warm water during cooking, if more is needed.

Martha Brookes Johnston

FRIED GREEN TOMATOES
4 to 6 servings.

3 large, firm green tomatoes	½ cup cornmeal
Sugar to taste	¼ cup flour
Salt and pepper to taste	¼ cup milk
2 eggs, beaten	

Slice tomatoes ½-inch thick; sprinkle with sugar, salt and pepper. Combine remaining ingredients, mixing well. Dip tomato slices into batter. Fry in ½-inch medium hot oil or shortening for 1 to 2 minutes per side, or until golden brown.

Eileen Welch
Ashdown, Arkansas

TOMATO CASSEROLE
6 to 8 servings.

5 medium tomatoes, peeled, sliced, and drained	¼ teaspoon pepper
½ cup mayonnaise	1 teaspoon basil
1 clove garlic, crushed	¼ cup Ritz cracker crumbs
½ cup grated Parmesan cheese	2 teaspoons butter

Arrange tomato slices in a greased 9 × 9-inch pan. Combine next 5 ingredients; spread mixture over tomatoes. Sprinkle with cracker crumbs; dot with butter. Bake 20 minutes at 425°. This may also be put into a baked 9-inch pie shell.

Jimmie Ann Simmons

OLD-FASHIONED TURNIPS
6 to 8 servings.

5 or 6 medium turnips	Sugar to taste
1 cup water	2 tablespoons butter, or bacon drippings
Salt and pepper to taste	

Wash, peel and cut turnips into slices. Put in covered sauce pan with water; cook over low heat until tender. Add seasonings and butter; simmer 5 to 10 minutes. Serve hot.

Eleanor Reeder Berry
Springfield, Illinois
Dorothy Shinn

THIS CAN'T BE TURNIPS
8 servings.

8 medium turnips	Grated Parmesan cheese
2 tablespoons butter	Slivered almonds, toasted
Salt and pepper to taste	

Boil whole, unpeeled turnips in salted water until barely tender; drain. Peel skins from turnips. With a teaspoon remove centers, being careful not to split sides of shell. Place centers in mixing bowl; mash; add butter, salt and pepper. Fill each shell with mashed turnips. Place filled shells in a greased 9 × 9-inch baking pan; sprinkle tops with cheese and then with almonds. Place under broiler and heat through just before serving.

Frank Lambright
Little Rock, Arkansas

TURNIP GREENS WITH CORNBREAD DUMPLINGS
8 to 10 servings.

3 to 4 pounds turnip greens	1 cup cornmeal
½ pound salt pork, sliced	½ teaspoon salt
2 quarts water	1½ cups boiling water
¼ cup bacon drippings	1 egg, beaten
2 tablespoons sugar	

Wash greens thoroughly, removing large stems. Tear large leaves into pieces, or cut with scissors or knife. In large pot bring water with salt pork to a boil; place greens in pot; add bacon drippings and sugar; reduce heat and simmer until tender, about 1 hour. Adjust seasonings. In small bowl, combine meal, salt, and boiling water, mixing well. Add egg; blend. Drop by spoonfuls over hot greens; cook over medium heat 15 to 20 minutes.

In memory of Mrs. Clenara Hankins
By Thelma Lee

MY ZUCCHINI
8 servings.

1 medium onion, chopped	Salt and pepper to taste
1 green pepper, chopped	Onion and celery salts to taste
2 tablespoons butter	6 to 8 medium zucchini,
1 (14½-ounce) can stewed tomatoes	unpeeled, sliced

Sauté onion and green pepper in butter until tender. Add remaining ingredients, seasoning to taste. Cover and simmer until zucchini is tender.

Bubbles Bush Florence
Arkadelphia, Arkansas

◇ *Judge Dexter Bush, Circuit Judge, 9th District, 1930-1951.*

ZUCCHINI MEDLEY
6 servings.

1 cup sliced onion rings	1 teaspoon seasoned salt
1 cup sliced green pepper	Dash of pepper
¼ cup butter	¼ cup Parmesan or grated Cheddar cheese
2 cups 1-inch zucchini slices	
4 fresh tomatoes, quartered	

In a large skillet sauté onion rings and green pepper in butter until lightly browned. Add zucchini and tomatoes; cook 10 minutes longer, or until vegetables are crisp-tender. Season with salt, pepper and cheese.

Mrs. Dale E. Murphy
Foreman, Arkansas
Mrs. J. P. McBeth
Arkadelphia, Arkansas

BASIC WHITE SAUCE
Yield: 1 cup.

2 tablespoons butter	½ teaspoon salt
2 tablespoons flour	1 cup milk

Melt butter over low heat; whisk in flour and salt; cook slowly, stirring until mixture is smooth, about 2 minutes. Do not brown. Gradually add milk; beat until smooth; bring to a boil over medium heat, stirring constantly; cook 1 minute.

Cheese Sauce: Stir ¾ cup grated cheese into cooked sauce until melted; add cayenne pepper to taste. Mushroom Sauce: Use ingredients of basic sauce but sauté ¾ cup sliced fresh mushrooms in butter before adding flour. To thickened sauce add ½ cup shredded American cheese. Yield: 1¾ cups.

Laura Jones

HOLLANDAISE SAUCE
Yield: ¾ cup.

½ cup butter	¼ teaspoon salt
3 egg yolks	**Dash white pepper**
1 tablespoon plus 1½ teaspoons lemon juice	

In a 2-cup glass measure, microwave butter on HIGH until melted, about 1 minute; do not boil. In a blender combine remaining ingredients; process until thick and lemon-colored. With blender running, add butter in a thin stream; process until thick.

La Nell Cox

To prevent white sauce from lumping, it is safer to have the milk hot when you add it to the roux (the flour and butter or oil mixture). Always cook a roux a few minutes before adding liquid.

To rescue a broken or curdled hollandaise or mayonnaise sauce, whisk in 1 or 2 teaspoons of boiling water, a drop at a time. If that doesn't work, put an egg yolk in a bowl; whisk in the sauce slowly; whisk until sauce is smooth.

BREADS

OLD-FASHIONED STONE-GROUND CORNBREAD
8 to 10 servings

- 1½ cups coarse stone-ground cornmeal
- 1 teaspoon salt
- 1 teaspoon baking soda
- 2 tablespoons flour
- 2 cups buttermilk
- 1 egg, beaten
- 2½ tablespoons bacon drippings

Combine dry ingredients with milk and egg; let batter rest about 20 minutes before baking. Melt drippings in an 8- to 10-inch iron skillet; grease should be warm, not hot; mix into batter. Heat well-greased skillet in oven until it smokes; remove; pour in batter. Bake 20 to 25 minutes, or until golden brown, at 425°.

Frank Lambright
Little Rock, Arkansas

◇ *James Francis Locke, one of the three brothers for whom the town of Lockesburg was named.*

BLUEBERRY-APPLE COFFEE CAKE
12 servings.

⅔ cup oil	1½ cups flour
1 egg	1 teaspoon baking soda
1 cup sugar	1 teaspoon salt
1 teaspoon cinnamon	2 cups blueberries
1 teaspoon vanilla	½ cup chopped nuts
1 teaspoon lemon juice	½ cup finely chopped apple

Mix first 6 ingredients in a mixing bowl, blending well. Add flour, soda, and salt. Fold in blueberries, nuts and apples. Bake in a greased and floured 9-inch square baking pan at 350° 40 minutes.

Era Friday Farmer
West Monroe, Louisiana

BLUEBERRY COFFEE CAKE
10 to 12 servings.

3 cups flour	¾ cup butter, softened
1½ teaspoons baking powder	1½ cups granulated sugar
¾ teaspoon baking soda	1 teaspoon vanilla
¼ teaspoon salt	4 eggs
¼ cup firmly packed light-brown sugar	1 cup sour cream
1 tablespoon flour	2 cups blueberries
½ teaspoon cinnamon	1 cup powdered sugar
	1 to 2 tablespoons milk

Sift together the first 4 ingredients; set aside. In small bowl, combine brown sugar, 1 tablespoon flour, and cinnamon; mix well. In a large bowl, at medium speed on electric mixer, beat butter with granulated sugar and vanilla until fluffy. Add eggs, one at a time, beating after each addition. At low speed, beat in flour mixture (in 3 additions) alternately with sour cream (in 2 additions), beating until combined. Pour ⅓ of batter into a lightly greased and floured 10-inch tube pan, spreading evenly. Sprinkly with ½ the blueberries and ½ the brown-sugar mixture. Repeat layers, topping with remaining batter. Bake at 350° 60 minutes, or until cake tester inserted in center comes out clean. Cool in pan on wire rack 20 minutes; gently remove from pan. Mix powdered sugar and milk until smooth; drizzle over cake.

Nelda Hooker

CRANBERRY YOGURT COFFEE CAKE
20 servings.

1	(18½-ounce) package yellow cake mix	1	cup unflavored yogurt
1	(13½-ounce) package vanilla instant pudding mix	¼	cup vegetable oil
		1	(16-ounce) can whole berry cranberry sauce
4	eggs	½	cup chopped nuts

In a large bowl blend first 5 ingredients; with electric mixer, beat on high 3 minutes, scraping bowl often. Spread ⅔ of the batter in a generously greased, lightly floured 9 × 13-inch pan. Spoon cranberry sauce evenly over batter; spoon remaining batter over sauce; sprinkle with nuts. Bake at 350° 55 to 60 minutes. Cool on rack 35 minutes.

Pearl Coulter

A featured recipe at Ocean Spray's Cranberry World Visitor' Center in Plymouth, Maine.

STREUSEL COFFEE CAKE
6 to 9 servings.

1½	cups sifted flour	1	teaspoon vanilla
3	teaspoons baking powder	½	cup brown sugar
¼	teaspoon salt	2	tablespoons flour
¾	cup sugar	2	teaspoons cinnamon
¼	cup shortening	2	tablespoons melted butter
1	egg, well beaten	½	cup chopped nuts
½	cup milk		

Sift baking powder, salt, and sugar with sifted flour into a mixing bowl; with pastry blender, cut in shortening until mixture is like fine cornmeal. Mix egg and milk; blend into flour mixture; add vanilla, stirring just to blend. Pour half the batter into a greased and floured 9-inch square baking pan. In small bowl, combine brown sugar, flour and cinnamon; blend in butter; stir in nuts. Sprinkle ½ streusel mixture over batter in pan; add remaining batter; sprinkle with remaining streusel mixture. Bake at 375° 25 to 30 minutes.

Glenda Williams

GRANDMA CHETTERBOX'S FLAP-JACKS
6 to 8 pancakes.

2 eggs, beaten	½ cup flour
½ cup milk	2 teaspoons sugar
1 teaspoon melted butter	⅛ teaspoon salt

In mixing bowl beat eggs, milk, and butter together; add dry ingredients; beat until smooth. For each pancake, pour ¼ cup batter into hot, lightly greased skillet; rotate pan to spread batter thin. Cook until top is bubbly; turn and brown on other side. Serve with powdered sugar, syrup, or jelly; originally were filled with cottage cheese, rolled jelly-roll fashion, and spread with jelly. Recipe doubles easily.

Mark Nation
Art Nation

WAFFLES
12 4-inch waffles.

1¾ cups flour	2 heaping tablespoons baking powder
¼ cup corn meal	2 eggs, beaten
½ teaspoon salt	2 cups milk
1 tablespoon sugar	¼ cup melted butter

In a large bowl combine dry ingredients, mixing well. Make a well in center; add remaining ingredients; beat until blended and smooth. Pour about 1¼ cups batter into a hot, lightly oiled waffle iron. Cook about 5 minutes or until done. Repeat until all batter is used. Serve hot with butter and warm syrup.

In memory of Howard Mottesheard
David Mottesheard
San Francisco, California

APPLESAUCE PANCAKES
12 pancakes.

1 cup pancake mix	½ cup applesauce
1 cup milk	⅛ teaspoon ginger
¼ cup molasses	⅛ teaspoon nutmeg
1 egg	⅛ teaspoon cinnamon
1 tablespoon melted shortening	

In a mixing bowl combine all ingredients; beat until smooth. Pour by ¼ cupfuls onto hot, lightly greased griddle. Turn when tops are covered with bubbles and edges look cooked. Serve hot with butter and applesauce.

Mary Lou Taylor

CINNAMON PANCAKES
20 2½-inch pancakes.

1 cup flour	½ teaspoon baking soda
1 cup milk	½ teaspoon cinnamon
1 egg	2 tablespoons olive oil
½ teaspoon baking powder	

In a mixing bowl blend all ingredients until more or less smooth, only slightly lumpy. Spoon onto a medium-hot, lightly buttered griddle in 2½-inch cakes. Turn when bubbles show on top. Serve hot with butter and syrup. To double, double all ingredients except the egg.

W. F. Rector, Jr.
Little Rock, Arkansas

◇ *Governor Henry Rector, 1860-1862*

BLENDER WHOLE WHEAT PANCAKES
8 pancakes.

1 egg	1 teaspoon wheat germ
1 cup apple juice	¼ teaspoon cinnamon
1 heaping cup whole wheat flour	

In a blender combine egg and juice. In a small bowl combine remaining ingredients; add to juice mixture a little at a time, blending with each addition. Allow batter to rest a few minutes to thicken. Pour by ¼ cupfuls onto hot, greased griddle; cook until top is bubbly and edges dry; turn and brown on other side. Batter can also be baked as waffles; makes 3 4-inch waffles.

Jane Norwood

EVER-READY BRAN MUFFINS
6 dozen.

1 (15-ounce) package Raisin Bran	2 teaspoons salt
5 cups flour	1 teaspoon cinnamon
3 cups sugar	½ teaspoon allspice
1 tablespoon plus 2 teaspoons baking soda	4 eggs, beaten
	1 quart buttermilk
	1 cup oil

In a large bowl combine all dry ingredients; make a well in center of mix. Add eggs, buttermilk, and oil; stir until well blended. Cover tightly; refrigerate until ready to bake; batter can be kept up to 6 weeks. To bake, stir batter down; fill greased muffin tins ⅔ full; bake at 400° 12 to 15 minutes, or until brown.

Aileen Arnett
Arkadelphia, Arkansas
Irene Daniels
Velma Owens

SPICED CHEESE MUFFINS
2 dozen.

2	cups flour	½	cup buttermilk
1	tablespoon baking powder	1	egg, beaten
½	teaspoon baking soda	¼	cup melted butter
½	teaspoon ginger	1	cup shredded Cheddar cheese
½	teaspoon allspice		
½	teaspoon salt	¼	cup chopped raisins or dates, optional
½	cup molasses		

Sift dry ingredients together in a mixing bowl. In a large bowl stir molasses and buttermilk into egg; add dry ingredients, butter, cheese, and raisins, stirring just until flour is moistened. Fill greased muffin tins ⅔ full; bake at 400° for 12 to 15 minutes.

Corliss Klinkner

HAM AND SAUSAGE MUFFINS
24 muffins.

3	tablespoons butter	1	teaspoon salt
½	cup minced green pepper	2	eggs
½	cup minced green onions with tops	2	cups buttermilk
		1	cup finely chopped ham
1	cup yellow cornmeal	1	cup finely chopped cooked sausage
1¼	cups flour		
2	teaspoons baking soda		

In a skillet sauté green pepper and onions in butter until soft, but not brown; set aside. In a large bowl sift cornmeal, flour, soda, and salt. In small bowl beat eggs; stir in buttermilk; add to flour mixture all at once, stirring only until blended. Fold in meats and sautéed vegetables. Spoon into well-greased muffin tins, filling tins ⅔ full. Bake at 400° for 30 minutes or until brown. Can be frozen and reheated.

Tommie Wright
Janie Clardy

PEACH MUFFINS
12 muffins.

1½ cups flour	1¼ cups coarsely chopped fresh, or drained canned peaches
¾ teaspoon salt	½ teaspoon vanilla
½ teaspoon baking soda	⅛ teaspoon almond extract
1 cup sugar	¼ cup chopped almonds, optional
2 eggs, well beaten	
½ cup salad oil	

In mixing bowl combine dry ingredients; make a well in center of mix. Add eggs and oil, stirring only until dry mix is moistened. Stir in remaining ingredients. Spoon ⅓ cup batter into greased muffin tins; bake at 350° for 20 to 25 minutes, or until muffins test done. (For Peach Bread, spoon batter into a greased and floured 5 × 9-inch loaf pan; bake at 350° for 1 hour, or until bread tests done.)

Clyta Tallman

WILLIAMSBURG SWEET POTATO MUFFINS
2½ dozen.

⅔ cup mashed sweet potatoes, pureed	½ teaspoon salt
4 tablespoons butter	½ teaspoon cinnamon
½ cup sugar	¼ teaspoon nutmeg
1 egg	½ cup milk
¾ cup flour	4 tablespoons chopped pecans
2 teaspoons baking powder	4 tablespoons chopped raisins

In mixing bowl cream butter and sugar; add egg and sweet potatoes; mix well. Sift flour with baking powder, salt, and spices. Add alternately with milk to potato mixture; do not overmix. Fold in nuts and raisins. Spoon into greased 1½-inch muffin tins, filling each ⅔ full. A little sugar and cinnamon may be sprinkled on top of each muffin, if desired. Bake at 400° for 25 minutes. Muffins can be frozen and reheated.

Carol Pullen Hill
Russellville, Arkansas

CHEDDAR-APPLE BREAD
1 loaf.

½ cup sugar	1 teaspoon salt
½ cup shortening	1 teaspoon baking soda
1 egg, beaten	1 teaspoon baking powder
1 (20-ounce) can apple pie filling	1 cup shredded Cheddar cheese
2½ cups sifted flour	½ cup chopped pecans

Cream sugar and shortening; add egg and mix well. Blend in pie filling. Sift dry ingredients together and add with cheese and nuts to batter. Pour into a greased and floured 5 × 9-inch loaf pan. Bake at 350° for 1½ hours, or until bread tests done.

Melanie Sikes

BUTTERMILK BISCUITS
15 biscuits.

2 cups flour, sifted	½ teaspoon salt
2 teaspoons baking powder	1 cup buttermilk
½ teaspoon baking soda	2 tablespoons oil

In mixing bowl combine dry ingredients; mix thoroughly. Add milk and oil, stirring until all flour is moistened. Turn out on floured board; knead 4 or 5 times; roll out; cut with 2-inch biscuit cutter. Lightly grease a 10-inch iron skillet or pie pan; as you place biscuits in pan, grease both sides of biscuits. Bake at 450° for about 15 minutes, or until golden brown.

Mrs. Melvin Smith
Siloam Springs, Arkansas
Ida Cox

VEGETABLE BUBBLE BREAD
1 10-inch loaf.

1 pound bacon	1 (2-ounce) jar diced pimentos, drained
2 sticks margarine	1 cup grated cheese
¾ cup chopped celery	3 (10-ounce) cans refrigerated biscuits
¾ cup chopped bell pepper	
¾ cup chopped onion	

Fry bacon; drain; crumble. In a skillet, sauté celery, bell pepper, and onion in margarine. Separate biscuits; cut each into quarters. In a large bowl, combine all ingredients; toss until biscuit pieces are coated. Turn into a greased and floured 10-inch Bundt pan; bake at 350° 30 to 40 minutes.

Doris James
Whiteface, Texas

SWEET POTATO BISCUITS
3 to 4 dozen.

2 cups hot mashed sweet potatoes	½ teaspoon baking soda
½ cup shortening	4 teaspoons baking powder
¾ cup sugar	1 teaspoon salt
6 or 7 tablespoons buttermilk	3 to 4 cups flour

In large bowl combine hot potatoes and shortening; stir until shortening melts. Add sugar and buttermilk. Sift in 3 cups flour and other dry ingredients; stir until blended. Sift in enough remaining flour to make a fairly stiff batter, blending as you add. Roll out on floured board to ½-inch thickness; cut with a small cutter. Bake at 450° about 20 minutes, or until lightly browned. Dough will freeze.

Mary Esther Herget
Paragould, Arkansas

◇ *Recipe brought from North Carolina in the 1800's by Mrs. Richard Jackson, mother of Mrs. Alfred Herget.*

"BACONIZED" CORNBREAD
6 servings.

1 cup cornmeal	1 egg
¼ cup flour	½ cup milk
1 tablespoon sugar	1 tablespoon bacon drippings
2 teaspoons baking powder	4 to 5 slices bacon, diced

Sift dry ingredients together in a mixing bowl; add egg and milk; mix well. Heat bacon drippings in a 9-inch iron skillet until hot but not smoking; pour in batter; dot batter with bacon pieces. Bake at 400° 15 minutes, or until brown.

Tommie Brown

FLUFFY CORNBREAD
8 servings.

1 cup flour	4 teaspoons baking powder
1 cup cornmeal	2 eggs
1 teaspoon salt	1 cup milk

Blend all ingredients thoroughly; bake in a greased 9-inch iron skillet at 425° for 20 minutes.

Joyce Wagner
Avis Wall

CORNBREAD DRESSING
8 to 10 servings.

10 cups crumbled cornbread	3 teaspoons instant chicken bouillon
4 slices bread, crumbled	4 ribs celery with tops, diced
1 teaspoon poultry seasoning	1 large onion, finely diced
⅛ teaspoon black pepper	5 cups chicken broth, divided
Sage to taste	6 hard boiled eggs, diced

In large bowl combine cornbread, bread, and seasonings. In a small sauce pan simmer celery and onion in 1 cup chicken broth until tender; add mixture to crumb mixture. Stir in broth to moisten; add eggs; mix well. Pour into a greased 9 × 13-inch baking pan; bake at 450° 25 to 30 minutes, or until browned. If desired, add chopped cooked chicken to mixture, or layer boned chicken on top.

Juanita Karr

JALAPEÑO CORNBREAD
6 to 8 servings.

1½ cups yellow cornmeal	1 cup grated cheese
1 cup buttermilk	1 small onion, chopped
½ cup oil	1 clove garlic, pressed
2 teaspoons baking powder	1 to 2 jalapeño peppers, seeded, minced
¼ teaspoon baking soda	
1 teaspoon salt	1 to 2 tablespoons bacon drippings
2 eggs, beaten	
1 cup cream-style corn	

Combine all ingredients except bacon drippings in a large mixing bowl; blend well. Heat bacon drippings in a 10-inch iron skillet until hot; pour batter into skillet; bake at 450° 20 to 30 minutes, or until golden brown.

Gladys Cowling

Sour Cream Variation: Omit onion, garlic, and buttermilk. Substitute 1 cup sour cream, 2 tablespoons chopped bell pepper; reduce oil to ¼ cup. Do not mix cheese with batter. Pour ½ batter into hot greased skillet; sprinkle with ½ cheese; repeat layers. Bake at 350° 35 to 40 minutes.

Ruth Whitley

CRANBERRY BREAD
1 loaf.

2 cups flour	¾ cup orange juice
1 cup sugar	3 tablespoons orange rind
½ teaspoon salt	1 egg, slightly beaten
½ teaspoon baking powder	1 cup sliced cranberries
1½ teaspoons baking soda	1 cup chopped nuts
2 tablespoons butter	

Sift flour, sugar, salt, baking powder, and baking soda into a mixing bowl. In a sauce pan heat butter, orange juice, and rind until butter melts; add to dry mixture with egg. Stir lightly until blended; add cranberries and nuts. Pour into a greased 5 × 9-inch loaf pan. Bake at 350° for 1 hour. Serve with cream cheese.

Mary Medaris, Director
Southwest Arkansas Regional Archives
Washington, Arkansas

BASIC CREPE BATTER
12 7-inch or 16 5-inch pancakes.

1 cup sifted flour	1 cup milk
½ teaspoon salt	2 tablespoons melted butter
2 eggs	

Combine flour, salt and eggs; mix well. Add milk and butter, beating until mixture is smooth. Refrigerate batter at least 2 hours. Brush crepe pan or a 6-inch skillet with oil; heat over medium heat until just hot but not smoking. Pour in 3 tablespoons batter, quickly tipping pan to cover entire bottom evenly and thinly. Cook crepe about 1 minute; lift edge to test for doneness. When lightly browned, flip over and cook about 30 seconds on other side. Stack crepes between layers of waxed paper to prevent sticking. Crepes freeze well. Stack; wrap in foil or plastic with edges tightly sealed. Defrost at room temperature before separating.

Harriett Aldridge
Food Editor, ARKANSAS GAZETTE
Little Rock, Arkansas

DATE-NUT BREAD
2 loaves.

8 ounces pitted dates, chopped	1 teaspoon salt
1½ cups boiling water	1 egg, beaten
2¾ cups flour	1 cup sugar
1 teaspoon baking powder	2 tablespoons butter
1½ teaspoons baking soda	1 teaspoon vanilla
	1 cup chopped walnuts

In a small bowl combine dates and boiling water; let cool to room temperature. Sift flour with baking powder, soda, and salt; set aside. In a mixing bowl beat eggs, sugar, butter and vanilla with rotary beater until smooth; add cooled date mixture, mixing well; add flour mixture; beat until well mixed. Stir in nuts. Turn into 2 greased and floured 5 × 9-inch loaf pans. Bake at 325° for 1 hour; cool in pans 10 minutes; turn out onto wire rack.

Mrs. Jack Dyer

OLD-FASHIONED CAKE DOUGHNUTS
About 2½ dozen.

4½ cups flour	1 cup sugar
4 teaspoons baking powder	1 cup milk
1¼ teaspoons salt	2 eggs, well beaten
¼ teaspoon nutmeg	Powdered sugar
3 tablespoons shortening	

Sift first 4 ingredients together 4 times. In a separate bowl cream shortening and sugar; add milk and eggs; combine with flour mixture. Turn onto well-floured board; knead lightly; roll out to ½-inch thickness; cut with floured doughnut cutter. Heat 2 to 3 inches oil to 375°; drop in 3 or 4 doughnuts at a time; cook about 1 minute or until golden on one side; turn and cook about 1 minute. Drain on paper towels; dust with powdered sugar.

Peggy Bryan

BLUEBERRY GINGERBREAD
12 servings.

½	cup oil	1	teaspoon cinnamon
1	cup sugar	½	teaspoon nutmeg
½	teaspoon salt	1	teaspoon baking soda
3	tablespoons molasses	1	cup blueberries, fresh or frozen
1	egg		
2	cups flour	1	cup buttermilk
½	teaspoon ginger	2	tablespoons sugar

With electric mixer beat together oil, sugar, salt and molasses; beat in egg. Combine flour, spices, and baking soda; dredge blueberries with 2 tablespoons of the flour mixture. Add remaining flour mixture to first mixture alternately with buttermilk, beating after each addition. Fold in blueberries. Pour into a greased and floured 8 × 12-inch baking dish; sprinkle top with remaining sugar. Bake at 350° for 35 to 40 minutes. Cut into squares; serve warm with butter or with whipped cream for a dessert.

Mary Ella Pool Roberts

HUSH PUPPIES
2 dozen.

1½	cups cornmeal	1	small onion, chopped
½	cup flour	2	eggs, beaten
2	tablespoons baking powder	¼	cup water, milk, or beer
1	teaspoon salt		

In mixing bowl sift dry ingredients together; add remaining ingredients; stir lightly to blend. Drop by teaspoonfuls into deep, hot fat, frying only a few at a time until golden brown. Drain on paper towels.

Don Campbell

Buttermilk Variation: Use 3 teaspoons baking powder, ¼ teaspoon baking soda, 1 egg, ½ cup buttermilk.

Nep Argenbright

BANANA-LEMON TEA BREAD
1 loaf.

⅔ cup shortening	2 cups flour
2 cups sugar	1 teaspoon baking soda
2 eggs	1 teaspoon salt
1½ cups mashed ripe bananas	1 tablespoon grated fresh lemon rind
6 tablespoons fresh lemon juice	Powdered sugar

In a large bowl cream shortening with sugar; beat in eggs, one at a time, beating well after each addition. Blend in bananas and lemon juice. Sift together flour, baking soda, and salt; blend into banana mixture; stir in lemon rind. Pour into greased, floured 5 × 9-inch loaf pan; bake at 325° for 1 hour, or until cake tester inserted in center comes out clean. Remove from pan; cool. Dust top with sifted powdered sugar.

Stella Lambert

APPLE OR PEAR BREAD WITH BROWN SUGAR TOPPING
2 loaves.

3 cups flour	3 eggs, slightly beaten
1 teaspoon baking soda	2 cups sugar
¼ teaspoon baking powder	2 cups grated pears or apples
1 teaspoon salt	2 teaspoons vanilla
1 tablespoon cinnamon	¾ cup flour
1 cup chopped pecans	¾ cup brown sugar
¾ cup vegetable oil	½ cup margarine

In a large bowl combine first 6 ingredients; make a well in the mixture. In a separate bowl combine oil, eggs, sugar, pears or apples, and vanilla; pour into well of dry mixture; stir just until well moistened. Spoon mixture into 2 greased 5 × 9-inch loaf pans. Combine ¾ cup flour and brown sugar; with a pastry blender or fork, work margarine into mixture until mixture is like coarse meal; sprinkle over batter. Bake at 325° for 1 hour and 15 minutes, or until bread tests done. Cool 10 minutes before removing from pans.

Mabel Morris
Ogden, Arkansas

PERSIMMON BREAD
1 loaf.

2 cups flour	¾ cup sugar
1 teaspoon baking powder	2 eggs, beaten
½ teaspoon salt	½ cup shortening
1 teaspoon baking soda	1 cup persimmon pulp
1 teaspoon cinnamon	1 teaspoon vanilla
½ teaspoon nutmeg	½ cup chopped nuts

Combine dry ingredients and spices; add eggs, shortening, and persimmon pulp; beat until well mixed. Add vanilla; stir in nuts. Pour into a greased and floured 5 × 9-inch loaf pan; bake at 375° for 50 to 55 minutes.

Rhonda Ryan

SWEET POTATO BREAD
3 loaves.

2 cups baked sweet potatoes, mashed	½ teaspoon nutmeg
3 cups sugar	⅔ cup orange juice
1 cup oil	1 teaspoon baking soda dissolved in ⅔ cup hot water
4 eggs, separated	1 cup chopped dates
3½ cups sifted flour	1 cup coconut
1½ teaspoons cinnamon	1 cup raisins
½ teaspoon cloves	1 cup chopped nuts
½ teaspoon salt	

In a large bowl blend potatoes, sugar, and oil, mixing well; beat in egg yolks. Combine flour, salt and spices; add alternately with orange juice and soda-water mixture. Add dates, coconut, raisins, and nuts. Beat egg whites until stiff; fold into mixture. Divide into 3 greased and floured 5 × 9-inch loaf pans; bake at 350° for 45 minutes, or until bread tests done.

Delta Sharp

LEMON-GLAZED PLUM BREAD
1 loaf.

2	cups flour	2	large eggs
2½	teaspoons baking powder	1	cup fresh plum pulp
½	teaspoon salt	1	tablespoon toasted sesame seeds
¼	cup butter		
¾	cup sugar	2	tablespoons sugar
1	teaspoon grated lemon rind	1	tablespoon lemon juice

In a bowl combine flour, baking powder, and salt; set aside. In a large bowl cream butter with sugar and lemon rind, beating with mixer until fluffy. Beat in eggs one at a time. Blend in flour mixture alternately with plum pulp; stir in sesame seeds. Batter will be quite stiff. Turn into a greased 5 × 9-inch loaf pan; bake at 350° for 55 to 65 minutes, or until bread tests done. Cool 10 minutes in pan; turn onto wire rack. Combine sugar and lemon juice; brush top of bread with lemon glaze.

Annie Quinn Dilday
Vancouver, British Columbia

BLACK WALNUT-PRUNE BREAD
3 loaves.

3	cups flour	2	cups sugar
1	teaspoon baking soda	1	cup buttermilk
1	teaspoon nutmeg	3	eggs
1	teaspoon cinnamon	1	cup cooked pitted prunes, chopped
1	teaspoon allspice		
Pinch of salt		2	cups chopped black walnuts
1	cup oil		

Sift flour with baking soda and spices. Combine sugar and oil; add flour mixture and milk alternately with eggs, blending well. Fold in prunes and nuts. Pour into 3 greased 4 × 8-inch loaf pans. Bake at 350° 30 to 35 minutes.

Patsy Purtell Thompson

PUMPKIN BREAD
2 loaves.

3 cups sugar	1 cup chopped pecans
3 cups flour	1 cup oil
2 teaspoons baking soda	4 eggs, beaten
1½ teaspoons salt	⅔ cup water
1 teaspoon nutmeg	1 cup canned pumpkin
1 teaspoon cinnamon	

Sift sugar, flour, soda, salt, and spices into a large bowl. Make a well in the center; add remaining ingredients; mix until blended well. Pour into 2 greased and floured 5 × 9-inch loaf pans; bake at 350° for 1 hour. (You can also use 3 coffee cans or 1 tube pan.)

Ann Coulter
Cary, North Carolina

DATE SCONES
About 2 dozen.

1¾ cups flour	¼ teaspoon salt
½ cup sugar	½ cup margarine, softened
2 teaspoons cream of tartar	½ cup chopped dates
1 teaspoon baking soda	2 eggs, slightly beaten

Combine dry ingredients; cut in butter; mix well. Add dates and eggs; stir until mixture forms a ball. On floured board roll dough to ½-inch thickness; cut with 2-inch biscuit cutter. Place on greased cookie sheet; bake at 400° about 15 minutes.

Allie Patrick
Arkadelphia, Arkansas

PUMPKIN SCONES

About 2 dozen 2-inch scones.

- ½ cup sugar
- 1 tablespoon butter
- 1 tablespoon hot water
- 1 egg
- 1 cup mashed pumpkin
- 2 cups self-rising flour
- Pinch of salt

Cream butter and sugar with hot water; add egg and beat well. Blend in pumpkin; add flour and salt. If too stiff, moisten with a little milk. Roll out on floured board to ½-inch thickness; cut with 2-inch biscuit cutter. Place on a baking sheet; bake at 450° for 10 minutes, or until lightly browned.

Shirley Philipps
Karridale, Western Australia

ZUCCHINI BREAD

2 loaves.

- 3 eggs
- 2 cups sugar
- 1 cup oil
- 2 teaspoons vanilla
- 3 cups flour
- 1 teaspoon salt
- 1 teaspoon baking powder
- 1 teaspoon baking soda
- 3 teaspoons cinnamon
- 2 cups shredded zucchini
- 1 cup chopped nuts
- 1 cup crushed pineapple, drained, optional

Beat eggs and sugar until light and fluffy; stir in oil and vanilla. Sift dry ingredients; combine with egg mixture. Add zucchini, nuts, and pineapple; blend well. Pour into 2 greased and floured 5 × 9-inch loaf pans. Bake at 350° for 1 hour.

Nita Green
Stockton, California
Henrietta Coulter
Los Angeles, California
Hazel Crews-Cohen

APRICOT BREAD
2 loaves.

3 cups whole wheat flour	¼ cup oil
½ cup whole bran cereal	¼ cup honey
2 packages yeast	1 egg
1 tablespoon salt	2 cups chopped walnuts
2½ cups water	3½ to 4 cups flour
1 cup dry milk powder	2 cups diced dried apricots

In a large bowl combine first 4 ingredients. In a sauce pan heat water, dry milk, oil, and honey until warm (115 to 120°), stirring constantly. Add, with egg, to yeast mixture. Beat, with mixer at low speed, 30 seconds, scraping sides of bowl constantly; increase speed to high; beat 3 minutes. With wooden spoon, stir in flour to make a moderately stiff dough. On lightly floured board knead until smooth and elastic, 8 to 10 minutes. Divide dough in half; roll each half to a 9 × 12-inch rectangle; sprinkle each with ½ the apricots. Roll up jelly-roll fashion, starting at short side; pinch ends to seal. Place in greased 5 × 9-inch loaf pans; cover; let rise in warm place until double, 40 to 45 minutes. Bake at 350° 40 minutes or until bread tests done. Remove from pans; cool on wire racks. (May substitute dates, dried peaches, or dried apples for apricots.)

Willa Gathright

BEIGNETS
5 dozen.

1 cup boiling water	½ cup sugar
¼ cup shortening	1 teaspoon salt
1 cup evaporated milk	2 eggs, beaten
1 package yeast	6 to 7 cups flour
½ cup lukewarm water	Powdered sugar

In a large bowl pour boiling water over shortening; add milk; cool. Dissolve yeast in lukewarm water; add to cooled mixture. Add sugar, salt, eggs, and enough flour for a soft dough. Pinch off a small amount; roll thin on a floured board. Cut into squares or triangles; fry in hot oil until golden brown. Drain on paper towels; sprinkle with powdered sugar; serve hot. Refrigerate any remaining dough in covered container; keeps well 1 week.

Mildred Etzkorn

BASIC ROLL DOUGH
2 dozen.

1 package yeast	¼ cup shortening
¼ cup warm water (120°)	1 teaspoon salt
1 cup milk, scalded	3½ cups sifted flour
¼ cup sugar	1 egg, beaten

In a small bowl soften yeast in warm water. In a large mixing bowl combine milk, sugar, shortening, and salt; cool to lukewarm. Add 1½ cups flour; beat well. Combine yeast mixture and egg; beat into mixture. Gradually add remaining flour to form a soft dough, beating well. Place in greased bowl, turning once to grease surface; cover; let rise about 2 hours. Turn out on lightly floured board; shape as desired; cover; let rise until doubled in bulk, about 30 to 45 minutes. Bake on greased baking sheet at 350° 12 to 15 minutes.

Josephine Murphy
Dallas, Texas
Novella B. Moon

Dissolve yeast in warm, not hot, water, 105° for cake yeast, 115° for dry. Test water on wrist as you would for a baby's bottle.

MOTHER'S ROLLS
About 6 dozen.

1 package yeast	1 cup cooked, mashed potatoes
½ cup warm water	2 eggs, well beaten
⅔ cup shortening	2 cups lukewarm water or milk
⅔ cup sugar	7½ cups sifted flour
1½ teaspoons salt	

In small bowl dissolve yeast in warm water. In large mixing bowl cream shortening, sugar, and salt; blend in potatoes, eggs, and yeast. Add ½ cup flour with lukewarm liquid; blend well. With hands, mix in remaining flour; knead in bowl until dough is smooth and elastic, about 8 minutes. Place in greased bowl, turning to grease top; cover; let rise until doubled in bulk. Punch down; cover tightly; refrigerate. To bake, work dough down; shape into rolls; place on greased baking sheet; let rise until doubled in bulk. Bake 15 to 20 minutes at 400°, or until brown.

In memory of Mrs. Ike Shinn
Magnolia, Arkansas
Ludie Shinn Anthes
Conway, Arkansas

Cinnamon Rolls: Roll dough out flat; brush with melted butter; sprinkle heavily with cinnamon and sugar; roll up jelly-roll fashion, starting at long side; pinch edge and ends to seal; slice into ½-inch rolls; let rise; bake as above.

Nancy Weber
Little Rock, Arkansas

ONE-RISE CINNAMON ROLLS
16 to 20 rolls.

1 cup heavy whipping cream (do not substitute)	1 cup hot tap water
1 cup brown sugar	2 tablespoons butter, softened
3 to 3½ cups flour, divided	1 egg
1 package yeast	½ cup sugar
¼ cup sugar	2 teaspoons cinnamon
1 teaspoon salt	½ cup butter, softened

Mix brown sugar and whipping cream; layer bottom of an ungreased 9 × 13-inch pan; set aside. In a large bowl blend 1½ cups flour and the next 6 ingredients; beat 3 minutes at medium speed on mixer. Stir in remaining flour; on floured board, knead 1 minute. Press or roll dough into a 15 × 7-inch rectangle. Mix ½ cup sugar, cinnamon and ½ cup butter; spread over dough. Starting at long side, roll tightly; seal edges. Cut into rolls; place cut side down on cream-brown sugar mixture. Cover; let rise until doubled in bulk, about 35 to 45 minutes. Bake at 350° for 20 to 25 minutes; cool 10 to 15 minutes before turning out on serving tray.

Nelda Hooker

CARMEL'S ROLLS
3 to 4 dozen.

1 cup milk	1 yeast cake
1 tablespoon sugar	3 tablespoons warm water
1 teaspoon salt	5 to 6 cups flour
2 tablespoons shortening	

In a sauce pan heat milk, sugar, salt and shortening until shortening melts; cool to lukewarm. Dissolve yeast in warm water; add to cooled mixture. Pour mixture into a large mixing bowl; gradually add 1 cup flour; beat well. Work in enough flour to form a stiff dough. Place in a greased bowl; turn once to grease top; cover; let rise until doubled in bulk. Make into desired shape; bake on greased cookie sheet at 425° for 10 minutes; reduce heat to 350°; bake until brown.

Carmel Humphrey

◇ *Oscar Humphrey, Arkansas State Auditor, 1937-1956.*

RED APPLE INN ROLLS
5 dozen.

1 cup boiling water	2½ yeast cakes
1 cup butter	1 cup warm water
⅔ cup sugar	2 eggs, beaten
2 teaspoons salt	6 cups flour

In large mixing bowl pour boiling water over butter, sugar, and salt; cool to lukewarm. In a small bowl dissolve yeast in warm water; add eggs. Add yeast-egg mixture to cooled mixture. Add flour; mix well. Cover; refrigerate overnight. Make into rolls 2 hours before baking; brush with melted butter or margarine, cover and let rise. Bake at 425° about 12 minutes.

RED APPLE INN
Heber Springs, Arkansas

Excellent Greers Ferry restaurant on romantic Eden Isle.

REFRIGERATOR YEAST ROLLS
about 2 dozen.

1 cup warm water	2 cups buttermilk
2 packages yeast	1 teaspoon baking soda
3 tablespoons sugar	5 cups self-rising flour
¾ cup vegetable oil	

In a large mixing bowl dissolve yeast in warm water; add sugar. Add in order, mixing well (may use electric mixer), oil, buttermilk, soda, and flour. Turn out onto a floured board; knead several times. Place in greased bowl; cover tightly; refrigerate; dough may be kept for a week. To bake, punch down; on lightly floured board, roll out to ½-inch thickness; cut with biscuit cutter. Place on slightly greased baking sheet; brush with melted butter; cover; let rise in warm place until double in bulk, about 1 hour. Bake at 425° 15 to 20 minutes, or until brown.

Wilma Cannon
Nelda H. Zachry
Lona Kitchens

DILLY BREAD
2 loaves.

1 package yeast	1 tablespoon minced onion
¼ cup warm water	1 teaspoon salt
1 cup creamed cottage cheese, at room temperature	¼ teaspoon baking soda
	2 teaspoons dill seed
	1 tablespoon melted butter
1 egg, beaten	2½ cups sifted flour
2 tablespoons sugar	

In small bowl dissolve yeast in warm water. In large bowl combine cottage cheese and egg; add yeast mixture and remaining ingredients; mix well. Cover; let rise in warm place until double in bulk. Punch down; divide in half; form into 2 loaves. Place in greased 5 × 9-inch loaf pans; cover; let rise again to double bulk. Bake 30 to 40 minutes at 350°.

Kay McBride

BROWN BREAD
5 loaves.

⅓ cup shortening	¾ cup sorghum, or honey
⅓ cup brown sugar	¼ teaspoon baking soda
4 teaspoons salt	1 tablespoon hot water
1 cup All Bran buds	½ cup cold water
3 tablespoons wheat germ	2 packages dry yeast
⅓ cup dry milk powder	½ cup lukewarm water
2 cups boiling water	7 cups whole wheat flour
1 (13-ounce) can evaporated milk, scalded	3 cups white flour
	Sesame seeds, optional

In a very large bowl cream first 6 ingredients; add boiling water and scalded milk; set aside to cool to lukewarm. In small bowl combine sorghum (or honey), baking soda, and hot water; whip until foamy; add to cooled mixture. Rinse small bowl with cold water; add to mixture. Dissolve yeast in lukewarm water; add to mixture. Add whole wheat and white flour until a very stiff dough is formed. Cover; let rise until double in bulk. Punch down (no need to knead); divide into 5 equal portions. Shape into loaves; place in greased 5 × 9-inch loaf pans; cover and let rise again until double. Bake at 400° for 10 minutes; reduce heat to 350° and bake until golden brown, about 25 minutes. If desired, sprinkle with sesame seeds before baking.

Jan Hale Barbo

CREAM CHEESE BRAID

4 12-inch loaves.

1 (8-ounce) container sour cream	2 packages yeast
½ cup butter	½ cup warm water (105-115°)
½ cup sugar	2 eggs, beaten
1 teaspoon salt	4 cups flour

In a sauce pan warm sour cream, butter, sugar, and salt until butter melts, mixing well; do not boil. In a large mixing bowl dissolve yeast in warm water. Stir in lukewarm sour cream mixture; add eggs, mixing well. Gradually stir in flour; dough will be soft. Cover tightly; chill overnight. Divide dough into 4 equal portions; knead each on a heavily floured board 4 or 5 times. Roll each portion into an 8 × 12-inch rectangle; spread ¼ of the filling over each, leaving ½-inch margin around edges. Roll up jelly-roll fashion, starting with long side; pinch ends tightly to seal; place seam-side down on greased baking sheets. Make 6 equally-spaced X-cuts across top of each loaf. Let rise until double. Bake 15 to 20 minutes at 375°.

Filling:

2 (8-ounce) packages cream cheese, softened	1 egg, beaten
¾ cup sugar	⅛ teaspoon salt
	2 teaspoons vanilla

Combine filling ingredients, beating until smooth.

Glaze:

2 cups sifted powdered sugar	2 teaspoons vanilla
¼ cup milk	

Blend glaze ingredients thoroughly. Spread over warm baked loaves.

Opal Ray
Ashdown, Arkansas

GERMAN BREAD
3 loaves.

3¾ cups warm water, divided	6 tablespoons sugar
1 cup dry milk powder	1 tablespoon salt
3 heaping tablespoons shortening	2 packages yeast
	5 to 6 cups flour

In a large bowl combine 3 cups warm water, shortening, sugar and salt; set aside. Dissolve yeast with ¾ cup warm water in small bowl; let stand 3 or 4 minutes. Add 5 cups flour to first mixture; then add yeast mixture; mix thoroughly. Add flour until dough is stiff enough to knead. On floured board, knead until dough is smooth and elastic, about 10 minutes. Place in greased bowl, turning once to grease top; cover with a damp cloth; set in a warm place; let rise until doubled in bulk, about 2 hours. Punch down; knead well again; divide into 3 equal portions; shape into loaves; place in greased 5 × 9-inch loaf pans. Cover; let rise until doubled in bulk, about 1½ hours. Bake at 350° until done and brown, about 30 minutes. This makes a heavy-type bread.

Wilma McCoy Warford

GOLDEN BUBBLE RING
28 rolls.

2 packages yeast	1 teaspoon salt
¼ cup warm water	2 eggs, beaten
½ cup scalded milk	4 to 4½ cups flour
1 cup sugar, divided	½ stick butter, melted
½ cup shortening	1 teaspoon cinnamon

In a small bowl soften yeast in warm water. In a large bowl combine milk, ½ cup sugar, shortening, and salt; cool to lukewarm. Add yeast mixture and eggs; mix well. Add 2 cups flour; beat until smooth. Mix in enough of remaining flour to make a soft dough. Knead on lightly floured board until smooth and elastic, 8 to 10 minutes. Place in greased bowl, turning to grease all surfaces; cover; let rise in warm place until double in bulk, 1½ hours. Punch down; cover; let rest 10 minutes. Shape into about 28 golf ball-size balls. Roll each in melted butter, then in mixture of cinnamon and remaining sugar. Arrange in a greased 9-inch tube pan; cover; let rise to double in bulk, about 1 hour. Bake at 350° for 35 to 40 minutes. Cool in pan; invert onto a rack.

Ealnor Coulter
Los Angeles, California
Linda Bowden

HONEY WHEAT BREAD
2 loaves.

4 to 5 cups bread flour, divided	8 ounces creamed cottage cheese
2 teaspoons salt	
2 packages yeast	2 eggs
1 cup water	1 cup whole wheat flour
½ cup honey	½ cup quick oats
¼ cup margarine	1 cup chopped nuts

In a large bowl combine 2 cups bread flour, salt and yeast; mix well. In sauce pan heat water, honey, margarine, and cottage cheese until very warm. With mixer at low speed, add warm liquid and eggs to flour mixture; beating until moistened; then beat 3 minutes at medium speed. Stir in whole wheat flour, oats, nuts, plus enough of remaining bread flour to form a soft dough. On floured board, knead dough about 10 minutes, or until smooth and elastic. Place in greased bowl, turning once to grease top; cover; let rise in a warm place away from draft until double in bulk. Punch down; divide in half; let rest, covered, 10 minutes. Shape into 2 loaves; place in greased and floured 5 × 9-inch loaf pans. Cover; let rise in warm place away from draft until double in bulk. Bake 35 minutes at 375°. Remove from pans immediately; cool on wire racks.

Lee Gierke
Ashdown, Arkansas

IRISH SODA BREAD
1 round loaf.

1 package yeast	1 tablespoon caraway seeds
¼ cup very warm water	½ teaspoon baking soda
2½ cups flour, divided	2 tablespoons butter
3 tablespoons sugar	¾ cup buttermilk
½ teaspoon salt	½ cup raisins

In small bowl dissolve yeast in warm water; set aside. In a large bowl combine 1 cup flour, sugar, salt, caraway seeds and soda; stir in dissolved yeast. Melt butter in small sauce pan; add buttermilk and beat well; add to flour mixture and incorporate. Add remaining flour to make a soft dough that leaves the sides of the bowl. Stir in raisins. Cover; let rise about 1 hour. Turn onto floured board; knead 20 to 30 times. Form into a smooth, rounded ball; place on greased baking sheet. Let rise to double bulk (50 minutes). Cut a ¼-inch-deep cross in center. Bake 30 minutes at 350°.

Vicki Masten

MORAVIAN SUGAR CAKE
2 round loaves.

1 package yeast	1 teaspoon salt
½ cup lukewarm water	2 eggs, beaten
1 cup hot mashed potatoes, unseasoned, 1 cup potato water, reserved	4½ cups flour Butter Brown sugar
1 cup sugar	Cinnamon
4 tablespoons soft butter	
½ cup shortening	

In a small bowl let yeast soak in warm water. In a separate bowl combine potatoes, sugar, butter, shortening, and salt; cool to lukewarm. Add yeast mixture and reserved potato water; mix well. Let rise in warm place, free from draft, until spongy, about 2 hours. Add eggs and sufficient flour to make a soft dough; cover; let rise until doubled in bulk. Turn out onto lightly floured board; punch down; knead lightly; divide in half. Spread into 2 greased 10 to 12-inch pizza pans; allow to partially rise again; when "light", make holes with fingers; fill with pieces of butter and plenty of brown sugar, using as much as possible. Dust with cinnamon. Bake at 375° 20 minutes.

Dolores Burchette Mottesheard
Jonesville, North Carolina

OATMEAL BREAD
2 loaves.

2 cups oatmeal	1 teaspoon sugar
2 cups boiling water	¼ cup warm water
2 teaspoons salt	⅓ cup brown sugar
1 tablespoon shortening	½ cup lukewarm water
1 package yeast	4½ cups flour

Stir oatmeal into boiling water; add salt and shortening; stir until smooth; cool to lukewarm. Dissolve yeast and sugar in warm water; combine with cooled oatmeal mixture. Add brown sugar dissolved in lukewarm water. Work in flour; knead. Place in greased bowl, turning once to grease top; cover with damp cloth; let rise to double in bulk. Turn out onto floured board for second kneading; if dough is too sticky, add ½ cup flour. Divide dough in half; press and shape into 2 greased 5 × 9-inch loaf pans; let rise to almost double. Bake 15 minutes at 425°; reduce heat to 375° and bake an additional 30 minutes.

Mary McCrory

ANADAMA (SQUAW) BREAD
2 loaves.

7 to 8 cups flour, divided
1¼ cups cornmeal
2½ teaspoons salt
2   packages yeast
⅓ cup softened margarine

2¼ cups very warm tap water (120° to 130°)
⅔ cup molasses, at room temperature

In a large bowl thoroughly mix 2½ cups flour, cornmeal, salt, and yeast; add margarine. Gradually add tap water and molasses to dry ingredients; beat 2 minutes at medium speed of electric mixer, scraping bowl occasionally. Add ½ cup flour; beat at high speed 2 minutes, scraping bowl occasionally. Stir in enough additional flour to make a stiff dough. Turn out onto lightly floured board; knead until smooth and elastic, about 8 to 10 minutes. Place in greased bowl, turning once to grease top; cover; let rise in warm place, free from draft, until doubled in bulk, about 1 hour. Punch down; divide in half. Roll each half into a 14 × 9-inch rectangle; shape into loaves; place in greased 5 × 9-inch loaf pans. Cover; let rise in warm place, free from draft, until doubled in bulk, about 45 minutes. Bake at 375° about 45 minutes, or until done. Remove from pans; cool on wire racks.

Can substitute ⅔ cup honey for molasses; flour can be divided 4 cups whole wheat and 3 cups white.

Ida M. Coulter Stone

DESSERTS

IRON SKILLET UPSIDE DOWN CAKE
6 to 8 servings

¼ cup butter	½ teaspoon salt
1 cup firmly packed brown sugar	½ cup oil
8 to 10 peach halves, drained	⅔ cup peach juice
1½ cups flour	1 teaspoon vanilla
¾ cup sugar	2 eggs, beaten
2 teaspoons baking powder	Maraschino cherries

Melt butter in a 10-inch iron skillet; remove from heat; sprinkle brown sugar evenly over butter; arrange peach halves over sugar; set aside. Sift dry ingredients together; add next 4 ingredients, blending well. Pour batter over peaches. Bake at 350° on oven rack slightly below center until cake pulls from sides of skillet, about 45 to 55 minutes. Remove from oven; let stand 5 minutes; turn out upside down onto cake platter. Garnish with maraschino cherries.

Martha Reeder Bell

BAKED APPLES
6 servings.

6 large cooking apples	1 teaspoon nutmeg
½ cup firmly packed brown sugar	3 tablespoons butter
	½ cup water
1 teaspoon cinnamon	

Core apples; slice a thin circle of peel from top of each; place in a shallow baking dish. Combine sugar and spices; spoon mixture into cavities of apples. Top each with ½ teaspoon butter. Pour water into baking dish; bake uncovered 30 to 45 minutes at 350° until tender, basting occasionally with pan juices.

Charles Karney Russell
Texarkana, Texas

CANDIED APPLES
16 apple halves.

8 tart apples, pared, cored, and halved	1½ cups water
2 cups sugar	½ teaspoon red food coloring

Combine sugar, water and food coloring in large heavy skillet; bring to a boil; simmer 5 minutes. Add apple halves, a few at a time; cook over low heat, basting with syrup until tender enough to pierce with a fork. When all apples are cooked, cook down liquid in pan to a heavy syrup; pour over apples; serve warm or chilled.

Sadie Jones

APPLE DIVINITY
8 servings.

6 cooking apples, pared, cored, thinly sliced	2 eggs
2 cups sugar, divided	1 cup flour
1½ teaspoons nutmeg	1 tablespoon baking powder
	2 tablespoons butter
	¼ teaspoon salt

Toss apple slices with 1 cup sugar and nutmeg; arrange in bottom of a greased 8 × 12-inch baking dish. In a bowl, combine remaining sugar and all other ingredients; dough will be stiff. By spoonfuls, dot dough over apples; dough will cover completely during baking. Bake at 350° about 25 minutes, or until lightly browned. Cool; serve with whipped cream.

Opal Turnage Eades
Snyder, Texas

APPLE FRITTERS
12-15 fritters.

1 egg, beaten	3 tablespoons sugar
⅓ cup milk	¼ teaspoon salt
1 cup flour	1 cup diced apples
1½ teaspoons baking powder	Peanut oil for frying

Sift flour, measure, and sift again with baking powder, sugar, and salt. Combine egg and milk; add dry mixture. Stir in apples. Drop by teaspoonfuls in deep hot oil (375°); fry until golden brown. Drain on paper towel. Serve with maple syrup, lemon sauce, or sprinkled with powdered sugar.

Nancy Van Der Linden

GLAZED APPLE SQUARES
25 squares.

3 cups flour	2 cups sugar
1 cup shortening	6 tablespoons flour
½ cup water	2 teaspoons cinnamon
1 egg, beaten	¼ teaspoon salt
1 tablespoon vinegar	½ cup chopped pecans
15 medium apples, pared, sliced	¼ cup butter

In mixing bowl cut shortening into flour until mixture resembles coarse meal. Combine water, egg and vinegar; blend into flour mixture. Divide dough in half; roll out one portion; line ungreased 10 × 15-inch jelly roll pan. Bake 10 minutes at 425°. Remove from oven; place apple slices over crust. Combine sugar, flour, cinnamon, salt and pecans; sprinkle over apples; dot with butter. Roll out remaining dough; place over apples; seal edges and cut vents slits in top of pastry. Bake 1 hour at 350°; cut into squares.

Glaze:

2 tablespoons melted butter	½ teaspoon vanilla
1 cup powdered sugar	Milk

Mix glaze ingredients, using enough milk for thin glaze; drizzle over warm apple squares.

Louneille Parker
Clinton, Iowa
Lucille Phillips
Arkadelphia, Arkansas

BLUEBERRY TORTE

12 servings.

- 1¼ cups graham cracker crumbs
- ½ cup melted margarine
- ½ cup firmly packed brown sugar
- 1 (8-ounce) package cream cheese
- 2 eggs
- ½ cup sugar
- 2 teaspoons lemon juice
- 1 (14- to 16-ounce) can blueberry pie filling
- 1 (8-ounce) container whipped topping

Combine first 3 ingredients; press firmly into bottom of a 9 × 13-inch baking pan. Beat until smooth next 4 ingredients; pour over crumb mixture. Bake 20 minutes at 300°; cool. Spread pie filling over baked crust; spread with whipped topping; chill.

Willie Jim Latimer Millwee

◇ *Minor M. Millwee, Associate Supreme Court Justice, 1945-1958.*

CHOCOLATE FOUR-LAYER DESSERT

10 to 12 servings.

- 2 cups flour
- 1 cup chopped nuts
- 2 sticks margarine, melted
- 1 (8-ounce) package cream cheese, softened
- 1 cup powdered sugar
- 1 (16-ounce) container whipped topping, divided
- 1 (6-ounce) package instant chocolate pie filling, prepared

Combine first 3 ingredients, mixing well; press into a 9 × 13-inch baking dish; bake at 400° until brown, about 10 minutes; cool. Combine cream cheese, sugar and 1 cup whipped topping; pour over crust. Pour pie filling over this mixture; cover with remaining whipped topping; chill. Garnish with chocolate curls or chopped nuts.

Ginger Dowdle
Sandra Jackson

PARTY CHOCOLATE DESSERT
18 servings.

1	cup flour	1	teaspoon vanilla
½	cup margarine, softened	2	egg whites, stiffly beaten
¼	cup powdered sugar	2	tablespoons water
¼	cup chopped pecans	1	cup chopped pecans
2	squares bitter chocolate	½	gallon pecan praline ice cream
⅔	cup butter		
2	cups powdered sugar, sifted	1	cup chopped pecans

For first layer, mix first 4 ingredients with hands to a soft dough; press firmly and evenly into bottom of a 9 × 13-inch baking dish. Bake 12 to 15 minutes at 400°, or until lightly brown; cool.

In sauce pan on low heat melt chocolate in butter; cool. Add sifted sugar, vanilla, water, and 1 cup pecans; fold in egg whites. Spread over baked crust; freeze 2 hours.

Soften ice cream; spread over frozen layer; top with remaining pecans; freeze. Cut into squares.

Mary E. Steel Allison

FRUIT COMPOTE
6 to 8 servings.

1	(8-ounce) can sliced pineapple, halved	2	tablespoons flour
1	(18-ounce) can peach halves	½	cup brown sugar
1	(16-ounce) jar apple rings, halved	1	stick butter
1	(16-ounce) can pear halves	1	cup sherry

Drain all fruit; arrange in alternate layers in a 2-quart casserole. In top of double boiler melt butter; stir in flour, sugar and sherry; cook until thickened. Pour over fruit; cover; chill overnight. Heat until hot and bubbly at 350°, about 20 minutes.

Edna Walden Bernard
Foreman, Arkansas

BAKED APPLE PUDDING WITH BRANDY SAUCE
8 servings.

⅓ cup softened butter	¼ teaspoon cinnamon
1 cup sugar	¼ teaspoon nutmeg
1 egg, beaten	1 teaspoon vanilla
1 cup flour	2 cups grated apples
1 teaspoon baking powder	½ cup chopped walnuts
¼ teaspoon salt	

Cream butter and sugar; add egg and beat well. Combine dry ingredients; add to creamed mixture, blending well. Blend in remaining ingredients. Spoon into a lightly-greased 8-inch square baking pan; bake at 350° 35 minutes, or until set.

Serve warm or cold with Brandy Sauce.

Brandy Sauce:

¼ cup softened butter	2 tablespoons brandy
1 cup powdered sugar	Dash of salt
1 teaspoon boiling water	

Cream butter and sugar until smooth; add remaining ingredients, beating until fluffy. Yield: ½ cup.

Patti Morris

PECAN DELIGHT
8 servings.

3 egg whites	1 cup chopped pecans
1 cup sugar	1 cup graham cracker crumbs

Beat egg whites until stiff; gradually add sugar. Fold in pecans and crumbs. Spoon into a heavily-buttered 9-inch pie pan. Bake at 325° 25 to 30 minutes; cool to room temperature; chill. Top with whipped topping.

Melaine Hickman
Cedar Hill, Texas

GRANDMA REVILS' BANANA PUDDING
10 to 12 servings.

1 cup plus 2 tablespoons sugar, divided	2 cups milk, divided
¼ cup flour	1 teaspoon vanilla
Pinch of salt	1 (12-ounce) box vanilla wafers
3 eggs, separated	4 to 5 bananas, sliced

In heavy sauce pan combine 1 cup sugar, flour and salt. Beat egg yolks with ¼ cup milk; blend into flour mixture. Add remaining milk; mix well. Cook over low heat, stirring constantly, until thick. Remove from heat; cool; add vanilla. Line a 9 × 13-inch dish with wafers; add alternate layers of pudding and bananas; another layer of wafers or wafer crumbs can be added in the center. Beat egg whites until stiff; gradually beat in remaining sugar; spread meringue over pudding. Bake 5 to 8 minutes at 425°, or until golden brown.

Jeannette Warren
DeWitt, Arkansas

SCALLOPED PINEAPPLE
8 servings.

1 cup butter	3 eggs, beaten
2 cups sugar	5½ slices bread, torn into small pieces
1 (19-ounce) can crushed pineapple	2 tablespoons milk

Cream butter and sugar; add crushed pineapple; mix well. Fold in eggs and bread pieces. Mix gently; pour into a buttered 8 × 12-inch baking dish. Spread milk on top to moisten. Bake 1 hour at 350°.

Sharon Johnson

CHERRY PUDDING
12 servings.

1 (16-ounce) can pie cherries, drained, juice reserved	2 eggs, beaten
1 teaspoon baking soda	1 tablespoon red food coloring
2 cups sugar	1 teaspoon vanilla
1½ cups plus 2 tablespoons flour, divided	1 cup chopped pecans
6 tablespoons butter, melted, divided	2 cups brown sugar
	2 cups hot water
	Pinch of salt

Mix soda with cherries; set aside. In separate bowl combine sugar with 1½ cups flour; make a well in mixture; add reserved juice, 4 tablespoons butter, eggs, food coloring, and vanilla; beat well. Fold in reserved cherries and nuts. Pour into a greased and floured 9 × 13-inch baking pan; bake 40 minutes at 325°. In sauce pan combine remaining butter and flour, brown sugar, water, and salt; cook until thickened. At end of baking time, remove pudding from oven; pour sauce over top; chill at least 12 hours before serving. Top with whipped cream.

Bennie Coulter

DATE PUDDING
6 servings.

1 cup chopped dates	1 egg, beaten
1 cup boiling water	2 tablespoons melted butter
1 teaspoon baking soda	1 cup flour
1 cup sugar	1 teaspoon vanilla
½ cup chopped nuts	

Combine first 3 ingredients in mixing bowl; set aside. In separate bowl combine sugar, nuts, egg and butter, blending well. Add flour and date mixture to sugar mixture; stir in vanilla. Pour into a greased 8 × 8-inch baking dish; bake at 350° 30 to 40 minutes, or until set. Serve with whipped cream.

Peg Gray
Evansville, Indiana
Betty Lindsey

THEODORE ROOSEVELT'S INDIAN PUDDING
10 to 12 servings.

6	cups milk, scalded	6	eggs, beaten
6	tablespoons cornmeal	½	pound raisins
½	cup dark brown sugar	1	teaspoon grated lemon rind
¼	pound butter	1	teaspoon ginger
1	teaspoon salt		

In mixing bowl combine milk and cornmeal; add sugar, butter and salt; cool. Add remaining ingredients; pour into a buttered 3-quart casserole. Set dish in a pan of hot water and bake at 300° 2 hours, or until set. Pudding will become firmer as it cools. Garnish with honey-glazed orange or lemon wedges. (Recipe was served December 18, 1902, at a dinner celebrating the renovation of the White House.)

Mrs. Buddy Slaton

ORANGE PUDDING
8 servings.

1	(3-ounce) box orange gelatin	1	(8-ounce) container whipped topping
1	(3-ounce) box tapioca pudding mix	1	(11-ounce) can mandarin oranges, drained
1	(3-ounce) box vanilla pudding mix	1	cup chopped nuts
2½	cups boiling water		

In sauce pan combine gelatin and pudding mixes; add water and boil until clear, about 5 minutes. Cool 30 minutes. Fold in remaining ingredients. Chill to set, at least 4 hours.

Thelma Gallaher

PERSIMMON PUDDING
8 to 10 servings.

1 cup persimmon pulp	1 cup flour
1 tablespoon butter, melted	1 teaspoon cinnamon
2 eggs, well beaten	1 teaspoon nutmeg
1½ cups milk	½ teaspoon salt
1 teaspoon vanilla	1 teaspoon baking powder
1 cup sugar	½ teaspoon baking soda

Combine first 6 ingredients, mixing well. Sift dry ingredients *twice*; blend into pulp mixture. Pour into a well-oiled 9 × 13-inch baking dish; bake at 350° about 1 hour or until set.

Mrs. Anthony Marthe
Green Forest, Arkansas

OLD-FASHIONED RAISIN PUDDING
6 servings.

1 cup brown sugar	2 tablespoons baking powder
2 cups water	½ cup brown sugar
2 tablespoons butter, divided	½ cup raisins
1 cup flour	½ cup milk

Combine sugar, water and 1 tablespoon butter; heat to boiling; boil 3 minutes. In a bowl, combine remaining butter and all other ingredients; mix well. Stir batter into boiling syrup; remove from heat; pour into a greased 2-quart casserole. Bake 30 minutes at 400°.

In memory of Myrtle Mcdonald
Delta Sharp

CREAM OF RICE PUDDING
6 to 8 servings.

¼ cup rice	¼ teaspoon cinnamon
4 cups milk, scalded	¼ teaspoon salt
¼ cup sugar	

Combine all ingredients; pour into a greased 1½-quart casserole. Bake at 300° about 2 hours, stirring every 15 to 20 minutes. When done, rice will have absorbed all liquid and will be soft and plump.

Mrs. Wilder Scroggins

FRESH STRAWBERRY MOUSSE

8 to 10 servings.

1 pint strawberries	¼ cup sugar
2 (3-ounce) packages strawberry gelatin	1 pint whipping cream, whipped

Crush strawberries and drain, reserving juice. Add enough water to juice to make 1½ cups. In sauce pan bring juice to a boil; stir in gelatin to dissolve; cool. Add strawberries and sugar; fold in whipped cream. Pour into a lightly-oiled 2-quart ring mold, or a 1½-quart souffle dish with a 2-inch collar. Chill several hours or overnight. (2 (10-ounce) packages frozen berries may be used; if used, omit sugar.)

Patricia Skinner Humphries
Benton, Arkansas

OREO COOKIE DESSERT

12 servings.

½ gallon vanilla ice cream, thawed until soupy	1 (8-ounce) container whipped topping
1 (16-ounce) package Oreo cookies, crushed into small bits	1 cup chopped pecans, optional

Combine all ingredients; pour into a 9 × 13-inch pan; freeze 2 to 4 hours. To serve, cut into squares; good with a little creme de menthe over the top.

Wanda Hampson
Little Rock, Arkansas
Frances Norwood Hampson

◇ M. L. Norwood, M. D., actively practiced in Lockesburg, 1896-1954

FRUITY CHEESECAKE CUPS
2 dozen.

2 (8-ounce) packages cream cheese	1 (12-ounce) box vanilla wafers
¾ cup sugar	24 foil baking cups
1 teaspoon vanilla	1 (21-ounce) can pie filling, any flavor
1 teaspoon lemon juice	
2 eggs	

Combine and beat thoroughly first 5 ingredients. Place baking cups in muffin pans; place 1 vanilla wafer in bottom of each; spread 1 tablespoon cheese mixture on top of each wafer; bake 12 minutes at 350°. Cool; spread pie filling over each baked crust; keep refrigerated.

Kay Hale
Bryan, Texas

FROZEN FRUIT CUPS
30 cups.

3 bananas, mashed	1 (6-ounce) can frozen orange juice with 1 can water
1 (13-ounce) can crushed pineapple	1 tablespoon lemon juice
2 (17-ounce) can apricot halves, drained, cut up	

Combine all ingredients; mix well. Pour into muffin tins, filling each tin ⅔ full; foil liners may be used. Freeze.

Billie Snow
Richardson, Texas

BANANAS FOSTER
8 servings.

12 tablespoons butter	2 ounces banana liqueur
1½ cups dark brown sugar	1 cup dark rum, warmed
1½ teaspoons cinnamon	1 quart vanilla ice milk or ice cream, frozen hard
6 bananas, halved lengthwise, then quartered	

In a flat skillet or flambe pan, over low heat, melt and stir together butter, sugar and cinnamon. When blended, add bananas and liqueur, cooking only to coat bananas and stirring gently. Add rum and ignite. Baste fruit with sauce until flame dies. Serve over ice cream.

Hope Norman Coulter
Little Rock, Arkansas

LUISE'S BREAD PUDDING
4 to 6 servings.

4 slices whole wheat bread, crumbled	½ cup brown sugar
1 (13-ounce) can evaporated milk	1 egg, slightly beaten
	½ cup melted butter

In mixing bowl combine bread and milk; add remaining ingredients, mixing lightly. Pour into a greased 1-quart casserole; bake at 325° 30 to 40 minutes, or until set. Serve warm with cream.

Luise Pride Thompson

PEACH DUMPLINGS
6 to 8 servings.

4 cups sliced fresh peaches	1½ teaspoons baking powder
⅔ cup sugar	2 tablespoons butter or shortening
4 tablespoons butter	⅓ to ½ cup milk
1 cup flour	
¼ teaspoon salt	

Use heavy pan with tight-fitting lid. Combine peaches, sugar and butter in pan; bring to a boil, uncovered. Sift dry ingredients into mixing bowl; cut in butter until mixture is like cornmeal. Add enough milk to make a drop biscuit dough. Drop dough by teaspoonfuls into boiling peaches. Reduce heat, cover tightly, and simmer 15 to 20 minutes until dumplings are cooked through. Serve hot with cream or ice cream.

Sarah Castleberry
Bearden, Arkansas

CHOCOLATE FUDGE SAUCE
2½ cups.

½ cup butter	1 (13-ounce) can evaporated milk
6 ounces chocolate	2 cups powdered sugar, sifted

Melt butter and chocolate in top of double boiler. Add milk and sugar alternately, stirring after each addition. Cook 1 or 2 hours, stirring occasionally. Sauce will be creamy and dreamy. Tightly covered, it will keep indefinitely in refrigerator; spoon out and heat amount desired.

Jeri Graves
Mabelvale, Arkansas

BASIC ICE CREAM
4 quarts.

6 eggs
2½ cups sugar
1 teaspoon vanilla
Milk and cream

Beat eggs about 20 minutes. (The secret of this ice cream is in this beating time). Gradually beat in sugar; stir in fruit. Pour into a 4-quart freezer; add milk and cream until mixture reaches fill line. Freeze. VARIATIONS: French Vanilla: use ½ pint whipping cream, 1 tablespoon vanilla. Chocolate: add 1 (6-ounce) can chocolate syrup. Strawberry: add 1 pint frozen whole berries, partially thawed. Banana: add 6 large, mashed bananas. Peach: add 6 to 8 very ripe, mashed peaches.

Cleve C. Turner, Jr.
Brinkley, Arkansas

HARLAN'S ICE CREAM
1 gallon.

2½ cups sugar
1 (14-ounce) can evaporated, or sweetened condensed milk
2 tablespoons vanilla
6 eggs, separated
2½ quarts milk
1 package powdered Junket ice cream mix, or 6 Junket tablets

With electric mixer, thoroughly mix canned milk, vanilla, and sugar. Add 1 quart milk; continue beating. Beat egg yolks until "lemony" in color. Fold into milk mixture. Beat egg whites until stiff; fold into mixture. Add remaining milk and Junket mix, beating thoroughly. "Secret to smooth blended homemade ice cream is using your mixer unsparingly."

Judge Harlan Weber
Little Rock, Arkansas

HOMEMADE ICE CREAM
1 gallon.

4 eggs	3 cups sugar
1 teaspoon salt	2 tablespoons vanilla
3 (8-ounce) containers half and half	2 (15-ounce) cans evaporated milk

Beat eggs until foamy; add other ingredients and beat well; pour into a 1-gallon freezer; freeze.

Murphy Cauthron
Ashdown, Arkansas

  ◇ *R. D. Murphy, Arkansas State Representative, 1860-1864.*

BUTTERFINGER ICE CREAM
1 gallon.

2 (14-ounce) cans sweetened condensed milk	4 large Butterfinger candy bars, crushed
½ (6-ounce) can chocolate syrup	Milk

Combine all ingredients in a 1-gallon freezer, adding enough milk to fill; freeze.

Judy Hall

LEMON ICE CREAM
1 gallon.

9 tablespoons lemon juice	2 quarts milk
3 cups sugar	1 pint cream

Combine lemon juice and sugar; let stand 10 minutes, or until sugar is dissolved. Add milk and cream; mix well; pour into 1-gallon freezer; freeze. For pineapple ice cream, add ⅔ cup orange juice and 1 (8-ounce) can crushed pineapple to recipe.

Mary Dale Coulter

STRAWBERRY-BANANA-NUT ICE CREAM
4 quarts.

6 eggs	1 (10-ounce) package frozen strawberries, or 1 pint fresh berries
1½ teaspoons lemon juice	
2 cups sugar	
1 (14-ounce) can sweetened condensed milk	2 bananas, mashed
	1 cup chopped pecans
1½ teaspoons vanilla	1 (8-ounce) container whipped topping
	Milk

Beat eggs with lemon juice; gradually beat in sugar. Add remaining ingredients except milk, in order given, folding in whipped topping. Pour into 4-quart freezer; add milk to bring mixture to fill line. Freeze; let ripen before serving.

Judge Perry V. Whitmore
Marjorie Corbell Whitmore
Little Rock, Arkansas

◇ Joseph A. Corbell, first County Judge of Howard County, 1874-1878.

MOM'S LEMON SHERBET
1 gallon.

1½ cups fresh lemon juice	1 (13-ounce) can evaporated milk
3⅓ cups sugar	
	Milk

Combine all ingredients in a 1-gallon ice cream freezer; add enough milk to fill freezer, and freeze. For different flavor, add to recipe 1 (20-ounce) can crushed pineapple, or 2 cups mashed peaches.

Sue Malcolm
Little Rock, Arkansas

FRESH APPLE CAKE
1 tube cake.

2	eggs, beaten	½	teaspoon cinnamon
2	cups sugar	½	teaspoon cloves
1	teaspoon vanilla	½	teaspoon nutmeg
1¼	cups oil	3	cups chopped apples
½	teaspoon salt	1	cup chopped pecans
3	cups flour	1	cup coconut, optional
1½	teaspoons baking soda		

In mixing bowl, combine eggs, sugar, vanilla and oil; blend well. Sift dry ingredients together; add to egg mixture. Stir in apples, pecans and coconut. Pour into greased and floured tube pan. Bake at 350° for about 1 hour and 30 minutes. Cool 15 minutes before removing from pan.

Bertha Christian
Connie Golden

APPLESAUCE CAKE
1 tube cake.

1	cup sugar or molasses	2½	cups flour
1	tablespoon cinnamon	1	cup raisins
1	tablespoon cloves	½	cup butter
2	teaspoons baking soda	½	cup chopped nuts
1½	cups unsweetened applesauce		

Combine first 3 ingredients; set aside. In mixing bowl stir soda into applesauce; let foam. Add sugar mixture and remaining ingredients; mix well. Pour into a greased, floured tube pan; bake at 350° 45 to 50 minutes, or until cake tests done. Cool; frost if desired.

In memory of Henrietta Burcham Milam
Vera Milam Ryker
Cecil, Arkansas

 Governor Jeff Davis, 1901-1907.

APRICOT NECTAR CAKE
1 tube cake.

1 (19-ounce) package lemon supreme cake mix	1 cup plus 2 tablespoons apricot nectar, divided
¾ cup oil	4 eggs
½ cup sugar	1 cup powdered sugar, sifted

Combine first 3 ingredients with 1 cup apricot nectar; beat until well blended. Add eggs, 1 at a time, beating well after each addition. Pour into a greased, floured tube pan; bake at 325° for 1 hour. Cool 10 minutes before removing from pan. Combine powdered sugar with 2 tablespoons apricot nectar; blend until smooth; spoon glaze over cake.

Judy Packnett
Clara Price

BANANA NUT CAKE
1 4-layer cake.

3 cups sugar	¾ teaspoon baking soda
1 cup oil	3 cups flour
4 eggs, beaten	¾ teaspoon salt
2 cups mashed bananas	2 teaspoons vanilla
½ cup buttermilk	2 cups chopped walnuts
1 teaspoon baking powder	

Combine first 4 ingredients, blending well; stir in milk. Combine dry ingredients; add to banana mixture; stir in vanilla and nuts. Pour into 4 greased, floured 8- or 9-inch pans; bake at 350° for 30 minutes. Cool completely before frosting.

Frosting:

1 stick margarine, softened	1 (16-ounce) box powdered sugar
1 banana, mashed	
2 teaspoons lemon juice	1 cup chopped walnuts

Combine first 3 ingredients; beat until smooth; add sugar; beat in well; stir in nuts.

Lea Polk
Rachel Satterfield
Vera Rodgers

CARROT CAKE

2 loaves or 1 tube cake.

1½ cups sugar	1 teaspoon nutmeg
1⅓ cups water	2½ cups sifted flour
2 large carrots, finely grated	2 teaspoons baking powder
1 cup raisins	1 teaspoon baking soda
1 tablespoon butter	½ teaspoon salt
1 teaspoon cloves	1 cup chopped nuts
1 teaspoon cinnamon	

In a sauce pan, combine sugar, water, carrots, raisins, butter, and spices; simmer for 5 minutes. Cover; let stand for 12 hours (a very important step). To bake, add remaining 5 ingredients to above mixture; blend well. Bake in 2 greased, floured 5 × 9-inch loaf pans or 1 tube pan at 275° for 2 hours.

Golda Gray

BOB BROOKES' CHEESECAKE

6 to 8 servings.

1 cup flour	1¼ teaspoons vanilla, divided
1½ cups sugar, divided	3 (8-ounce) packages cream cheese, softened
1 teaspoon grated lemon rind	
½ cup butter	4 egg whites
1 egg yolk, slightly beaten	

Combine flour, ¼ cup sugar, and lemon rind; cut in butter until mixture is crumbly. Add egg yolk and ¼ teaspoon vanilla; mix well. Pat ⅓ dough on bottom of a 9-inch springform pan, sides removed. Bake at 400° 8 minutes; cool. Butter sides of pan; attach to bottom; pat remaining dough about 1¾ inches up sides of pan. Beat cream cheese and 1 teaspoon vanilla until fluffy. In separate bowl beat egg whites until foamy; add 1 cup sugar in thirds, beating after each addition; beat until stiff. Fold egg whites gently into cheese; pour into crust. Bake at 350° 25 minutes; center will be soft. Cool; chill 4 hours. To serve, remove from pan; cut and serve with fresh fruit or fruit sauce.

Frances Brookes

DELUXE CHEESECAKE WITH RASPBERRY SAUCE
10 servings.

1½ cups graham cracker crumbs	3 (8-ounce) packages cream cheese, softened
6 tablespoons butter, melted	3 eggs
1½ teaspoons cinnamon	1 teaspoon vanilla, divided
1 cup plus 5 tablespoons sugar, divided	1 (16-ounce) container sour cream

Combine first 3 ingredients with 2 tablespoons sugar; mix well; press into a 10-inch springform pan; set aside. In mixing bowl beat cream cheese until soft and creamy; gradually add 1 cup sugar, beating until fluffy. Add eggs, 1 at a time, beating after each addition; stir in ½ teaspoon vanilla. Pour over crust; bake at 375° for 25 to 35 minutes, or until set. Beat sour cream on medium speed of electric mixer 2 minutes; add remaining sugar and vanilla; beat 1 minute; spread over cheesecake. Bake at 500° 5 to 8 minutes, or until bubbly; cool; chill 8 hours or overnight. To serve, remove from pan; cut and top each serving with Raspberry Sauce.

Raspberry Sauce:

1 (10-ounce) package frozen raspberries, thawed, drained, liquid reserved	1 tablespoon cornstarch
	2 tablespoons Cointreau or orange flavored liqueur

Combine raspberry liquid, cornstarch, and Cointreau; cook over low heat until thickened; add raspberries; blend. Chill.

Jean Wickstrom Liles
Foods Editor, SOUTHERN LIVING

Topping Variation: Instead of sauce, substitute blueberry or cherry pie filling.

Viola Thornton Thomason
Broken Bow, Oklahoma

CARROT-COCONUT CAKE
12 to 15 servings.

2	cups sugar	2	teaspoons baking soda
1½	cups oil	2	teaspoons cinnamon
4	eggs	3	cups finely grated carrots
2	cups flour	1	cup finely chopped nuts
1	teaspoon salt	½	cup coconut

Mix sugar, oil and eggs. Add flour, salt, baking soda and cinnamon. Stir in carrots, nuts and coconut. Pour into a greased and floured 9 × 13-inch cake pan. Bake at 350° for 50 to 60 minutes.

Minnie Hopkins

FOOLPROOF BUTTERMILK CHOCOLATE CAKE
20 servings.

1	stick margarine	2	eggs, beaten
½	cup oil	1	teaspoon baking soda dissolved in ½ cup buttermilk
1	cup water		
2	cups sugar		
2	cups flour	1	teaspoon vanilla
4	tablespoons cocoa		

Heat margarine, oil, and water to boiling point; pour over combined sugar, flour, and cocoa; cool. Add remaining ingredients; mix well. Pour into a greased, floured 12 × 15-inch pan; bake 20 minutes at 400°. Remove from oven; pour hot frosting over cake in pan; cover immediately; cool.

Frosting:

1	stick margarine	3½	cups powdered sugar
⅓	cup buttermilk	½	cup nuts
4	tablespoons cocoa		

Bring margarine, buttermilk, and cocoa to a boil; boil 2 minutes; remove from heat. Pour over sugar and nuts; mix well.

Mrs. Dan (Baby) Futrell
Hot Springs, Arkansas

◇ *Governor J. M. Futrell (1933-1937) signed the bill to establish horse racing in Hot Springs.*

CHERRY DUMP CAKE
12 servings.

- 1 (21-ounce) can cherry pie filling
- 1 (20-ounce) can crushed pineapple, drained
- 1 (19-ounce) package yellow cake mix
- 2 sticks margarine
- 1 cup chopped pecans
- 1 (3-ounce) can coconut, optional

Combine pie filling and pineapple; spread evenly in an ungreased 9 × 13-inch pan. Crumble dry cake mix evenly over filling. Dot with margarine; sprinkle with nuts and coconut. Bake at 350° until a light or medium brown crust has formed, about 45 minutes. Serve warm with whipped topping or ice cream.

Lucille Westbrook
Nashville, Arkansas
Bonnie Hogg

MOTHER'S GERMAN CHOCOLATE TORTE
1 6-layer torte.

- 2 cups sugar
- 1 cup shortening
- 6 egg yolks
- 1 (4-ounce) bar German sweet chocolate
- ½ cup boiling water
- 2¼ cups flour
- 1 cup buttermilk
- 1 teaspoon baking soda
- 1 teaspoon vanilla
- Pinch of salt
- 6 egg whites, stiffly beaten

Cream sugar and shortening; add egg yolks, 1 at a time. Melt chocolate in boiling water; add to mixture. Add flour alternately with buttermilk, with baking soda dissolved in ¼ cup of the buttermilk. Add vanilla and salt; fold in egg whites. Pour into 6 9-inch cake pans; you may use 3 pans, slicing layers in half when cooled. Bake 30 minutes at 350°; cool. Spread frosting between each of the layers and over the top.

Frosting:

- 2 cups sugar
- 2 cups evaporated milk
- 2 sticks butter
- 6 egg yolks, beaten
- 1 (14-ounce) package flaked coconut
- 2 cups chopped pecans
- 2 teaspoons vanilla

In double boiler cook, stirring constantly, sugar, milk, butter, and egg yolks; cook until thickened. Add remaining ingredients; mix well.

Melinda Coulter Taggart

SCOTCH FUDGE
8 to 10 servings.

1 cup water	2 eggs
2 sticks margarine	½ cup buttermilk
3 tablespoons cocoa	1 teaspoon baking soda
2 cups sugar	1 teaspoon cinnamon
2 cups flour	1 teaspoon vanilla

In a sauce pan bring water, margarine, and cocoa to a boil. In a mixing bowl combine remaining ingredients. Combine the 2 mixtures, blending well. Pour into a buttered 9 × 13-inch pan. Bake at 375° for 30 minutes; cake is done when it pulls away from sides of pan. Pour frosting over warm cake in pan. Cool; cut in squares.

Frosting:

1 stick butter	1 (16-ounce) box powdered sugar
3 tablespoons cocoa	½ cup chopped pecans
1 teaspoon vanilla	
6 tablespoons milk	

Melt butter with cocoa in a sauce pan over low heat. Remove from heat; add vanilla, milk, and powdered sugar, beating until smooth. Stir in pecans.

Barbara Pryor
Little Rock, Arkansas

◇ *David Pryor, Governor 1975-1979;*
U.S. Senator 1979-1991.

FUDGE CAKE
12 servings.

1 cup sugar	1 (16-ounce) can chocolate syrup
1 cup oil	1 teaspoon vanilla
4 eggs, beaten	1 cup flour
1 teaspoon baking powder	

Combine all ingredients, blending well. Pour into a greased, floured 9 × 13-inch pan. Bake at 350° for 30 to 35 minutes; do not overcook. Frost only if desired.

Joyce Matheson
Marlene Bevill
Sue Krieder

FUDGE CAKE OF 1920
12 servings.

2 cups sugar	2 teaspoons baking powder
2 heaping tablespoons cocoa	1 cup buttermilk
½ cup butter	3 cups flour
2 eggs	1 teaspoon vanilla
2 teaspoons baking soda	1 cup hot water

Mix sugar and cocoa well. Add butter and eggs; cream. Mix baking soda and baking powder in milk. Add this mixture and remaining ingredients to first mixture. Bake in greased and floured 9 × 13-inch pan at 350° for 45 minutes. Cool and frost.

Fudge Frosting:

1¼ cups sugar	¼ cup milk
¼ cup cocoa	1 teaspoon vanilla

Bring to a boil. Remove from heat; stir until cool. Makes a soft spread.

Alice Smalley

CHOCOLATE CREAM CAKE
1 3-layer cake.

1 (8-ounce) package cream cheese, softened	¼ cup shortening
1 (3-ounce) package cream cheese, softened	3 eggs
	1 teaspoon salt
2 sticks margarine, softened	2¼ cups flour
¼ cup hot water	1 teaspoon baking soda
2 (16-ounce) boxes powdered sugar	1 cup buttermilk
	1 teaspoon vanilla
1 (16-ounce) package semi-sweet chocolate chips	

In large bowl cream first 3 ingredients, beating until fluffy. Melt chips in hot water; add to mixture with powdered sugar; blend well. Divide mixture in half; reserve half for frosting; to the other half, beat in shortening, eggs, and salt. Stir in flour, baking soda, and buttermilk. Add vanilla; blend well. Spoon into 3 greased, floured 8-inch cake pans; bake at 350° for 35 minutes; cool. Spread reserved frosting mixture between layers and over top and sides.

Aurora Brent

COLA CAKE
12 servings.

- 1 cup margarine
- 3 tablespoons cocoa
- 1 cup cola
- 2 cups sugar
- 2 cups flour
- 1 teaspoon baking soda
- 2 eggs, beaten
- ½ cup buttermilk
- 1 teaspoon vanilla
- 4 cups miniature marshmallows

Combine margarine, cocoa and cola; bring to a boil. Combine sugar, flour and baking soda. Pour cola mixture into dry mixture. Add eggs, buttermilk, vanilla and marshmallows; mix well. Pour into a greased and floured 9 × 12-inch cake pan; bake at 350° for 30 to 35 minutes.

Frosting:

- ½ cup margarine
- 3 tablespoons cocoa
- 6 tablespoons cola
- 1 (16-ounce) package powdered sugar
- ½ cup nuts

Heat margarine, cocoa and cola; bring to a boil. Combine sugar and nuts. Pour hot mixture into sugar-nut mixture. Ice cake while hot. Cover at once.

Lynn Chism
Nashville, Arkansas
Felix Bell

CHOCOLATE CHERRY BAR CAKE
10 to 12 servings.

1 (19-ounce) package devil's food cake mix	1 teaspoon almond extract
1 (21-ounce) can cherry pie filling	2 eggs, beaten

In a large bowl combine all ingredients, stirring by hand until well mixed. Pour into greased and floured 9 × 13-inch pan. Bake 25 to 30 minutes (or until toothpick inserted into center comes out clean) at 350°. Pour frosting over warm cake in pan.

Frosting:

1 cup sugar	⅓ cup milk
5 tablespoons margarine	1 cup semi-sweet chocolate pieces

In a small pan combine sugar, margarine and milk. Boil, stirring constantly for 1 minute. Remove from heat; stir in chocolate pieces until smooth.

Blanche Scott
Nashville, Arkansas

ITALIAN CREAM CAKE
1 3-layer cake.

2 cups sugar	2 cups flour
½ cup shortening	1 cup angel flake coconut
½ cup oil	½ teaspoon butter flavoring
5 eggs, separated	½ teaspoon vanilla
1 teaspoon baking soda	1 cup chopped pecans, optional
1 cup buttermilk	

Cream sugar, shortening, and oil; add egg yolks, 1 at a time, beating after each addition. Stir baking soda into buttermilk; add buttermilk alternately with flour to batter. Fold in coconut. Beat egg whites; fold in; add flavorings. Pour into 3 greased, floured 9-inch cake pans. Bake at 350° for 25 minutes. Cool before frosting.

Frosting:

1 (8-ounce) package cream cheese	½ teaspoon butter flavoring
½ cup margarine	½ teaspoon vanilla
1 (16-ounce) box powdered sugar	1½ cups chopped pecans

Cream cheese and margarine; gradually beat in sugar; add flavorings. Stir in nuts.

Elaine Hickman
Cedar Hill, Texas
Roberta Dillahunty
Los Angeles, California
Judy Jones

COCONUT CAKE
1 3-layer cake.

½ cup shortening	1 cup milk
1¼ cups sugar	2 egg yolks
¼ cup oil	1 egg
2 cups self-rising flour	1 teaspoon vanilla

Cream together first 3 ingredients, beating until fluffy. Add remaining ingredients; beat 4 minutes. Pour into 3 greased, floured 8-inch cake pans. Bake at 350° for 40 minutes, or until cake tests done. Cool 10 minutes in pan; remove; cool completely before frosting.

Frosting:

1½ cups sugar	⅓ cup water
2 egg whites	1 teaspoon vanilla
¼ cup light corn syrup	Coconut to garnish

Combine all ingredients but coconut in top of a double boiler. Cook and beat until fluffy.

Grace Cross

LEMON LOVERS' DELIGHT
12 servings.

1 (19-ounce) package yellow cake mix	¾ cup mashed apricots
1 (3-ounce) package lemon gelatin	2 cups powdered sugar, sifted
4 eggs	½ cup lemon juice
½ cup oil	

Blend first 5 ingredients thoroughly. Bake in a greased, floured 9 × 13-inch pan at 350° for 40 minutes. Blend powdered sugar and lemon juice until smooth. While cake is still hot, punch holes with a fork; spoon lemon glaze over cake; cool.

Glennda Refeld Fread
Almyra, Arkansas

◇ ReFeld: Believed to be Arkansas County's oldest continuing family, dating from Charles Re-he-feld, an established merchant at Arkansas Post in 1794.

FRIENDSHIP CAKE
1 tube cake.

1 cup butter, melted	¼ teaspoon nutmeg
1¾ cups sugar	2 eggs
3 cups flour	2 cups brandied fruit, coarsely chopped*
1 teaspoon baking soda	
1 teaspoon cinnamon	1 cup chopped pecans
½ teaspoon salt	½ cup brandied fruit juice*
¼ teaspoon ground cloves	

Combine butter and sugar in a large bowl; beat well. Combine next 6 ingredients; add to butter mixture, beating well. Add eggs; beat well. Add brandied fruit, pecans and juice; mix well. Pour batter into well-greased and floured 10-inch tube pan. Bake at 350° for 1 hour. Cool in pan 10 minutes; remove; cool completely on wire rack. Sprinkle with powdered sugar. (*See Index for recipe.)

Burrow Eloth (Bus) Friday

◆ *Architect of the Public Employees Retirement System 1957-1969*

FRUIT COCKTAIL CAKE
12 servings.

2 cups flour	2 eggs, beaten
1½ cups sugar	1 teaspoon vanilla
2 teaspoons baking soda	¾ cup firmly packed brown sugar
1 teaspoon salt	
1 (16 to 17-ounce) can fruit cocktail	½ cup chopped pecans

Combine first 7 ingredients; mix well; pour into greased and floured 9 x 13-inch pan. Mix remaining ingredients; sprinkle over batter. Bake at 350° 30 to 40 minutes. Spoon frosting over warm cake in pan.

Frosting:

1 stick margarine	1 (3-ounce) can angel flake coconut
1 cup evaporated milk	
1 teaspoon vanilla	

Combine margarine and milk; boil 10 minutes. Add vanilla and coconut.

Mrs. King Ebbert Doss

 King Ebbert Doss, County Judge, Sevier County, 1947-1953.

FRUIT CAKE
1 tube cake.

1½ cups candied cherries	1 cup butter
1½ cups candied pineapple	6 eggs, separated
3 cups seedless raisins	¾ teaspoon baking soda
1½ cups currants	2 teaspoons baking powder
1½ cups almonds or walnuts	1 teaspoon nutmeg
2 cups pecans	1 teaspoon cinnamon
1 cup rum, divided	1½ teaspoons mace or nutmeg
2 cups coconut	1½ teaspoons ginger
1 cup fig preserves	1 cup orange juice
2½ cups flour, divided	½ cup grape jelly
1¾ cups sugar	

Place first 6 ingredients in mixing bowl; mix well with ½ cup rum; let stand overnight. Add coconut and preserves to marinated mixture; toss with ½ cup flour. In large bowl, cream sugar and butter; add egg yolks, one at a time, beating well. Sift together 2 cups flour, baking soda, baking powder, and spices; gradually add to creamed mixture. Beat in orange juice, ½ cup rum, and jelly; add fruit mixture. Beat egg whites until firm peaks form; fold into batter. Spoon into a greased, paper-lined tube pan. Bake 2½ hours at 250°. Keep in tightly covered container; douse occasionally with ½ cup rum.

Mattie Bell
Lillian Wesson
Los Angeles, California

LEMON FRUIT CAKE

1 tube cake.

1	pound margarine	2	ounces candied pineapple, chopped
3	cups sugar		
1	teaspoon baking soda in 2 tablespoons water	2	ounces candied cherries, chopped
6	eggs, separated	1	pound white raisins
5	cups flour, divided	1	quart pecans, chopped
		2	ounces lemon extract

Cream margarine and sugar; add egg yolks; beat well. Add baking soda water; beat. Dredge fruit and nuts in 2 cups flour; add remaining flour to batter; beat until smooth. Add extract; mix. Stir in fruit-nut mixture. Beat egg whites; fold into batter. Pour into a large, greased, floured tube pan; bake at 250° for 3 hours. Cool; remove from pan; place fresh apple slices on cake; wrap in cloth soaked in apple cider.

Martha Turner Mitchell
Inola, Oklahoma
Kathryn Mize
Mineral Springs, Arkansas

PEAR FRUIT CAKE

1 tube cake.

1	teaspoon cinnamon	3	eggs
3	cups flour	4	medium apples, finely chopped
½	teaspoon salt		
2	cups sugar	4	medium pears, finely chopped
½	teaspoon baking powder		
2	teaspoons baking soda	2	cups coconut
1½	cups oil	1	cup chopped nuts
2	teaspoons vanilla		

Sift together dry ingredients; add oil, vanilla, and eggs; beat until smooth. Stir in fruit, coconut, and nuts. Pour into a greased, floured tube pan; bake at 300° for 1 hour; increase temperature to 325° and bake 30 minutes. Cool; wrap in foil; refrigerate. Let age several weeks.

Mildred Thornton Bismark
Cove, Arkansas
Shelby Zachry Murphy
Moore, Oklahoma

VANILLA WAFER FRUIT CAKE
1 tube cake.

1	(13½-ounce) package vanilla wafers, crushed	2	eggs, beaten
1	pound pecans	½	cup sugar
½	pound cherries	1	(6-ounce) can evaporated milk
½	pound candied pineapple	⅛	teaspoon salt
¼	pound raisins		

Chop fruit and nuts. Keep out 4 whole cherries, 16 pecan halves and 2 slices pineapple. Mix chopped nuts and fruit with vanilla wafers. Beat eggs well; add sugar, salt and milk. To this mixture add fruit, nuts and vanilla wafers; blend well; let stand a few minutes. Line tube pan with waxed paper. Push batter into pan. Decorate top with cherries, pineapple and nut halves. Bake at 325° for 1 hour.

Beth Ann Gressett
Sanger, Texas

Jackson Cookie Company, Inc., North Little Rock.

WHITE FRUIT CAKE
1 tube cake.

½	pound butter	1	pound white seedless raisins
2	cups sugar	1	pound pecans, chopped
6	eggs, separated	1	pound candied cherries, chopped
1	cup whiskey	1	pound candied pineapple
4	cups sifted flour	½	pound citron, chopped (optional)
1	teaspoon nutmeg		
1	teaspoon baking powder		

Cream butter and sugar. Add egg yolks, whiskey and sifted dry ingredients. Fold in beaten egg whites. Add nuts and fruits. Pour into greased and floured tube pan. Bake at 275° 2½ to 3 hours, or until cake tests done.

Mrs. Eula Terral Julian
Pine Bluff, Arkansas

◇ *Governor Thomas J. Terral - 1925-1927*

ARKANSAS MINCEMEAT CAKE
1 tube cake.

1 pint pear mincemeat mix*	2½ cups flour
1 cup boiling water	2 teaspoons baking soda
⅔ cup oil	½ teaspoon salt
2 cups sugar	

Stir first 4 ingredients together, blending well. Sift flour, baking soda, and salt together; add to mincemeat mixture. Pour into a greased, floured tube pan; bake at 350° 1 hour, or until cake tests done. Cool on rack until partially cooled; frost. (*See Index for recipe.)

Frosting:

¾ cup sugar	1 teaspoon vanilla
1 stick margarine	1 cup flaked or shredded coconut
½ cup evaporated milk	

In a sauce pan boil sugar, milk, and margarine 1 minute; remove from heat; add vanilla and coconut.

Bell Cain Morrow
Caddo Gap, Arkansas
Blanche Mitchell Reid
New Hope, Arkansas

Cocoa as a substitute for chocolate: 3 tablespoons cocoa plus 1 tablespoon shortening equals 1 ounce unsweetened baking chocolate. 6 tablespoons cocoa plus 7 tablespoons sugar plus ¼ cup shortening equals 1 cup semi-sweet chocolate chips or 6 ounces semi-sweet baking chocolate. 3 tablespoons cocoa plus 4½ tablespoons sugar plus 2¾ tablespoons shortening equals 1 bar (4 ounces) sweet baking chocolate.

JAM CAKE
1 3-layer cake.

1	cup butter	1	teaspoon nutmeg
2	cups sugar	1	teaspoon baking soda
5	eggs, separated	1	cup buttermilk
1½	cups jam (any flavor)	1	cup chopped nuts
3	cups flour		

Cream butter and sugar; add egg yolks and jam; blend well. Mix dry ingredients; add to creamed mixture alternately with buttermilk, beating well. Fold in stiffly beaten egg whites and nuts. Pour into 3 greased, floured 8-inch cake pans. Bake 30 to 40 minutes at 350°. Cool; remove from pans; frost.

Frosting:

3	cups sugar	1	teaspoon vanilla
2	cups milk	1	cup chopped pecans
½	cup butter		

In a sauce pan, over medium heat, bring sugar and milk to a boil, stirring constantly. Reduce heat; continuing to stir, cook until mixture reaches soft ball stage (234°); remove from heat; stir in butter and vanilla. Beat until slightly thickened; add nuts.

Mary Corbell Williamson
Irving, Texas

MOUND CAKE
12 to 16 servings.

1	(19-ounce) box chocolate cake mix	1	(7-ounce) jar marshmallow creme
1	(13-ounce) can evaporated milk	1	(14-ounce) package flaked coconut
1	stick butter	1	(1-pound) can fudge frosting
1	cup sugar		

Mix and bake cake mix according to package direction, baking in 2 9-inch layers; cool and split layers in half to make 4 layers. In a sauce pan, over low heat, stir and blend remaining ingredients except coconut and frosting. Remove from heat; add coconut. Spread between cake layers; frost top and sides with fudge frosting.

Zula Mae Cooper
Texarkana, Arkansas
Naye Dean Dowdle

PEANUT BUTTER CAKE

1 3-layer cake.

½ cup shortening	1¼ cups flour
1 cup sugar	½ teaspoon baking soda
2 eggs	3 teaspoons baking powder
½ cup peanut butter	1 cup milk
1 teaspoon vanilla	

Cream shortening; add sugar; cream into shortening. Add eggs, beating well. Add peanut butter and vanilla; blend. Sift flour, baking soda and baking powder; add to creamed mixture a small amount at a time alternating with a little milk. Continue beating until all is combined. Pour into 3 8-inch greased and floured cake pans; bake at 375° 25 to 30 minutes. Remove from pan; cool and frost.

Frosting:

3 cups powdered sugar	⅓ cup peanut butter
3 tablespoons cocoa	Dash salt
⅓ stick margarine	Milk
1 teaspoon vanilla	

Combine all ingredients, mixing with enough milk to make spreading easy.

Katherine Hargis

PERSIMMON CAKE

1 loaf cake.

1 egg	1¾ cups flour
¾ cup sugar	3 teaspoons baking powder
3 tablespoons butter	½ teaspoon salt
½ cup milk	¾ cup persimmon pulp

Beat egg, sugar, and butter until well blended; add milk; beat well. Stir in dry ingredients, mixing thoroughly. Add pulp; blend. Pour into a greased, floured 5 × 9-inch loaf pan. Bake at 350° 25 to 30 minutes, or until lightly brown and cake tests done.

Esther Daniel

PIÑA COLADA CAKE
1 tube cake.

1 (8-ounce) can crushed pineapple, drained	½ cup plain yogurt
1 (19-ounce) package yellow pudding cake mix	4 eggs
½ cup canned cream of coconut	⅓ cup oil
	⅓ cup water

Spoon drained pineapple evenly over bottom of a greased, floured tube pan. In mixing bowl blend remaining ingredients on low speed of electric mixer; beat 3 minutes on medium speed. Spoon batter into pan; bake at 350° 55 minutes, or until cake tests done. Remove from oven; with a fork, poke deep holes in cake about 1-inch apart; slowly pour syrup over cake. Cool in pan 30 minutes; invert; cool completely. Spoon glaze over cooled cake.

Syrup:

¼ cup sugar ¼ cup light rum
¼ cup water

In sauce pan boil sugar and water 2 minutes; remove from heat; add rum. Keep syrup warm.

Glaze:

¼ cup canned cream of coconut 1 (3-ounce) package cream cheese

In small mixer bowl gradually beat cream of coconut into cream cheese until smooth.

Lennie Crenshaw
Winthrop, Arkansas
Pauline Luttrell Merideth

PINEAPPLE SHEET CAKE

12 servings.

2	cups flour	2	teaspoons baking soda
2	cups sugar	1	teaspoon vanilla
2	eggs	¼	teaspoon salt
½	cup oil	1	(20-ounce) can crushed pineapple

Combine all ingredients; stir until well blended. Bake in a greased, floured 9 × 13-inch pan at 350° for 25 to 30 minutes. Frost while warm.

Frosting:

1	stick margarine, melted	1	(8-ounce) can flaked coconut
⅔	cup evaporated milk	1	cup chopped pecans
1	cup sugar	1	teaspoon vanilla

In a sauce pan combine margarine, milk, and sugar; boil 5 minutes. Remove from heat; add remaining ingredients.

Bertha Clinton Crager
Grannis, Arkansas
Donna Cox

HEAVENLY PINEAPPLE CAKE

1 tube cake.

1	(8-ounce) can unsweetened crushed pineapple, drained, juice reserved	1	tablespoon baking powder
		½	teaspoon salt
		1	teaspoon almond extract
6	eggs, separated	½	teaspoon cream of tartar
2	cups flour	1	cup sugar, divided

To reserved pineapple juice, add water to measure ¾ cup; set aside. Beat egg yolks until thick and lemon-colored. Add ½ cup sugar and pineapple juice mixture; beat 3 minutes. Combine flour, baking powder and salt; add to egg mixture, mixing well. Add almond extract. Beat egg whites (at room temperature) with cream of tartar until soft peaks form; gradually add ½ cup sugar, beating until stiff. Fold egg whites and pineapple into batter. Spoon into ungreased 10-inch tube pan. Bake at 350° for 50 to 55 minutes. Invert cake and cool one hour.

Vida Traywick

HUMMINGBIRD CAKE
1 3-layer cake.

3	cups flour	3	eggs
2	cups sugar	1½	teaspoons vanilla
1	teaspoon salt	1	(8-ounce) can crushed pineapple
1	teaspoon baking soda		
1	teaspoon cinnamon	1	cup chopped nuts
1½	cups oil	2	cups chopped bananas

Combine dry ingredients in a large bowl. Add oil and eggs; stir, do not beat. Add vanilla, pineapple, nuts and bananas; stir. Spoon batter into 3 greased and floured 9-inch cake pans. Bake at 350° for 25 or 30 minutes. Cool in pans 10 minutes. Remove from pan and frost.

Frosting:

2	(8-ounce) packages cream cheese, softened	2	teaspoons vanilla
		1	cup chopped nuts
1	cup butter, softened		
2	pounds powdered sugar		

Combine all ingredients except nuts; beat until smooth; stir in nuts.

Maudie M. Doss
Texarkana, Arkansas
Fannie Pope
Patsy Havins

POPPY SEED CAKE
1 tube cake or 2 loaves.

2	cups sugar	3	cups sifted flour
1½	cups vegetable oil	1	(13-ounce) can evaporated milk
4	eggs		
1	tablespoon vanilla	1	teaspoon baking soda
1	cup chopped nuts	1	(2-ounce) box poppy seeds
½	teaspoon salt		

Combine all ingredients in a large bowl; beat until smooth. Pour into a greased and floured 10-inch tube pan or 2 5 × 9-inch loaf pans. Bake tube cake 1 hour and 10 minutes at 350°; loaves for 45 to 50 minutes. Cool; remove from pan.

Maxine Phelps
Arkadelphia, Arkansas

PUMPKIN PIE CAKE
12 servings.

1 (16-ounce) can pumpkin	1 (13-ounce) can evaporated milk
3 eggs, beaten	1 teaspoon salt
¾ cup sugar	1 (19-ounce) package yellow or white cake mix
¾ cup brown sugar	2 sticks butter, melted
2 teaspoons pumpkin pie spice	1 cup broken pecans

Combine first 7 ingredients; blend thoroughly. Pour into an ungreased 9 × 13-inch pan. Spread dry cake mix over batter in pan. Pour butter evenly over cake mix; sprinkle with pecans. Bake at 350° for 1 hour and 15 minutes; cool; cut in squares.

Mamie Lula Sparks
Talladega, Alabama

HAWAIIAN PINEAPPLE CAKE
12 servings.

1 (19-ounce) package yellow cake mix	1 (3¾-ounce) box instant vanilla pudding
1 (20-ounce) can crushed pineapple, drained	1 cup milk
1 (8-ounce) package cream cheese, softened	2 cups whipped topping
	1 cup coconut, or chopped nuts

Mix cake according to package directions. Bake in a greased, floured 9 × 13-inch pan at 350° 40 to 50 minutes; cool completely. Punch large holes over top of cake; spread pineapple evenly over top of cake. Beat cream cheese, pudding mix, and milk until thick enough to spread; spread over pineapple layer. Spread layer of whipped topping over cake; sprinkle with coconut or nuts. Refrigerate at least 1 hour before serving.

Bessie Walker Roach
Jacksonville, Texas
Ida Ellen Snow

PUMPKIN WALNUT CAKE
1 tube cake.

3 cups sifted flour	4 eggs
2 teaspoons baking powder	2 cups sugar
2 teaspoons baking soda	1½ cups oil
1 teaspoon salt	1 (16-ounce) can pumpkin, or
3½ teaspoons cinnamon	1½ cups mashed, cooked sweet potatoes
	1 cup chopped walnuts

Sift first 5 ingredients together. In large mixing bowl, at high speed, beat eggs until whites and yolks are combined; gradually add sugar, beating until thick and lemon-colored. Add oil, beating constantly. At low speed, add dry ingredients, alternating with pumpkin, beginning and ending with dry ingredients; beat until smooth after each addition. Stir in nuts. Bake in ungreased tube pan at 350° for 1 hour and 10 minutes. Cool completely in pan on rack before removing; frost.

Frosting:

½ cup butter	1 (16-ounce) box powdered sugar
1 (8-ounce) package cream cheese	1 teaspoon vanilla

Cream butter and cheese; gradually add sugar, beating until light and fluffy. Stir in vanilla.

Mary Rafferty
Wheaton, Illinois
Minnie Hankins

WHIPPING CREAM POUND CAKE
1 tube cake.

3 cups sugar	2 cups flour
1 cup butter	1 cup whipping cream
6 eggs	2 teaspoons vanilla

Cream sugar and butter. Add eggs and flour alternately, beating well after each addition. Add cream and vanilla; mix well. Pour into a greased and floured tube pan. Place in cold oven, turn to 325°. Bake 1 hour and 25 minutes. Do not open oven door until done. Cool in pan for 10 minutes.

Ella Honnel Steel

FIVE FLAVOR BUTTERMILK POUND CAKE
1 tube cake.

1 cup margarine	2 teaspoons lemon extract
2 cups sugar	3 teaspoons coconut extract
4 eggs	1 teaspoon butter-flavored extract
1 cup buttermilk	
½ teaspoon baking soda	1 teaspoon almond extract
3 cups flour	½ teaspoon salt
2 teaspoons vanilla	

Cream margarine and sugar well. Add eggs, one at a time, beating well after each addition. Stir baking soda into buttermilk. Add to batter alternately with flour. Add flavorings and salt; beat thoroughly to blend flavors. Bake in a well greased and floured tube pan at 325° for 1 hour. (Try this with ½ whole wheat and ½ regular flour.)

Tina Raine
Texarkana, Arkansas
Eunice Bell

LEMON POUND CAKE
1 tube cake.

1½ cups butter, softened	1 tablespoon plus 1½ teaspoons lemon juice
3 cups sugar	
8 eggs	1 tablespoon plus 1½ teaspoons lemon extract
3 cups flour	

Cream butter; gradually add sugar, beating until light and fluffy. Add eggs, one at a time, beating well after each addition. Add flour, mixing well. Add lemon juice and extract; beat to blend flavor. Pour into greased and floured 10-inch tube pan. Bake at 350° for 1 hour and 15 minutes. Cool in pan.

Loretta McRae
Bessie Stuart

RUM CAKE
12 servings.

½ cup chopped pecans	½ cup light rum
1 (19-ounce) package yellow cake mix	½ cup water
	½ cup oil
1 (3¾-ounce) package vanilla instant pudding mix	4 eggs

Sprinkle nuts in bottom of a greased, floured 9 × 13-inch pan. In mixing bowl, combine remaining ingredients, blending well; beat 2 minutes. Pour into pan; bake at 325° 50 to 60 minutes. Cool 10 minutes; remove from pan; pour hot glaze over cake (will cause cake to settle).

Hot Rum Glaze:

1 cup sugar	¼ cup light rum
1 stick butter	¼ cup water

In a sauce pan bring glaze ingredients to a boil; boil 2 or 3 minutes.

Tressie Williams
Los Angeles, California
Agnes Gilmore

Blackberry Variation: Substitute 1 (3-ounce) package blackberry gelatin and ¾ cup blackberry wine for pudding mix and rum. Blend 2 cups powdered sugar and ½ cup blackberry wine; bring to a boil; cool to consistency to thick syrup; use as glaze over cooled cake.

Polly Crisp

CORA LOCKE'S SPICE CAKE
12 servings.

1 cup sugar	1½ cups flour
¾ cup shortening	Pinch of salt
1 cup buttermilk	½ teaspoon cinnamon
2 eggs	¼ teaspoon allspice
1 teaspoon baking soda	¼ teaspoon ground cloves
2 tablespoons cocoa	

Cream sugar and shortening; add milk and slightly beaten eggs. Sift together all dry ingredients; beat into mixture. Pour into a greased and floured 9-inch pan. Bake at 350° for 25 to 30 minutes. This cake is usually served warm with whipped cream.

Mrs. Susie Phillips Smith

◇ *An old recipe given to her neighbor, Mrs. Smith, by Cora Davis Locke.*

CREAM CHEESE POUND CAKE
1 tube cake.

¾ pound butter, softened	3 cups flour
1 (8-ounce) package cream cheese, softened	6 eggs
3 cups sugar	1 teaspoon vanilla

Cream butter and cream cheese; beat well. Combine sugar and flour; add alternately with eggs, one at a time, beating well after each addition. Pour into greased and floured tube pan. Place in cold oven and turn to 350°. Bake for 1 hour and 20 minutes. Cool 10 minutes.

Emma Butler
Marguerite Russell

BLACK WALNUT CAKE
12 servings.

Made with Arkansas' black walnuts, naturally!	½ teaspoon salt
2 cups brown sugar	2 cups flour, reserve 1 tablespoonful
½ cup butter	⅔ cup milk
1 teaspoon vanilla	1 cup finely chopped or ground black walnuts, dredged in reserved flour
3 eggs, separated	
2 teaspoons baking powder	

Cream sugar, butter and vanilla. Add egg yolks one at a time, beating well after each addition. Sift dry ingredients; add to creamed mixture alternately with milk. Add nuts; mix well. Fold in stiffly beaten egg whites. Pour into greased and floured 9 × 13-inch pan. Bake at 350° for 1 hour or until cake tests done.

Frosting:

2 tablespoons thick cream	2 cups powdered sugar
2 tablespoons butter	2 or 3 tablespoons finely chopped black walnuts
1 teaspoon vanilla	

Blend cream, butter, vanilla and powdered sugar. Fold in nuts. Spread on cake. This can be wrapped in foil and stored for about a week before cutting.

Gerry Spradlin
Russellville, Arkansas

Black Walnut Caramel Frosting:

2 cups evaporated milk	¼ teaspoon salt
2 cups sugar	½ cup ground black walnuts
1 teaspoon black walnut flavor	2 tablespoons butter

Cook first 4 ingredients over low heat; stir until sugar dissolves. Cook to a soft ball stage (236°); remove from heat and add black walnuts and butter; mix well. Spread over cake.

In memory of Etta Simmons.

There is a large black walnut shelling and processing plant in Gravette.

NEVER SAY "NEVER FAIL" DIVINITY
about 3 dozen.

2½ cups sugar	2 egg whites
½ teaspoon salt	2 teaspoons vanilla
½ cup water	1 cup chopped nuts
½ cup light corn syrup	

In heavy sauce pan cook first 4 ingredients, stirring constantly, until sugar dissolves. Continue cooking, without stirring, until candy thermometer reads 248°. Beat egg whites until stiff, but not dry; with electric mixer on HIGH, pour ½ of the syrup into the beaten egg whites. Cook remaining syrup to 272°; with mixer on HIGH, pour slowly into egg-syrup mixture; continue beating until the mixture starts holding its shape; add vanilla. With mixer on LOW, or with wooden spoon, continue beating until mixture forms peaks; add nuts. Push, by teaspoonfuls, onto waxed paper to make nice puffed peaks; cool.

Mrs. Gunter England

EASY DIVINITY
16 squares.

2 cups sugar	1 teaspoon vanilla
½ cup water	1 cup nuts
1 (7-ounce) jar marshmallow creme	

Boil sugar and water until mixture threads when dropped in cold water; add marshmallow creme; beat well. Blend in vanilla and nuts thoroughly; pour into a buttered 8-inch square pan; chill until set; cut in squares.

Emma Lee Mickle

ALMOND BARK CANDY
about 4 pounds.

3 pounds almond bark	2 cups Rice Krispies cereal
2½ cups dry roasted peanuts	2 cups peanut butter cereal
2 cups miniature marshmallows	

Melt almond bark over low heat, stirring constantly. Add remaining ingredients. Mix well; drop by spoonfuls onto waxed paper.

Jo Porter
Ashdown, Arkansas

BAKED FUDGE
6 to 10 servings.

4 eggs, at room temperature, well beaten	½ cup cocoa
2 cups sugar	1 cup melted butter
½ cup flour	1 cup chopped pecans
	2 teaspoons vanilla

Beat eggs and sugar until mixture forms ribbons when beaters are lifted; sift in blended flour and cocoa; blend. Stir in remaining ingredients. Spread evenly in a 9-inch square baking pan; place pan into a larger pan; add boiling water to larger pan to a 1-inch depth. Bake at 350° 45 to 60 minutes, or until knife inserted in center comes out moist but clean. Fudge should be firm like custard and crusty on top. Cut into squares; serve with whipped cream.

Joyce Fugitt
Berniece Stinnett

SEES FUDGE
16 squares.

4½ cups sugar	2 cups chopped walnuts
1 (13-ounce) can evaporated milk	1 pint marshmallow creme
3 to 6 ounces semi-sweet chocolate chips	½ pound butter
	1 teaspoon vanilla

In large sauce pan bring sugar and milk to a boil; boil 12 minutes. In a large bowl, combine remaining ingredients; pour in hot milk mixture; stir until well blended. Pour into a buttered or waxed paper-lined 9 × 13-inch pan. Chill until firm; cut into squares.

Ruby Bonvillain

FAST CHOCOLATE FUDGE
16 pieces.

2½ to 3 cups semi-sweet chocolate chips
1 (14-ounce) can sweetened condensed milk
¼ cup butter
1 cup chopped pecans
1 teaspoon vanilla

Microwave chips, milk and butter on 50% to 70% power until chocolate melts, 3 to 5 minutes, stirring several times. Stir in nuts; pour into a buttered 9-inch square baking dish. Refrigerate until set. Cut into squares.

Ruby Ellen Steel Burkhead

PEANUT BUTTER FUDGE
16 squares.

4 cups sugar
1⅔ cups evaporated milk
½ cup butter
1 (7-ounce) jar marshmallow creme
1 teaspoon vanilla
1 (18-ounce) jar chunky peanut butter

Boil sugar, milk and butter to soft ball stage. Add marshmallow creme, vanilla and peanut butter; mix well. Spread in buttered 9 × 13-inch pan. Chill until set; cut in squares.

Katie Sue Smiley

REESE CUPS
24 squares.

1 (16-ounce) box powdered sugar
1½ cups peanut butter
1 tablespoon vanilla
¾ cup graham cracker crumbs
2 sticks butter, melted
1 (12-ounce) package semi-sweet chocolate chips

Combine first 5 ingredients; press into a buttered 9 × 13-inch pan. Melt chocolate chips; pour over peanut butter mixture. Chill until chocolate hardens; cut in squares.

Marsha Higgins

MIMI MATTESON'S CHOCOLATE PEANUT CLUSTERS
30 clusters.

1   (11½-ounce) package milk chocolate chips
1   (6-ounce) package butterscotch chips
2   tablespoons smooth peanut butter
1   ounce paraffin
3   cups roasted Spanish peanuts

In a double boiler melt first 4 ingredients, stirring until smooth and blended; add peanuts. Drop by spoonfuls onto waxed paper; cool.

Beverly Matteson
Foreman, Arkansas

MATTESON FARMS, *shipping peanuts around the world daily.*

BUCKEYE BALLS
8 dozen.

1½ cups peanut butter
½   cup butter
1   teaspoon vanilla
1   (16-ounce) package powdered sugar
1   (6-ounce) package semi-sweet chocolate pieces
2   tablespoons shortening

In a bowl mix first 4 ingredients to form a smooth dough; shape into ½-inch balls; place on waxed paper-lined baking sheet; chill. In top of double boiler, over simmering, not boiling, water, melt chocolate with shortening; remove from heat; insert a toothpick into candy ball; dip ¾ of the ball into melted chocolate; place on waxed paper until set; repeat until all are coated.

Joan Root Johnson
Arlington, Virginia
Sandra K. Taylor

PECAN CLUSTERS
12 dozen.

1 (7-ounce) jar marshmallow creme	1 (13-ounce) can evaporated milk
1½ pounds chocolate kisses	½ cup butter
5 cups sugar	6 cups pecan halves

In a large bowl combine marshmallow creme and kisses; set aside. In a sauce pan bring sugar, milk, and butter to a boil; cook for 8 minutes; pour over creme and kisses; stir until thoroughly blended; add pecans; stir. Drop by teaspoonfuls onto waxed paper; cool.

Kathyrn Wilson

LAZY MILLIONAIRES
4 dozen.

2 (14-ounce) packages vanilla caramels	1 cup semi-sweet chocolate chips
1 tablespoon evaporated milk	⅓ bar paraffin
	8 cups chopped pecans

In a heavy sauce pan melt first 4 ingredients; stir in pecans; drop on greased waxed paper; cool.

Suzanne and Gary Green

BOURBON NUT LOG
1 candy log.

2 tablespoons bourbon	1 cup chopped candied pineapple
1 (14-ounce) can sweetened condensed milk	1 cup chopped pecans
1 cup chopped candied cherries	1 (12-ounce) box vanilla wafers, crushed
	Powdered sugar

Stir bourbon into milk; add candied fruits, nuts, and wafers; shape into a log; roll in powdered sugar. Wrap in waxed paper; freeze 1 hour; cut into slices. Store, covered, in refrigerator.

Patricia Andrews
Nashville, Arkansas

PEANUT BRITTLE
1 pound.

1 cup sugar	2 cups raw peanuts
½ cup white corn syrup	½ teaspoon baking soda

In deep heavy sauce pan, stirring constantly, cook sugar and syrup until sugar dissolves. Add peanuts; continue cooking and stirring until peanuts pop and turn brown as if roasted. When mixture turns to caramel (285° on candy thermometer), quickly add baking soda; stir rapidly. When mixture expands and bubbles, pour quickly onto greased cookie sheet or platter; cool completely, break into pieces.

Mrs. C. L. Williams
Port Neches, Texas
Nellie DeShazo

BUTTERMILK PRALINES
30 pralines.

1 cup buttermilk	¼ cup margarine
2 cups firmly packed dark brown sugar	1 teaspoon vanilla
¼ teaspoon salt	2 cups pecans

In heavy sauce pan combine first 3 ingredients; boil, stirring constantly, until mixture reaches soft ball state (234°); remove from heat. Add margarine and vanilla; do not stir; cool, without stirring, to lukewarm (150°); stir in pecans; beat. Drop by spoonfuls onto waxed paper; cool.

Mrs. Lowell Clements
Bryan, Texas
Mary Culp

PEPPERMINT BARK
36 squares.

1 pound white chocolate	4 to 7 drops red food coloring
½ cup crushed peppermint candies	

Melt chocolate in heavy saucepan over low heat. Stir in candies and food coloring. Spread in foil covered 12 × 15-inch baking sheet; let stand until firm; cut in squares.

Raeann Refeld
Almyra, Arkansas

◇ *Pierre Jardelas, original Spanish land grant owner of land upon which Arkansas Post was laid out in 1819.*

ROCKY ROAD BARS
48 bars.

12 double graham crackers	½ cup butter
2 cups miniature marshmallows	½ cup firmly packed dark brown sugar
1 (6-ounce) package semi-sweet chocolate chips	1 teaspoon vanilla

Arrange crackers in a single layer on a 10 × 15-inch jelly-roll pan; sprinkle with marshmallows, then chips. In a sauce pan, cook butter and brown sugar over low heat, stirring constantly, until sugar dissolves; add vanilla; drizzle evenly over crackers. Bake 10 to 12 minutes at 350°; cool; cut into bars.

L'Jon Hill
High Ridge, Missouri

ROCKY ROAD
36 pieces.

1 (12-ounce) package chocolate chips	1 (10-ounce) package miniature marshmallows
1 (14-ounce) can sweetened condensed milk	1 pound dry roasted unsalted peanuts

Mix chocolate chips and milk; bring to a boil. Remove from heat; stir in marshmallows and peanuts. Spread in a 10 × 15-inch jellyroll pan; cool; cut in squares.

Jennifer Gail Stafford
Hamburg, Arkansas
Wilma Morris

CARAMEL CRUNCH
8 quarts.

5 quarts popped popcorn	½ cup light corn syrup
2 sticks butter	1 teaspoon salt
2 cups firmly packed dark brown sugar	½ teaspoon baking soda
	2 cups toasted nuts, optional

Keep popcorn warm and crisp in a shallow pan in 250° oven. In a heavy 2-quart sauce pan, combine butter, sugar, syrup, and salt; bring mixture to a boil, stirring constantly. Boil over medium heat to soft ball stage (234°), stirring constantly. Remove from heat; stir in baking soda. Combine popcorn and nuts in a large bowl; gradually pour hot syrup over mixture, stirring well to coat. Turn mixture into greased 10 × 15-inch jelly-roll pans; bake at 250° 20 minutes; stir well; bake an additional 20 minutes. Cool completely in pans; break into pieces; store in airtight containers in cool place.

Donna Sims
Houston, Texas
Freda Huntsberger
Mrs. Bill Phillips

BANANA NUT COOKIES
4 dozen.

½ cup shortening
½ cup butter
1½ cups sugar
2 eggs
1 cup ripe, mashed bananas
½ cup buttermilk
1 teaspoon vanilla
3 cups flour
1½ teaspoons baking soda
½ teaspoon salt
1 teaspoon cinnamon, optional
1 cup chopped nuts, optional

Mix first 4 ingredients, beating well; stir in bananas, buttermilk, and vanilla; thoroughly blend in dry ingredients. Stir in nuts. Chill 1 hour; drop by teaspoonfuls onto lightly greased cookie sheet; bake at 375° 10 minutes, or until browned.

Mrs. Allan Baker

BROWN SUGAR KISSES
2 dozen.

1 egg white
½ teaspoon salt
1 cup light brown sugar
1 cup chopped pecans

Beat egg white until foamy; add salt; beat until stiff. Beating, gradually add sugar; beat until stiff and glossy; fold in nuts. Drop by teaspoonfuls 2 inches apart on a greased brown paper-covered cookie sheet. Bake at 325° about 20 minutes, or until set and delicately browned. Loosen immediately with spatula; cool.

Mrs. Allan Baker

BROWN SUGAR COOKIES
8 dozen.

⅔ cup shortening
⅔ cup softened margarine
1 cup sugar
1 cup firmly packed brown sugar
2 eggs, beaten
2 teaspoons vanilla
3¼ cups flour
1 teaspoon baking soda
1 teaspoon salt

Cream first 4 ingredients together; add eggs and vanilla, beating well. Sift dry ingredients together; add to creamed mixture; stir to blend; chill. Drop by teaspoonfuls onto cookie sheet, placing 2 inches apart. Bake 12 to 15 minutes at 375°; cool. Dough will keep, refrigerated, 1 week.

Bertha Christian

RANGER MACAROONS
"A Bunch".

1 cup butter	1 teaspoon baking powder
1 cup brown sugar	1 teaspoon baking soda
1 cup sugar	2 cups dry oats
2 eggs	2 cups corn flakes
1 teaspoon salt	1 cup coconut
1 teaspoon vanilla	1 cup chopped nuts
2 cups flour	

Combine all ingredients, blending well; drop by teaspoonfuls onto a cookie sheet; press lightly with fork. Bake 10 minutes at 375°, or until light brown.

Ruth Hinton Pilger
Mountain Home, Arkansas

VANILLA CRISPS
5 dozen.

¼ cup shortening	1½ teaspoons vanilla
¼ cup butter	1⅓ cups flour
1 cup sugar	1 teaspoon baking powder
2 eggs, beaten	½ teaspoon salt

Cream first 2 ingredients; add sugar; cream well again. Add eggs; beat until fluffy; stir in vanilla. Combine dry ingredients; stir into mixture, mixing well. Drop by teaspoonfuls onto a flour-dusted baking sheet; bake at 400° about 8 minutes, or until light brown.

Katherine Hargis

FROSTED CARROT COOKIES
6 to 7 dozen.

1 cup sugar	1 teaspoon vanilla
¾ cup shortening	1 cup mashed cooked carrots
1 egg	2 tablespoons grated orange rind
2 cups flour	2 tablespoons butter, melted
1 teaspoon baking powder	1 (16-ounce) box powdered sugar
¼ teaspoon salt	Orange juice

Cream sugar and shortening; add egg, beating well. Sift dry ingredients together; blend into creamed mixture; stir in vanilla and carrots. Drop by teaspoonfuls onto cookie sheet; bake about 15 minutes at 350°; cool. Combine rind, butter, and sugar; add enough orange juice to make right consistency to spread; frost cooled cookies.

Jan Hendrix
Morene Akers

CHEESECAKE COOKIES
16 squares.

⅓ cup brown sugar	¼ cup sugar
1 cup flour	1 egg
½ cup chopped walnuts	2 tablespoons milk or cream
⅓ cup melted butter	1 tablespoon lemon juice
1 (8-ounce) package cream cheese	1 teaspoon vanilla

Combine first 3 ingredients; stir in butter; mix well. Reserving ¾ cup for topping, pat remaining mixture in an 8-inch square baking pan; bake 15 minutes at 350°; cool. Beat cream cheese and sugar until smooth; beat in remaining ingredients; pour into baked crust; top with reserved crumbs; bake for 25 minutes. Cool thoroughly; cut into squares; keep refrigerated.

Anna Belle Gore
Stringtown, Arkansas

CHRISTMAS FRUIT COOKIES
4 to 5 dozen.

¼ cup butter	4 ounces fruit juice or brandy
½ cup brown sugar	½ teaspoon soda dissolved in
2 eggs, well beaten	1½ teaspoons milk
1½ cups flour	½ pound raisins
½ teaspoon allspice	1 pound candied cherries, chopped
½ teaspoon cinnamon	¼ pound candied mixed fruits, chopped
½ teaspoon nutmeg	2 cups chopped pecans

Cream butter and sugar; add eggs and dry ingredients; mixing well; stir in remaining ingredients. Drop by teaspoonfuls onto greased cookie sheet; bake 12 to 15 minutes at 350°. Better if made ahead to age; store with an apple or brandy-moistened cloth in an airtight container.

Ruby Ellen Steel Burkhead

BLOND BROWNIES
35 squares.

1 (16-ounce) box brown sugar	2⅔ cups flour
⅔ cup melted butter	2½ teaspoons baking powder
3 eggs	½ teaspoon salt
1 tablespoon vanilla	½ cup chopped nuts

Cream sugar and butter; add eggs and vanilla, mixing well. Sift dry ingredients together; blend well into creamed mixture; stir in nuts. Pour into a greased, floured 10 × 15-inch jelly roll pan; bake about 20 minutes at 350°. Cool; cut into squares.

Brenda Presson
Wilma Cannon

BROWNIE FUDGE SQUARES
35 squares.

1½ cups butter
1 cup cocoa
6 eggs, beaten
3 cups sugar

1½ cups flour
1 teaspoon vanilla
2 cups chopped pecans

Cook butter and cocoa over medium heat, stirring frequently, until butter melts; set aside. Thoroughly beat eggs with sugar; add flour and vanilla, mixing well. Add chocolate mixture, beating until just blended; stir in nuts. Pour into a greased, floured 10 × 15-inch jelly roll pan; bake at 325° for 40 to 50 minutes, or until toothpick inserted in center comes out clean; cool; cut into squares.

Ada Joyce Coleman

ELEGANT FROSTED BROWNIES
16 squares.

1 cup margarine
2 cups sugar
4 eggs, beaten

4 (1-ounce) squares unsweetened chocolate
2 teaspoons vanilla
1 cup flour

Thoroughly cream margarine and sugar; add eggs, beating in well. Melt chocolate in top of double boiler; blend into creamed mixture with vanilla and flour. Pour into a greased 8 × 12-inch baking pan; bake 35 minutes at 350°; cool; frost; cut in squares; refrigerate.

Frosting:

1 (1-ounce) square unsweetened chocolate
1 teaspoon margarine
2 sticks margarine, melted

1 (16-ounce) box powdered sugar
4 tablespoons milk
2 teaspoons vanilla

Melt first 2 ingredients in top of double boiler; set aside. Combine remaining ingredients; spread over brownies. Spread chocolate mixture evenly on top.

Gordon Hale
Arkadelphia, Arkansas

EASY CHOCOLATE COOKIES
4½ dozen.

1¼ cups softened butter	¾ cup cocoa
2 cups sugar	1 teaspoon baking soda
2 eggs, beaten	½ teaspoon salt
2 teaspoons vanilla	1 cup finely chopped nuts
2 cups flour	

Cream butter and sugar; add eggs and vanilla, blending well. Combine dry ingredients; stir into creamed mixture; stir in nuts. Drop by teaspoonfuls onto ungreased cookie sheet; bake 8 to 9 minutes at 350°. Do not overbake; cookies will be soft. Cool 1 minute before removing from baking sheet.

Betty Currence

MAGIC COOKIE BARS
16 bars.

1½ cups corn flake or graham cracker crumbs	1 cup coarsely chopped walnuts
3 tablespoons sugar	1⅓ cups flaked coconut
1 stick melted margarine	1 (14-ounce) can sweetened condensed milk
1 cup semi-sweet chocolate morsels	

Combine crumbs, sugar, and margarine; in bottom of a 9 × 13-inch baking pan, press mixture evenly and firmly to form crust. In order given, sprinkle layers of morsels, nuts, and coconut over crumb base; pour milk evenly over top. Bake at 350° about 25 minutes, or until lightly browned around edges; cool; cut in bars.

Verl McAdams
Ashdown, Arkansas
Myrtle Murphy

NEITHER CAKE NOR CANDY
18 squares.

1½ squares bitter chocolate	2 eggs, beaten
2 tablespoons butter	½ cup flour
1 cup sugar	1 cup chopped nuts
1 teaspoon vanilla	½ cup chopped dates or raisins

In double boiler melt chocolate and butter; add sugar and vanilla, mixing well. Beat in eggs. Dredge nuts and fruit with sifted flour; add to chocolate mixture. Bake in a well-greased 8 × 12-inch baking pan 20 minutes at 350°; cool; cut in squares.

Juaveeta Hanson

FAMOUS AMOS (RAISIN-FILLED) CHOCOLATE CHIP COOKIES
6 dozen.

1 cup softened margarine	2½ cups sifted flour
¾ cup firmly packed light brown sugar	1 teaspoon baking soda
	½ teaspoon salt
¾ cup sugar	2 cups raisins
1 teaspoon vanilla	1 (12-ounce) package semi-sweet chocolate chips
1 teaspoon water	
2 eggs	

Beat first 6 ingredients together until creamy. Combine dry ingredients; add to creamed mixture, blending well. Fold in raisins and chips. Drop by spoonfuls onto cookie sheet, placing 1½-inches apart; bake at 375° for 8 minutes, or until brown.

Cora Coulter

STIR AND SPOON FUDGE DROPS
4 dozen.

2	tablespoons butter	1½	cups semi-sweet chocolate chips
⅔	cup evaporated milk	1	teaspoon vanilla
1⅔	cups sugar	½	cup chopped walnuts
½	teaspoon salt	½	cup raisins
2	cups miniature marshmallows	½	cup chopped candied fruit

In heavy sauce pan, over medium heat, bring first 4 ingredients to a boil; cook 4 to 5 minutes (start timing when mixture starts bubbling around edges of pan); stir constantly. Remove from heat; add remaining ingredients; stir vigorously until marshmallows melt and blend. Drop by teaspoonfuls onto waxed paper; cool.

Ruth Wilson

MAGIC GRANOLA BARS
24 to 30 squares.

½	cup melted margarine	¾	cup butterscotch chips
1½	cups crushed graham crackers	1	cup granola mix*
1⅓	cups flaked coconut	1	(15-ounce) can sweetened condensed milk
¾	cup chocolate chips		

Pour margarine into bottom of a 9 × 13-inch baking pan; sprinkle with crushed crackers, then with coconut. Combine chocolate and butterscotch chips; layer over coconut; sprinkle with granola mix. Drizzle milk evenly over top; bake at 350° until edges are browned, about 25 minutes; cool; cut in squares. (*See Index for recipe.)

Rhoda Smith

ANGEL GRAHAM BARS
4 to 5 dozen.

- 1 (16-ounce) box graham crackers
- 3 cups sugar, divided
- ½ cup evaporated milk
- 1 cup margarine
- 1 egg, beaten
- 1½ teaspoons vanilla, divided
- 1 cup finely chopped nuts
- 1 cup flaked coconut
- 1 cup graham cracker crumbs
- ½ stick margarine, melted
- Milk

Layer whole graham crackers on a cookie sheet. In sauce pan, combine 1 cup sugar and next 3 ingredients; bring to a boil; cook until thickened; add 1 teaspoon vanilla, nuts, coconut, and crumbs; mix well. Spread over whole crackers; top with another layer of crackers. Combine 2 cups sugar with melted margarine and ½ teaspoon vanilla; add enough milk to make right consistency to spread. Spread frosting on crackers; chill; cut into squares; keep refrigerated.

Geraldine Smith
Myrtle Sims

COCONUT BARS
18 squares.

- ½ cup butter
- ½ cup sugar
- 1 cup flour
- 2 eggs, lightly beaten
- 1 cup firmly packed brown sugar
- 1 teaspoon baking powder
- 1 cup coconut
- 2 tablespoons sifted flour
- 1 teaspoon vanilla
- 1 cup chopped nuts

Combine first 3 ingredients; spread over bottom of a 9-inch square pan; bake 10 minutes at 350°; cool. Combine remaining ingredients; spread over cooled crust; bake 25 minutes at 350°; cool; cut into squares.

Gladys Dodson
Dallas, Texas

GERMANTOWN OATMEAL COOKIES
10 dozen.

1 pound butter	2 teaspoons baking powder
2 cups firmly packed brown sugar	2 teaspoons baking soda
1 cup sugar	½ teaspoon salt
4 eggs	2 cups rolled oats
5 cups flour	2 cups coconut

Cream butter until light and fluffy; add sugars and eggs, beating well. Sift together next 4 ingredients; add to creamed mixture 1 cup at a time; stir in oats and coconut. Using rounded teaspoonfuls, shape dough into balls; place 3 inches apart on ungreased cookie sheet; do not flatten. Bake 8 to 10 minutes at 350°, or until golden brown. Cool on rack.

Jeri Graves
Mabelvale, Arkansas
Linda Hickman
Cedar Hill, Texas

BEST EVER COOKIES
3 to 4 dozen.

½ cup sugar	½ teaspoon baking soda
½ cup brown sugar	½ teaspoon cream of tartar
½ cup softened margarine	½ cup uncooked oats
½ cup oil	½ cup coconut
1 egg	½ cup crushed corn flakes or Rice Krispies
½ teaspoon vanilla	½ cup chopped nuts
1¾ cups flour	1 cup chocolate chips, optional
½ teaspoon salt	

Cream first 6 ingredients together, beating well. Combine flour with next 3 ingredients; add to creamed mixture; stir until well blended. Stir in remaining ingredients. Drop by teaspoonfuls onto greased cookie sheet; flatted with a moistened fork; bake 10 to 12 minutes at 350°.

Lucille Allen
Balch, Arkansas
Kathy Hickman
Cedar Hill, Texas

DATE PINWHEEL COOKIES
5 dozen.

1 pound dates, chopped	3 eggs
2 cups sugar, divided	4 cups flour
½ cup water	1 teaspoon baking soda
1 cup chopped pecans	1 teaspoon salt
1 cup margarine	1 teaspoon cinnamon
1 cup brown sugar	

Combine dates, 1 cup sugar, and water; cook over low heat until very thick; add pecans; set aside. Cream margarine, remaining sugars, and eggs; add dry ingredients, mixing well. Divide into 3 balls; roll each out on waxed paper; spread date filling over dough; roll up; wrap in waxed paper; chill thoroughly. Cut in slices ¼-inch thick; place on greased cookie sheet; bake 10 to 12 minutes at 350°. May be frozen unbaked.

Maylene Alexander

GRAPENUT COOKIES
5½ dozen.

1¾ cups sifted flour	¾ cup butter
½ teaspoon baking powder	1 cup sugar
1 teaspoon baking soda	1 egg
½ teaspoon salt	1 cup thick sweetened applesauce
1 teaspoon cinnamon	
½ teaspoon cloves	1 cup grapenuts
½ teaspoon nutmeg	½ cup raisins or nuts

Sift first 7 ingredients together; set aside. Cream butter and sugar; beat in egg. Add dry ingredients alternately with applesauce, mixing well. Stir in grapenuts and raisins or nuts. Drop by teaspoonfuls onto greased cookie sheet. Bake 10 minutes at 375°. (Pureed canned apricots can be used for applesauce.)

Lee Gierke
Ashdown, Arkansas
Dot Cummings
Longview, Texas

LEMON BARS
18 bars.

1 (19-ounce) package lemon cake mix	8 ounces cream cheese, at room temperature
3 eggs, divided	1 teaspoon vanilla
1 stick margarine, melted	Coconut or powdered sugar
1 (16-ounce) box powdered sugar	

Stir cake mix, 1 egg and margarine until blended; press mixture into a greased, floured 9 × 13-inch baking pan. Beat remaining eggs, sugar and cheese until blended; add vanilla; pour over cake mixture; sprinkle with coconut or powdered sugar. Bake 30 to 40 minutes at 350°; cool; cut into squares.

Ann Miller

Pecan Surprise Variation: Reserve 1 cup cake mix. Combine remaining mix, 1 egg, ½ cup butter; press into pan; bake 15 minutes at 350°. Filling: Beat 2 minutes at medium speed the reserved mix, ½ cup firmly packed brown sugar, ½ cup dark corn syrup, 1 teaspoon vanilla, 3 eggs; stir in 1 cup chopped pecans. Bake 25 to 30 minutes at 350°.

Mildred Thornton Bismark

ORANGE CHEWS
30 chews.

1 (16-ounce) box brown sugar	2 cups plus 2 tablespoons flour, divided
4 eggs, beaten	12 candy orange slices, chopped
1 teaspoon vanilla	1 cup chopped pecans
½ teaspoon salt	Powdered sugar

Mix thoroughly first 4 ingredients with 2 cups flour; dredge orange slices in remaining flour; mix with dough; add pecans. Batter will be very stiff. Press into a greased, floured 9 × 13-inch baking pan; bake about 40 minutes at 350°. Cool; cut in small squares; sprinkle with powdered sugar.

Jean Sutton
Broaddus, Texas

PECAN SANDIES
5 to 6 dozen.

- 1 cup margarine
- 1 cup oil
- 1 cup sugar
- 1 cup powdered sugar
- 2 eggs, well beaten
- 4 cups flour
- 1 teaspoon salt
- 1 teaspoon baking soda
- 1 teaspoon cream of tartar
- 1 teaspoon vanilla
- 2 cups chopped pecans

Cream margarine; blend in oil, sugars, and eggs, mixing well. Sift dry ingredients; stir into mixture. Add vanilla; mix well; stir in nuts. By teaspoonfuls, shape small balls of dough; place on greased cookie sheet; flatten by pressing with bottom of small glass, bottom moistened and dipped in powdered sugar. Bake 12 to 15 minutes at 350°, until edges begin to brown.

Ruth Caldwell
Arkadelphia, Arkansas
Velma Daniels

RICE KRISPIE AND CORN FLAKE TREAT
18 squares.

- 1 cup sugar
- 1 cup white corn syrup
- ½ stick margarine
- 1 cup peanut butter
- 1 teaspoon vanilla
- 4 cups corn flakes
- 2 cups Rice Krispies
- 1 cup salted peanuts, optional

Boil first 3 ingredients 1 minute; remove from heat; stir in peanut butter and vanilla; stir in remaining ingredients. Press into a 9 × 13-inch pan; cool; cut in squares.

Annie Faye Sharp
Vanessa Fisk

SUGAR COOKIES
5 to 6 dozen.

2 cups sugar	1 teaspoon baking soda
1 cup shortening	½ cup buttermilk
2 eggs	3 cups flour
1 teaspoon vanilla	¼ teaspoon salt

Cream sugar and shortening; beat in eggs and vanilla, mixing well. Add soda to buttermilk; set aside. Combine dry ingredients; add alternately with buttermilk to creamed mixture, blending well. Dough should be stiff; add more flour if needed. Roll out on floured board; cut with 2-inch cookie cutter; place on greased cookie sheet; bake 10 to 12 minutes at 400°. May vary by using half whole wheat flour and half brown sugar.

Opal Turnage Eades
Snyder, Texas

DROP SUGAR COOKIES
2½ dozen.

½ cup shortening	1 teaspoon vanilla
½ cup margarine	2½ cups flour
1 cup sugar	¾ teaspoon salt
1 egg, beaten	½ teaspoon baking soda

Cream first 3 ingredients; add eggs and vanilla; beat until fluffy; add dry ingredients, mixing well. Drop by teaspoonfuls onto ungreased cookie sheet; flatten with bottom of a small glass, bottom moistened and dipped in sugar. Bake about 12 minutes at 350°.

Nelda Gathright

CHOCOLATE PEANUT BUTTER COOKIES
4 dozen.

½ cup softened butter	1 cup flour
⅓ cup creamy peanut butter	½ teaspoon baking soda
⅔ cup sugar	¼ teaspoon salt
⅓ cup firmly packed brown sugar	1 cup crushed Rice Krispies
1 egg	1 cup semi-sweet chocolate chips
½ teaspoon vanilla	

Cream first 4 ingredients together; thoroughly blend in egg and vanilla. Combine flour, soda, and salt; add to creamed mixture, mixing well; add remaining ingredients. Drop by level tablespoonfuls onto greased baking sheet; bake 8 to 10 minutes at 350°, or until bottoms are lightly browned. Cool 1 minute on baking sheet before removing to rack. Can be frosted.

Rose Nash
Tena Nash
Maxine Tabler

PINEAPPLE COOKIES
3 dozen.

½ cup shortening	2 cups flour
1 cup plus 2 tablespoons sugar, divided	1 teaspoon baking soda
½ cup crushed pineapple	1 teaspoon baking powder
1 egg	½ teaspoon salt
½ teaspoon vanilla	1 tablespoon nutmeg

Cream shortening and 1 cup sugar; beat in pineapple, egg, and vanilla; stir in flour, soda, baking powder, and salt. Drop by teaspoonfuls onto greased cookie sheet; bake 7 to 10 minutes at 375°. Remove from baking sheet; combine remaining sugar and nutmeg; sprinkle over cookies; cool.

Ruby Friday

SAND TARTS
3 to 4 dozen.

1 cup butter	2¾ cups flour
1 tablespoon shortening	1 teaspoon vanilla
6 heaping tablespoons brown sugar	½ cup finely chopped nuts

Cream together first 5 ingredients until well mixed and smooth; stir in nuts. Shape into small balls; place on cookie sheet; depress and garnish with a pecan half or a bit of jelly. Bake at 350° 10 to 12 minutes, or until brown.

Bubbles Florence
Arkadelphia, Arkansas

SWEDISH SHORTBREAD COOKIES
3 dozen.

2 sticks margarine, softened	2 cups flour
½ cup sugar	

Cream butter; gradually add sugar, beating until light and fluffy. Gradually add flour, mixing well. Shape dough into a roll; wrap in waxed paper; chill thoroughly. Cut in ¼-inch slices; bake at 300° for 18 to 20 minutes, or until lightly browned. Remove immediately to rack to cool.

Tommye Spigner Penney
D. R. Penney

◇ *James Penney, County Clerk, Sevier County, 1840-1849.*

OLD-FASHIONED TEA CAKES
4 dozen.

1 stick butter	½ teaspoon vanilla
1 cup sugar	1¾ cups flour
1 egg, beaten	½ teaspoon salt
2 tablespoons milk	2 teaspoons baking powder

Cream butter and sugar; add egg, milk and vanilla, beating well. Sift dry ingredients together; add to creamed mixture, blending well. Shape into a roll; wrap in waxed paper; chill. Cut in ¼-inch slices; place on ungreased cookie sheet; bake at 375° 12 minutes, or until brown.

Belva Zachry
Hellena Little Thornton

APPLE LEMON PIE
1 (9-inch) pie.

5 large tart apples, cored, sliced, unpeeled	Cinnamon to taste
¼ cup lemon juice	Nutmeg to taste
1 teaspoon molasses	1 stick margarine
1 cup sugar	Pastry for 2-crust pie

Place apple slices in a bowl; mix lemon juice and molasses; pour over apples; stir to coat; spread evenly in crust. Combine sugar and spices; sprinkle over apples; dot with margarine. Top with full pastry; cut steam slits in top crust; or cut pastry into strips and lattice. Bake at 350° for 40 minutes, or until browned.

Dorothy Burleson

APPLE PECAN PIE
1 (9-inch) pie.

1 cup sugar	1½ cups grated Cheddar cheese
1 tablespoon flour	1 egg, beaten
1 teaspoon cinnamon	6 tablespoons melted butter
Dash of salt	1 (9-inch) unbaked pie shell
4 cups coarsely grated apples	1 cup chopped pecans

Combine first 4 ingredients; add apples and cheese; toss gently. Stir in egg and butter; spoon mixture into pastry shell; sprinkle with pecans. Bake 10 minutes at 400°; reduce heat to 350°; bake 50 minutes. (If using food processor to prepare apples, do not peel.)

Adrienne Taggart Gillispie

GREEN APPLE PIE
1 (9-inch) pie.

5 cups sliced green apples	1 teaspoon cinnamon
½ stick butter	¼ teaspoon nutmeg
1 teaspoon salt	2 tablespoons flour
1 cup sugar	Pastry for 2-crust pie

In sauce pan cook first 6 ingredients over low heat until apples are slightly tender; remove from heat; stir in flour, mixing well; pour into pie crust. Cover with top crust; cut steam slits. Bake 15 minutes at 375°; reduce heat to 325°; bake 30 minutes.

Mrs. Ted Pumphrey

SOUR CREAM APPLE PIE
1 (9-inch) pie.

6¼ tablespoons flour, divided	¼ teaspoon nutmeg
⅛ teaspoon salt	2¼ cups diced tart apples
1¼ cups sugar, divided	1 (9-inch) unbaked pie shell
1 egg	1¼ teaspoons cinnamon
1¼ cups sour cream	4 tablespoons softened butter
1¼ teaspoons vanilla	

Combine 2¼ tablespoons flour and salt; add 1 cup sugar, egg, sour cream, vanilla, and nutmeg; beat until smooth; fold in apples. Pour into pie shell; bake 15 minutes at 400°; reduce heat to 350°; bake 30 minutes. Combine ¼ cup flour, 4 tablespoons sugar, cinnamon, and butter; crumble with pastry blender. Remove pie from oven; sprinkle with topping; bake 10 minutes at 400°.

Naomi Hale

MIMI'S APRICOT PIE
1 (10-inch) pie.

1 (6-ounce) package dried apricots	8 canned apricot halves, drained
1¾ cups warm water	2 ounces butter
1½ cups plus 3 tablespoons sugar, divided	1 tablespoon flour
1 tablespoon cornstarch	1 teaspoon cinnamon, divided
¼ cup water	Pastry for 2-crust pie

Soak dried apricots in warm water 30 minutes; simmer 30 minutes or until very soft; remove from heat; stir in 1½ cups sugar mixed with cornstarch and ¼ cup water; cook 1 minute; cool. Sprinkle bottom crust with a mixture of flour and 1 tablespoon sugar; dot crust with butter; pour in cooled filling. Place canned halves on filling, in center and 6 to 7 more encircling but not too close to edge of filling. Mix remaining sugar and cinnamon; sprinkle filling with ½ of mixture. Cover pie with lattice strips; sprinkle top with remaining sugar-cinnamon mixture. Bake 15 minutes at 400°; reduce heat to 375° for 15 minutes, or until edges begin to bubble; reduce heat to 350° and cook until medium brown, about 15 minutes.

June Knight Allison

APRICOT TARTS
18 tarts.

1 (4-ounce) package cream cheese	⅛ teaspoon salt
1 cup flour	½ cup apricot preserves
1 stick margarine	1 egg white

With pastry blender combine first 4 ingredients, blending well; wrap in waxed paper; chill. Roll pastry out thin; cut into 2-inch circles. Drop 1 teaspoon preserves on a circle; top with another circle; seal edges with egg white; place on a cookie sheet. Bake 10 minutes at 400°.

Phyllis Wittman

MARION BENSON'S BLUEBERRY PIE
1 (9-inch) pie.

1 (3-ounce) package cream cheese	1 (21-ounce) can blueberry pie filling
½ cup powdered sugar	1 tablespoon lemon juice
½ teaspoon vanilla	1 (9-inch) baked pie shell
1 cup heavy cream	

Cream until smooth cheese, sugar, and vanilla. Whip cream until stiff, but not dry; fold into cheese mixture; spread evenly in pastry shell. Blend pie filling and lemon juice; spoon over filling; chill.

Patricia McGoldrick
Rockford, Illinois

OLD TIME BUTTERMILK PIE
1 (9-inch) pie.

½ cup butter, softened	1 teaspoon vanilla
1½ cups sugar	¼ teaspoon salt
3 rounded tablespoons flour	Dash of nutmeg
5 eggs, beaten	1 (9-inch) unbaked pie shell
1 cup buttermilk	

Cream butter and sugar; add flour and eggs; beat until fluffy; stir in remaining pie ingredients. Pour into pie shell; bake 45 to 50 minutes at 350°; cool.

Molein Zachry
Inez Harrison

Lemon Buttermilk Variation: Add 1 teaspoon each cinnamon and grated lemon rind, 2 teaspoons lemon juice, ¼ teaspoon cloves. Separate eggs, folding stiffly beaten egg whites into batter.

J. B. Summers
The Old County Jail
Washington, Arkansas

BLUEBERRY CHIFFON PIE

1 (9-inch) pie.

2 cups fresh blueberries, divided	1 (8-ounce) container whipped topping
1 jigger Kirsch or cherry-flavored brandy	1 (9-inch) graham cracker crust
1 (8-ounce) container peach flavored yogurt	

Soak 1 cup berries in brandy for a few minutes; combine with yogurt and whipped topping in a blender or food processor, until blended. Spoon into crust; garnish with remaining berries; chill.

Flo Pullen
Little Rock, Arkansas

CARAMEL NUT PIE

1 (9-inch) pie.

1 cup firmly packed brown sugar	3 eggs, well beaten
½ cup sugar	2 tablespoons milk
1 tablespoon flour	1 teaspoon vanilla
1½ cups light corn syrup	1 (9-inch) unbaked pie shell
½ cup butter, melted	1½ cups coarsely chopped pecans or walnuts

Combine sugars and flour, mixing well; add remaining pie ingredients, stirring until well blended. Pour into pie shell; sprinkle with nuts. Bake at 350° for 50 minutes, or until set.

Dorothy Shinn
Edith Frachiseur

NO-BAKE REGAL CHEESE PIE
1 (8-inch) pie.

1 (8-ounce) package cream cheese	1 teaspoon vanilla
½ cup sugar	⅛ teaspoon salt
½ cup milk	4½ ounces whipped topping
1 teaspoon lemon juice	1 (8-inch) vanilla wafer crust

Beat cream cheese until smooth and fluffy; gradually add sugar, beating well. Blend in milk, juice, vanilla, and salt; fold in whipped topping. Spoon into crust; chill until set, at least 4 hours.

Ruth P. Maxwell
Texarkana, Arkansas

CHERRY COBBLER
12 servings.

2 cups sugar, divided	½ cup milk
1 cup flour	3 tablespoons butter, melted
¼ teaspoon salt	1 (14- to 16-ounce) can cherries
2 teaspoons baking powder	2 tablespoons red food coloring

Combine 1 cup sugar with next 5 ingredients, mixing well; spread into bottom of a buttered 9 × 13-inch baking pan. In a sauce pan, bring cherries, 1 cup sugar, and food coloring to a boil; pour over crust mixture. Bake at 350° for 30 to 45 minutes, or until golden.

Ruby White

CHERRIES IN THE SNOW
1 (9-inch) pie.

1	(3-ounce) package cream cheese	½	pint whipping cream, whipped
½	cup sugar	1	(21-ounce) can cherry pie filling
1	teaspoon vanilla		
1	cup miniature marshmallows	1	(9-inch) graham cracker crust

Beat first 3 ingredients together until fluffy; fold in whipped cream and marshmallows; pour into crust. Pour pie filling evenly over top; chill well before serving.

Melba Taylor
Caruthersville, Missouri
Glenda Campbell

OUT OF THIS WORLD PIE
2 (9-inch) pies.

1	(21-ounce) can cherry pie filling	1	(3-ounce) package cherry gelatin
¾	cup sugar	4	bananas, sliced
1	(20-ounce) can crushed pineapple	1	cup chopped pecans
		2	(9-inch) baked pie shells
1	tablespoon cornstarch		
1	teaspoon red food coloring	1	(16-ounce) container whipped topping

In sauce pan combine first 5 ingredients; cook, stirring, until thick; remove from heat; add gelatin; stir to blend; cool. Fold in bananas and nuts; pour into pie shells; cover with whipped topping. Chill before serving.

Doris Cannon Williamson

CHESS PIE
1 (9-inch) pie.

1 (8-ounce) package cream cheese, at room temperature	3 eggs
1 stick butter, softened	1 teaspoon vanilla or lemon flavoring
1½ cups sugar	1 (9-inch) unbaked pie shell

Cream cheese and butter until smooth; add remaining ingredients, beating in well. Pour into pie shell; bake at 325° for 50 minutes, or until set.

Mrs. Robert Watson

PINEAPPLE CHESS PIE
1 (9-inch) pie.

2 cups sugar	1 teaspoon vanilla
4 eggs, beaten	1 cup angel flake coconut
1 stick margarine, melted	1 (8-ounce) can crushed pineapple
1 tablespoon flour	
1 tablespoon cornmeal	1 (9-inch) unbaked pie shell

Combine all pie ingredients, blending well. Pour into pie shell; bake at 350° for 45 to 50 minutes, or until slightly firm in center.

Betty Locke Taylor

◇ Matthew Washington Locke donated the land for the city of Lockesburg, founded in 1878.

SOUTHERN CHESS PIE
1 (9-inch) pie.

1 cup firmly packed brown sugar	2 tablespoons milk
½ cup sugar	1 teaspoon vanilla
1 teaspoon flour	1 cup chopped pecans
2 eggs	1 (9-inch) unbaked pie shell
½ cup butter, melted	

Mix flour and sugars; beat in next 4 ingredients; fold in nuts. Pour into pie shell; bake at 375° for 40 to 45 minutes, or until set.

Mildred Hodges

CHOCOLATE CHESS PIE
1 (9-inch) pie.

1¼ cups sugar	1 tablespoon white vinegar
3 tablespoons cocoa	1 stick margarine, melted
3 eggs, well beaten	1 tablespoon vanilla
5 tablespoons evaporated milk	1 (9-inch) unbaked pie shell

Combine dry ingredients; beat into eggs; stir in remaining pie ingredients, blending well. Pour into pie shell; bake at 350° about 40 minutes, or until set.

Mrs. Thelma Walker Kent
Fort Worth, Texas

GOLD BRICK PIE
2 (8-inch) pies.

2½ sticks margarine	2 cups chopped pecans
1⅓ cups sugar	2 (8-inch) butter-crumb pie crusts
4 ounces unsweetened chocolate, melted	1 (16-ounce) container whipped topping
6 eggs	1 square semi-sweet chocolate, slivered
1 tablespoon vanilla	

Cream margarine and sugar; stir in chocolate. Add eggs, 1 at a time, beating well after each addition; stir in vanilla and nuts. Pour into crusts; spread with whipped topping; sprinkle with slivered chocolate. Chill 3 hours; freezes well.

Juanita Bell

Pastry flour can be "made" by combining 3 parts bleached all-purpose flour with 1 part cake flour; or 4 parts regular all-purpose flour and 1 part cake flour.

MICROWAVE CHOCOLATE PIE
1 (9-inch) pie.

1	cup sugar	3	egg yolks, beaten
3	tablespoons cocoa	½	stick margarine
3	tablespoons cornstarch	1	teaspoon vanilla
⅛	teaspoon salt	1	(9-inch) baked pie shell
2	cups milk	1	(8-ounce) container whipped topping

In 1½-quart glass bowl mix dry ingredients well; add milk gradually, stirring until smooth; microwave at HIGH 8 to 9 minutes, stirring every 2 minutes, until smooth and thickened. Stir ½ hot mixture into egg yolks; then stir yolk mixture back into hot mixture; microwave at HIGH 1 to 2 minutes, until mixture is thick and glossy. Stir in margarine and vanilla; pour into pie shell; spread with topping; chill.

Helen Hubbard Jones
Mineral Springs, Arkansas

CHOCOLATE CHIP PIE
1 (9-inch) pie.

2	eggs, beaten	1	(6-ounce) package semi-sweet chocolate chips
1	cup sugar		
½	cup flour	½	cup chopped nuts
1	stick margarine, melted	½	cup coconut, optional
1	teaspoon vanilla	1	(9-inch) unbaked pie shell

Combine first 3 ingredients, mixing well; stir in remaining ingredients. Pour into pie shell; bake 35 to 40 minutes at 350°. Serve with whipped cream.

Rebecca Stevens
Rhonda Honea

CHOCOLATE MERINGUE PIE
1 (9-inch) pie.

1½ cups plus 6 tablespoons sugar, divided	4 eggs, separated
2 tablespoons cornstarch	1 tablespoon butter, melted
3 teaspoons cocoa	1 teaspoon vanilla
3 cups evaporated milk or half and half	1 (9-inch) baked pie shell

In top of double boiler combine 1½ cups sugar with next 3 ingredients; cook slowly, stirring, so mixture thickens gradually. Beat egg yolks until thick and lemon-colored; beat in butter; stirring, add ½ cup hot mixture to eggs; stirring, pour back into hot mixture; cook until thick. Remove from heat; add vanilla; cool; pour into pie shell. Beat egg whites until stiff; add sugar gradually, beating until meringue is stiff and glossy. Spread on pie to seal edges; bake at 425° 5 to 8 minutes, or until golden brown.

Mrs. Roy Dwade Norwood Holleman
Chidester, Arkansas
Jackson Norwood
Murfreesboro, Arkansas

◇ *C. Miles Norwood: the only labor candidate for governor in Arkansas history (Election of 1888).*

DRUM ROLL PIE
1 (9-inch) pie.

½ cup flour	1 cup chocolate chips
1 cup sugar	1 teaspoon vanilla
2 eggs, slightly beaten	1 cup chopped pecans
1 stick margarine, melted	1 (9-inch) unbaked pie shell

Combine flour and sugar; stir in eggs and margarine; add remaining ingredients, mixing well. Pour into pie shell; bake 30 minutes at 350°. Serve warm with whipped cream.

Brenda Dickerson

COCONUT CREAM PIE
1 (9-inch) pie.

1¼ cups sugar, divided	1¼ cups coconut, divided
⅓ cup flour	1 teaspoon vanilla
1 cup evaporated milk	2 tablespoons margarine
1 cup water	1 (9-inch) baked pie shell
2 eggs, separated	Dash of cream of tartar

Combine 1 cup sugar with next 3 ingredients; add well beaten egg yolks; cook, stirring, until slightly thickened. Stirring constantly, over medium heat, boil slowly a few minutes; remove from heat. Add 1 cup coconut and next 2 ingredients, stirring until margarine melts; pour into pie shell. Beat egg whites until foamy; beating, slowly add cream of tartar and remaining sugar; beat until stiff and glossy. Spread meringue over filling, sealing edge of pastry. Sprinkle with remaining coconut. Bake at 400° until golden brown, 8 to 10 minutes.

Corine Hooker
Paula Hooker

CUSTARD PIE
1 (9-inch) pie.

¾ cup sugar	⅛ teaspoon salt
2 tablespoons butter	1 teaspoon vanilla
3 eggs, beaten	¼ teaspoon nutmeg
2 cups milk	1 (9-inch) unbaked pie shell

Cream sugar and butter; add eggs and beat until fluffy; add remaining ingredients, blending well. Pour into pie shell; bake 10 minutes at 425°; reduce heat to 325°; bake about 30 minutes, or until set and lightly browned.

Anna Bell Duggan
Leta Pearl Piggee
Jodie Higginbotham

LEMON MERINGUE PIE

1 (9-inch) pie.

1⅓ cups sugar, divided	¼ cup lemon juice
5 tablespoons cornstarch	2 tablespoons lemon rind
⅛ teaspoon salt	1 (9-inch) baked pie shell
1½ cups boiling water	¼ teaspoon cream of tartar
3 eggs, separated	

Combine 1 cup sugar, cornstarch, and salt, mixing well; add water, and cook over low heat, stirring constantly, until thickened. Combine egg yolks, juice, and rind; beat well; gradually stir ¼ hot mixture into yolks; add to remaining hot mixture, stirring constantly. Cook, stirring constantly, 8 to 10 minutes, or until smooth and thickened; pour into pie shell. Beat egg whites with cream of tartar until soft peaks form; gradually add ⅓ cup sugar, beating until stiff and glossy. Spread over filling, sealing edges; bake at 425° 5 to 8 minutes, or until golden brown.

Grace Stuart
Mineral Springs, Arkansas

LUSCIOUS LEMON PIE

1 (9-inch) pie.

1 cup sugar	½ cup fresh lemon juice
3 tablespoons cornstarch	1 cup milk
1 tablespoon grated lemon rind	3 egg yolks, beaten
	1 cup sour cream
4 tablespoons butter	1 (9-inch) baked pie shell

In heavy sauce pan combine first 7 ingredients; cook over medium heat, stirring constantly, until thick and smooth; mixture will be very thick; cover and cool. Fold in sour cream; pour into pie shell; chill at least 2 hours before serving. Top with whipped cream.

Jeri Graves
Mabelvale, Arkansas

Substitute 1 teaspoon lemon juice for cream of tartar when making meringues for lemon and lime pies.

OLD-FASHIONED LEMON MERINGUE PIE
1 (9-inch) pie.

1 cup plus 4 tablespoons sugar, divided	2 eggs, separated
1 teaspoon salt	2 tablespoons lemon rind
¼ cup flour	1 tablespoon butter
2 tablespoons cornstarch	¼ cup lemon juice
1½ cups water	1 (9-inch) baked pie shell

In heavy sauce pan combine 1 cup sugar with next 4 ingredients; bring to a boil, stirring constantly; boil 1 minute. Remove from heat; pour about ⅓ mixture into slightly beaten egg yolks, stirring constantly. Stirring, pour mixture back into sauce pan. Add lemon rind; bring to a boil; boil 1 minute. Remove from heat; add butter; then gradually add lemon juice. Pour into pie shell. Beat egg whites until fluffy; add remaining sugar, beating, 1 tablespoon at a time; beat until stiff. Spread over filling, touching pastry with meringue mixture all around. Bake at 325° until meringue is light brown.

Mrs. A. M. Owen
Paragould, Arkansas
Freda Huntsberger

MUSCADINE AND PECAN PIE
1 (9-inch) pie.

1½ quarts stemmed muscadines	1 teaspoon butter
1½ cups sugar	⅛ teaspoon salt
3 tablespoons quick-cooking tapioca	½ cup chopped pecans
	Pastry for 2-crust pie

Remove pulp from muscadines; reserve skins. Place pulp in sauce pan; bring to a boil; remove from heat; sieve to remove seeds. Add enough pulp to reserved skins to make 3½ cups; combine with remaining pie ingredients, mixing well. Pour into pie shell; cover with pastry; cut vent slits in top crust. Bake 15 minutes at 425°; reduce heat to 400°; bake 30 minutes, or until brown. (Concord grapes may be substituted for muscadines.)

Barbara Anderson

OSGOOD PIE
1 (9-inch) pie.

1	cup sugar	1	teaspoon cloves
1	tablespoon vinegar	1	teaspoon cinnamon
1	cup raisins	1	teaspoon allspice
1	tablespoon butter, melted	½	cup nuts
2	eggs, separated	1	(9-inch) unbaked pie shell

Combine all ingredients except egg whites, blending well. Beat egg whites until stiff; fold into mixture. Pour into pie shell; bake 50 to 60 minutes at 350°. Serve with whipped cream.

Mrs. Paul L. Stone

PARTY PEACH PIE
1 (9-inch) pie.

2	cups sliced fresh peaches	2	eggs, lightly beaten
⅔	cup sugar, divided	1	tablespoon butter
3½	tablespoons cornstarch	1	teaspoon vanilla
¼	teaspoon salt	1	(9-inch) vanilla wafer crust
1	cup evaporated milk	½	cup vanilla wafer crumbs
1	cup peach syrup		

Sprinkle peaches with ½ of the sugar; chill overnight; drain; reserve juice (add water to make 1 cup). In sauce pan, combine cornstarch, salt, and remaining sugar; gradually add milk and peach juice. Stirring, cook until thickened; simmer 10 minutes longer; then remove from heat. Pour ½ cup of hot mixture into eggs, stirring constantly. Stir egg mixture back into hot mixture; return to heat; cook 5 minutes; add butter and vanilla; cool covered. Pour ½ of filling into pie crust; add ½ of the peaches; add remaining filling; top with peaches. Sprinkle top with crumbs. Chill 3 hours.

Mrs. Tom Vertrees, Sr.
Fort Smith, Arkansas

◇ *Governor John Sebastian Little, 1907-1909.*

PEANUT BUTTER PIE

1 (9-inch) pie.

1 (8-ounce) package cream cheese	½ cup milk
1 cup powdered sugar	1 (8-ounce) container whipped topping
½ cup peanut butter	1 (9-inch) baked pie shell

Beat cream cheese until fluffy; beat in sugar and peanut butter; gradually add milk, beating; fold in whipped topping. Pour into pie shell; chill before serving.

Bonnie Moore
Tex Hanna

PEACH COBBLER

12 servings.

1½ cups sifted self-rising flour	2 to 3 cups sliced fresh peaches
½ cup shortening	2 cups sugar
⅓ cup milk	2 cups water
1 stick margarine	

Cut shortening into flour to crumb consistency; add milk; stir until dough leaves sides of bowl; turn on to floured board; roll to ¼-inch thickness. With margarine, thoroughly grease a 9 × 13-inch baking dish; line bottom with dough; keep remainder of dough to strip for lattice top. Cover bottom with peaches; mix sugar and water; pour over peaches; cover with dough lattice. Bake at 350° about 1 hour; turn off oven; let set until ready to serve.

Jo Billings
Center Point, Arkansas

PECAN PIE

1 (9-inch) pie.

1 cup sugar	1 tablespoon lemon juice, optional
1 cup light corn syrup	
3 eggs, beaten	1 teaspoon lemon extract, optional
⅓ stick butter, softened	
1 teaspoon vanilla	1½ cups coarsely chopped pecans
	1 (9-inch) unbaked pie shell

Combine all pie ingredients except pecans, mixing well. Sprinkle pecans evenly over pie shell; pour syrup mixture over pecans. Bake at 375° for 45 minutes, or until set.

Thelma Kelly
Mineral Springs, Arkansas
Lucerne Payne
Louise Lacefield

PECAN-CREAM CHEESE PIE

1 (9-inch) pie.

1 (8-ounce) package cream cheese, softened	1 (9-inch) unbaked pie shell
4 eggs, divided	1¼ cups coarsely chopped pecans
⅓ cup plus ¼ cup sugar, divided	1 cup light corn syrup
2 teaspoons vanilla, divided	¼ teaspoon salt

Beat cream cheese, 1 egg, ⅓ cup sugar and 1 teaspoon vanilla at medium speed until smooth; spread into pie shell; sprinkle with pecans. In large bowl, beat remaining eggs until frothy; add syrup, salt, and remaining sugar and vanilla; beat until well blended; pour over pecans. Bake at 375° about 40 minutes, or until center tests done.

Betty Frazier

PECAN-SOUR CREAM PIE
1 (9-inch) pie.

2 eggs, separated	¼ teaspoon lemon extract
1 cup sugar	¼ teaspoon salt
¼ cup flour	1 (9-inch) baked pie shell
1 cup sour cream	1 cup brown sugar
	1 cup chopped nuts

Cream egg yolks with next 5 ingredients; place in top of double boiler; cook mixture, stirring constantly, until thickened. Pour into pie shell. Beat egg whites until foamy; gradually add sugar, beating until stiff peaks form; fold in nuts; spread meringue over filling, sealing to edge of pastry. Bake at 350° 12 to 15 minutes, or until golden brown.

Ruth Ward

MILLION DOLLAR PIE
1 (9-inch) pie.

1 (8-ounce) package cream cheese	½ cup pecans
1 cup sugar	1 (8-ounce) can crushed pineapple
1 (8-ounce) container whipped topping	1 (9-inch) graham cracker crust

Blend cream cheese and sugar; fold in remaining ingredients; pour into pie crust; freeze. Remove from freezer 15 minutes before serving.

Bobby Harrison

SOUR CREAM RAISIN PIE
1 (9-inch) pie.

1 cup raisins	1 cup sour cream
1 cup plus 1 teaspoon sugar, divided	3 teaspoons vinegar
	1 teaspoon vanilla
2 cups water	Pinch of salt
3 teaspoons flour	1 (9-inch) baked pie shell
2 egg yolks	

Cook raisins, 1 cup sugar, and water until raisins are plump. Beat egg yolks with flour and 1 teaspoon sugar; stir into raisins; cook, stirring, until mixture thickens. Remove from heat; add remaining ingredients; blend well. Pour into pie shell; cool. May be topped with meringue or whipped topping.

Glady Clinton Crockett
Grannis, Arkansas

TINY RUSSIAN MINT PIES
18 pies.

1 cup butter	18 paper baking cups
2 cups sifted powdered sugar	18 vanilla wafers
4 squares unsweetened chocolate, melted	1 cup heavy cream, whipped
	Chopped nuts
4 eggs	Maraschino cherries
1 teaspoon peppermint flavoring	
2 teaspoons vanilla	

Cream butter and sugar; blend in chocolate; add eggs, 1 at a time, beating well; blend in flavorings. In each baking cup, place 1 vanilla wafer; spoon ¾ full with chocolate mixture; top with dollop of whipped cream; sprinkle with nuts; garnish with cherry half. Chill. Freezes well; place in muffin tins to freeze; store frozen pies in plastic bags.

Marian Matlock
Annette Currie
Arkadelphia, Arkansas

PEAR MINCE PIE
1 (9-inch) pie.

1 pint pear mincemeat*   **Pastry for 2-crust pie**

Pour mincemeat into pie shell; cover with pastry; cut steam slits in top crust. Bake at 350° for 40 minutes, or until golden brown. (*See Index for recipe.)

Elverna Sykes

SWEET POTATO PIE
1 (9-inch) pie.

¾ cup sugar	Dash of allspice
2 eggs, beaten	2 cups mashed cooked sweet potatoes
½ cup softened margarine	
½ cup milk	1 (9-inch) unbaked pie shell

Blend first 5 ingredients well; beat in sweet potatoes until well mixed; pour into pie shell. Bake at 350° about 40 minutes, or until knife inserted in center comes out clean. Cool completely.

Daisy Zachry

BAKED ALASKA PIE
6 servings.

1 (8-inch) graham cracker crust	3 egg whites
1 quart vanilla ice cream	Dash of salt
½ cup chocolate syrup	¼ cup sugar

Scoop half of ice cream into pie shell; drizzle ¼ cup syrup over ice cream; repeat layers; cover; freeze. To serve: Beat egg whites with salt until soft peaks form; gradually beat in sugar; beat until stiff peaks form; spread over ice cream. Bake at 425° for 4 to 5 minutes, or until meringue is golden brown. Serve at once.

Lynn Clayborn Ross

Brownie Alaskas: Substitute brownies cut in 3-inch squares for pie crust; top with scoops of ice cream; freeze. To serve, top with meringue, sealing edge of brownie; bake 2 to 3 minutes at 500°.

Margaret Mottesheard Tyser
Spartanburg, South Carolina

CREAMY PUMPKIN PIE

1 (9-inch) pie.

1 (16-ounce) can pumpkin	½ teaspoon ginger
1 (14-ounce) can sweetened condensed milk	½ teaspoon nutmeg
	½ teaspoon cloves
2 eggs, beaten	½ teaspoon allspice
1 teaspoon cinnamon	1 (9-inch) unbaked pie shell
½ teaspoon salt	

Combine all ingredients, beating until smooth and well mixed; pour into pie shell. Bake 15 minutes at 425°; reduce heat to 350°; continue baking 35 to 40 minutes, or until knife inserted comes out clean. Cool thoroughly; serve topped with whipped cream.

Mrs. Fred Pendergrass

VANILLA PIE

1 (9-inch) pie.

1 cup sugar	3 egg yolks
3 tablespoons cornstarch	1 teaspoon vanilla
Dash of salt	1 tablespoon butter
2 cups milk	1 (9-inch) baked pie shell
1 cup evaporated milk	

Combine first 3 ingredients in a sauce pan; gradually add milks; bring to a boil; boil about 3 minutes. Pour ½ cup of hot mixture into slightly beaten egg yolks, beating well; pour back into hot mixture; cook, stirring, until thick. Remove from heat; add vanilla and butter. Pour into pie shell; chill before serving. Serve plain or topped with sliced strawberries, bananas, or kiwi fruit.

Bonnie Landes
Hope, Arkansas

CRUST FOR FRIED PIES
about 15 crusts.

5 cups flour	1 cup shortening
1 teaspoon baking powder	1 egg, lightly beaten
2 tablespoons sugar	1 (13-ounce) can evaporated milk
2 teaspoons salt	

Combine dry ingredients; cut in shortening. Combine egg and milk; add to dry mixture, mixing well. Roll out to desired thickness; cut in saucer-size circles; fill with fruit. Fold over; crimp edges with fork; fry in deep, hot oil.

Christine Crawford
Mineral Springs, Arkansas
Eva Morris

NEVER-FAIL FLAKY PIE CRUST
2 (9-inch) pie crusts.

1 cup shortening	1 egg, lightly beaten
1 teaspoon salt	1 tablespoon vinegar
1 teaspoon sugar	5 tablespoons ice water
3 cups flour	

Cut shortening into combined dry ingredients with pastry blender. In small bowl, add vinegar and water to egg; add to dry mixture; mix well. Roll out on floured board.

Patsy Stemple
Louise Thornton Clay

EASY PIE CRUST
1 pie crust.

½ cup oil	¼ cup milk
½ teaspoon salt	1½ cups flour

Pour all ingredients in pie pan; with fork, mix until flour is moistened; shape into ball. With fingers, press dough to fit pan.

Janet McDonald
Sanger, Texas

OATMEAL PIE CRUST
1 (9-inch) pastry shell.

1 cup flour	½ cup shortening
1 teaspoon salt	½ cup regular oats
¼ cup sugar	3 to 4 tablespoons water

In mixing bowl, combine flour, salt, and sugar; cut in shortening until mixture resembles coarse meal; stir in oats. Sprinkle water evenly over surface; stir with fork until all ingredients are moistened. Shape dough into a ball; chill. To use, roll out on floured board.

Nola Pope

Microwave Variation: Combine ⅓ cup each butter and brown sugar with 2 cups quick-cooking oats; press into pie plate; cook on HIGH 2 or 3 minutes, rotating twice.

Kathy Latimer

PEANUT BUTTER-GRAHAM CRACKER PIE CRUST
1 (9-inch) crust.

¼ cup smooth, or crunchy, peanut butter	¼ cup sugar
2 cups finely crushed graham cracker crumbs	2 tablespoons water

Blend peanut butter into combined crumbs and sugar; add water and knead mixture gently. Press into bottom and sides of a well-buttered 9-inch pie pan. Chill thoroughly before filling.

Sissi Slabaugh

PRESERVING HINTS

Though home canners who use correct methods in processing foods have no reason to worry about BOTULISM, as an extra precaution, boil all low acid foods for 15 minutes before tasting. Thick masses, such as greens, should be stirred while boiling.

Acid and pectin, necessary for the formation of jelly, are contained in varying amounts in fruit, depending on the type of fruit and the degree of ripeness. Pectin is at its highest quality in just-ripe fruit; acid content is higher in underripe fruit. For the best jellied product, three-fourths of the fruit should be just ripe with the remaining fourth slightly underripe. If the fruit is naturally low in acid, add lemon juice.

Increasing the size of jelly recipes is not recommended. Better success is obtained by making two separate batches of a recipe rather than doubling the size.

To cut down on foaming when cooking jelly, add ¼ cup margarine to jelly mixture at the time you add the powdered pectin.

Processing in boiling water baths is now recommended for all jellies and fruit spreads except for freezer fruit spreads. Place in canner rack with water hot to gently boiling covering jars by 1 to 2 inches. Cover; begin processing time when water returns to a boil. Process 5 minutes for jellies, honeys and butters, 10 minutes for jams and marmalades, and 15 minutes for preserves.

Soft spreads tend to thicken as they cool, so how thick the finished spread will be is hard to judge when it is still hot. Generally, jams, conserves, marmalades and preserves should be boiled until the temperature is 8°F above the boiling point of water in your area. A firm spread will result when cooked to this temperature; for a softer spread, shorten the cooking time, and for a firmer one, lengthen it.

A sweet syrup for your canned or frozen fruit can be made with honey instead of sugar. Choose a light-flavored honey so the honey taste doesn't overpower the flavor of the fruit. For a medium syrup blend 2 cups honey with 4 cups very hot water; for a thin syrup blend 1 cup honey with 3 cups very hot water. To prevent the fruit from darkening, pack fruit in hot honey syrup as soon as it is peeled and sliced.

Store peanuts in a cool, dry place. In the refrigerator peanuts in the shell keep about 9 months; shelled peanuts keep about 3 months. Peanuts in the shell or shelled peanuts in tight containers store indefinitely at 0°F or lower. Peanuts can be used immediately upon removal from frozen storage and may be refrozen without loss of quality.

Some foods do not freeze will: custards and cream pie fillings (get watery, lumpy); egg whites and meringues (become tough and rubbery); soft frostings and cake icings made with egg whites; mayonnaise (not in salads)(separates); macaroni, spaghetti and some rice when frozen separately (gets mushy, has warmed over flavor); Irish potatoes cooked in stews (get mushy, darken); fried foods (get soggy) (exceptions: French fried potatoes and onion rings). Some seasonings (pepper, onions, cloves, synthetic vanilla) become strong and bitter when used in frozen prepared food.

PRESERVING

CANNED GREEN BEANS
Yield: 6 quarts

1	gallon water	½	cup salt
½	cup sugar	1	gallon snapped green beans
½	cup vinegar		

In a large canning kettle bring first 4 ingredients to a boil; add beans; cook 6 to 8 minutes. Ladle into hot sterilized jars; seal. To cook, drain beans and rinse thoroughly; cook as you would fresh beans but do not add additional salt. Do not can in jars larger than quart size.

Nina McCoy

APPLE BUTTER

6 to 7 pints.

2	dozen medium tart apples, cored, quartered (about 6 pounds)	2	tablespoons cinnamon
		1	teaspoon cloves
		¼	teaspoon mace
2	quarts unsweetened apple cider	½	teaspoon allspice
3	cups sugar		
¼	cup firmly packed brown sugar		

In food processor, using steel knife, process apple quarters; do not peel. In canning kettle cook apples with cider until soft. In a blender, in batches, puree cooked apple mixture. Return to kettle; add sugars and spices; cook over low heat, stirring often, until thick, at least 1 hour. Ladle hot mixture into hot sterilized jars, leaving ¼-inch head space; seal. Process 10 minutes in hot water bath.

Suzanne Allison Wray

APRICOT-WALNUT CONSERVE

5½-pint jars.

1	pound dried apricots	3	tablespoons lemon juice
1½	cups orange juice	3½	cups sugar
2	tablespoons grated orange rind	¾	cup chopped walnuts

Cover apricots with water in a heavy stainless steel or enamel sauce pan; simmer uncovered about 20 minutes, or until tender. Drain; chop. Return chopped apricots to sauce pan; combine with orange juice, orange rind, lemon juice and sugar. Bring to a boil; cook until mixture is thick, stirring constantly. Remove from heat; stir in nuts. Fill hot sterilized jars; seal; process in hot water bath 20 minutes.

Mothers' League
Longview, Texas

BRANDIED FRUIT STARTER
6 cups.

1 (15¼-ounce) can pineapple chunks	1 (10-ounce) jar maraschino cherries, drained
1 (16-ounce) can sliced peaches, drained	1½ cups sugar
1 (17-ounce) can apricot halves, drained	1¼ cups brandy

Combine all ingredients in a clean, non-metal bowl; stir gently; cover and let stand at room temperature for 3 weeks, stirring twice a week. Serve over ice cream, or use in Friendship Cake recipe (See Index). Reserve at least 1 cup starter at all times; to replenish, add 1 cup sugar and 1 of the first 4 ingredients every 1 to 3 weeks, alternating fruits each time; stir gently. Cover; let stand 3 days before using.

Burrow Eloth (Bus) Friday

CANNED APPLE PIE FILLING
7 quarts.

4 cups sugar	8 cups water
¼ teaspoon nutmeg	3 tablespoons lemon juice
2 teaspoons cinnamon	8 quarts pared, sliced tart apples
¾ cup cornstarch	

In canning kettle combine all ingredients except apples; cook until mixture thickens, stirring often. Add apples; continue cooking to boiling; boil 5 minutes. Pack in hot sterilized jars; seal. Process 30 minutes in hot water bath.

Ilene Snow

CHOW-CHOW
6 pints.

- 3 cups chopped onions
- 3 cups chopped green tomatoes
- 3 cups seeded, chopped sweet green peppers
- 2 hot green peppers, seeded, chopped
- 2½ cups vinegar (5% acidity)
- 1 large cabbage, shredded
- 2 tablespoons salt
- 1½ cups sugar
- 2 teaspoons celery seed
- 2 teaspoons dry mustard
- 1 teaspoon mustard seed
- 1 teaspoon turmeric
- 2 tablespoons pickling spices, tied in a bag

Combine chopped vegetables; sprinkle with salt; let stand overnight; drain. In canning kettle combine vinegar, sugar, and spices; bring to a boil; simmer 10 minutes. Add vegetables; simmer 10 minutes; bring to boiling; remove spice bag. Pack, boiling hot, into hot sterilized jars. Process 10 minutes in hot water bath.

Dora Tennessee Campbell

CORN RELISH
6 pints.

- 2 quarts whole kernel corn
- 6 large onions, chopped
- 1 large cabbage, chopped
- 6 large ripe tomatoes, peeled, chopped
- 4 ribs celery, chopped
- 3 hot peppers, seeded, chopped
- 3 pints vinegar
- 4 cups sugar
- 1 teaspoon turmeric
- 2 tablespoons dry mustard
- 1 (6-ounce) can pimentos (optional)

In a large pan combine all ingredients except turmeric. Boil for 20 minutes; add turmeric; stir; pour into hot sterilized pint jars; seal.

Enice Sharp
Athel Ayers

CUCUMBER PICKLES
1 gallon.

3 medium onions, chopped	4 cups vinegar
3 bell peppers, chopped	¼ cup salt
Cucumbers, thinly sliced (enough to fill 1 gallon jar)	1 teaspoon celery seed
4 cups sugar	1½ teaspoons turmeric

Pack peppers, onions and cucumbers in a gallon jar. Boil remaining ingredients to dissolve; cool; pour over cucumbers. Shake vigorously once a day for 7 days. Start eating after 7 days. Does not have to be sealed.

Isabel Boyce Webb
Washington, Arkansas

DILLED OKRA
4 to 5 pints.

3 to 3½ pounds small okra pods	1 quart water
3 small hot peppers, seeded, sliced	1 pint vinegar (5% acidity)
1 pod garlic, sliced	2 teaspoons dill seed
⅓ cup salt	

Pack okra pods with slices of garlic and hot pepper (to taste) in hot sterilized jars, leaving ¼-inch head space. In a sauce pan combine remaining ingredients; bring to a boil. Pour boiling brine in each jar to cover, leaving above head space. Seal; process 10 minutes in hot water bath. For a sweeter okra, add 6 teaspoons celery seed and ½ cup sugar to brine.

Dorothy Shinn

PRESERVED CHILDREN

Take one large field, half a dozen children, two or three small dogs, a pinch of brook, and some pebbles. Mix the children and dogs well together. Put them on the field, stirring constantly. Pour the brook over the pebbles; sprinkle the field with flowers; spread all over a deep blue sky, and bake in the sun. When brown, set away to cool in the bath tub.

Edith Frachiseur
Anna Freeman

HONEY WATERMELON RIND PRESERVES
8 pints.

5 pounds peeled chopped watermelon rinds	14 cups sugar
1 gallon water	1¾ quarts water
1 tablespoon baking soda	1 cup light corn syrup
	1 lemon, seeded, sliced

In large container soak rinds in 1 gallon water and soda overnight; drain; wash in 2 clear water rinses. Place in canning kettle; add enough water to immerse rinds; cover; cook 1 hour. Add 1¾ quarts water and sugar; bring to a boil; gently boil 2 hours. Add syrup and lemon; cook slowly 2 hours. Ladle into hot sterilized jars; seal.

Necie Roberts

HOT DOG RELISH
10 to 12 pints.

1½ gallons green tomatoes, halved, seeded	6 cups sugar
6 large onions, quartered	2½ tablespoons salt
2 large green peppers, quartered	1 quart vinegar (5% acidity)
½ pod red sweet pepper	1 (1¼-ounce) box pickling spices, in spice bag

With food grinder or food processor, grind tomatoes, onions, and peppers. In canning kettle, bring sugar, vinegar, and salt to a boil; add vegetables and spice bag. Boil gently 1 hour, stirring often. When desired consistency is reached, and relish takes on a shiny appearance, ladle into hot sterilized jars; seal. Process 15 minutes in hot water bath.

Winona Skelton

IT'S PECAN SEASON

Pecans in the shell: Stored at 70° or lower, remain edible 4 months. Refrigerated, keep 18 months; frozen in sealed, moisture-vapor-proof containers, store 6 to 7 years.

Cracked Pecans: Shell immediately; place nutmeats in shallow pans to air dry 10 to 14 days. May be oven dried at 105° for 1 to 2 hours. Air drying is preferred. Pecan halves at 70° or lower remain edible 2 months; refrigerated, keep 1 year. Frozen as above will store equally as well as pecans in shell.

Lois Thomas

PEACH HONEY
1 pint.

2 cups peaches, peeled and mashed
1¾ cup firmly packed light brown sugar

Combine peaches and sugar; cook over low heat until sugar melts. Bring to boil; then reduce heat; simmer for about 30 minutes or until mixture is thick and clear, stirring often. Seal in hot sterilized jars.

Jo Billings
Center Point, Arkansas

TOMMIE'S PEAR MARMALADE
3 pints.

4 cups pears, grated
4 cups sugar
1 (15-ounce) can crushed pineapple with liquid
2 to 3 tablespoons lemon juice
1 (1¾-ounce) package powdered fruit pectin

Combine pears, sugar, pineapple, and lemon juice in a large sauce pan. Cook over medium heat, stirring often, until pears are done, about 20 minutes. Stir in pectin; bring to boil again; boil 1 minute. Spoon mixture into hot sterilized jars. Adjust lids. Process in boiling water bath for 5 minutes.

Betty Williams

BLANCHE'S PEAR MINCEMEAT
12 pints.

2 gallons cut-up pears
4 oranges, unpeeled, seeded
2 (1-pound) boxes raisins
5 cups coconut
1½ cups vinegar
6 cups sugar
1 teaspoon cinnamon
1 teaspoon nutmeg
1 teaspoon cloves
1 teaspoon allspice

Grind pears, oranges, and raisins; place in large canning kettle; add remaining ingredients; bring to a boil; remove from heat. Pour into hot, sterilized pint jars; seal. Not necessary to process; may also be frozen.

Bell Cain Morrow
Caddo Gap, Arkansas

PEAR RELISH
6 pints.

24 medium pears, cored	6 red bell peppers, seeded
12 medium onions, quartered	1 quart vinegar (5% acidity)
6 hot peppers, seeded	3 cups sugar
6 green bell peppers, seeded	2 (12-ounce) jars prepared mustard
	Salt to taste

With food grinder or food processor, grind (or finely chop) pears, onions, and peppers. In canning kettle combine with remaining ingredients; boil for 40 minutes. Ladle into hot sterilized jars; seal.

Verda Coulter
Ashdown, Arkansas
Dorothy Coulter Fraser
Hot Springs, Arkansas

PICANTE SAUCE
5 pints.

6 cups peeled, chopped tomatoes	1½ teaspoons salt
1½ cups seeded, finely chopped jalapeño peppers	3 cloves garlic, pressed
	1½ cups vinegar (5% acidity)
1½ cups chopped onion	

Combine all ingredients; bring to a boil; cover; simmer 5 minutes. Pack into hot sterilized jars; seal. Process 30 minutes in hot water bath.

Bea Phillips
Foreman, Arkansas

PICKLED GREEN BEANS
6 pints.

3 pounds green beans, stemmed	6 bunches dillweed
6 cups vinegar (5% acidity)	6 cloves garlic
2 cups water	6 red hot peppers
1 cup salt	

Pack 1 piece dillweed, 1 pepper pod, 1 clove garlic, and raw green beans, leaving 1-inch head space, in each hot sterilized jar. Heat vinegar, water, and salt to boiling; pour over beans; remove air bubbles; seal. Store at least 4 weeks before opening.

Doris James

TACO SAUCE
4 or 5 pints.

3 quarts peeled, chopped ripe tomatoes	6 hot or jalapeño peppers, seeded, chopped
4 medium onions, chopped	2 teaspoons red pepper
1 sweet pepper, seeded, chopped	¼ cup sugar
	¾ cup vinegar (5% acidity)
	1½ tablespoons salt

Combine all ingredients; cook until thick, or reduce to one half. stirring occasionally to prevent sticking. Ladle into hot sterilized jars; seal. Process 10 minutes in hot water bath.

Dana Newberg
Nashville, Arkansas

RIPE TOMATO RELISH
4 pints.

6 medium onions, chopped	1 tablespoon black pepper
4 medium red sweet peppers, chopped	1 tablespoon cinnamon
1 small stalk celery, chopped	1½ teaspoons cloves
4 quarts chopped ripe tomatoes	1½ teaspoons cayenne pepper
	1 cup sugar
¼ cup salt	1 quart vinegar (5% acidity)

Combine first 5 ingredients; mix well; let stand overnight. Drain; add spices, sugar, and vinegar; mix well. Pack into hot sterilized jars; seal immediately. Do not cook.

Mary Roper
Ridgeway, Texas

HONEY MUSTARD
about 6 cups.

1 pound mustard powder	½ cup prepared horseradish
1¾ cups cider vinegar	2 cups oil
1 cup honey	8 teaspoons salt

Beat all ingredients for 5 minutes with an electric mixer. Spoon into hot sterilized jars; seal. Store in cool, dry place for 3 months before using.

Annie Quinn Dilday
Vancouver, British Columbia

YELLOW SQUASH RELISH
6 pints.

12 cups grated or chopped yellow squash	5 tablespoons salt
4 cups chopped onions	2½ cups vinegar (5% acidity)
2 sweet red peppers, seeded, chopped	2 teaspoons pickling spices, tied in a bag
2 sweet green peppers, seeded, chopped	1 teaspoon celery seed
1 (4-ounce) jar pimentos, optional	1 teaspoon turmeric
	6 cups sugar

Combine first 5 ingredients; sprinkle with salt; cover; let stand overnight. Drain mixture; rinse with cold water. In canning kettle bring vinegar and spices to a boil; boil 10 minutes; add sugar; stir until sugar dissolves. Remove spice bag; add squash mixture; bring to a good boil. Pack in hot sterilized jars; seal. Process 10 minutes in hot water bath.

Beth Friday

ZUCCHINI-PINEAPPLE
(Mock Crushed Pineapple)
about 4 cups.

8 cups coarsely-shredded, peeled zucchini	¾ cup lemon juice
3 cups pineapple juice	1½ cups sugar

Bring all ingredients to a boil; cook 20 minutes. Fill hot sterilized jars to within ½-inch of top; seal; process 15 minutes in hot water bath. Mixture freezes well; cool; spoon into freezer bags; freeze. Can be used in any recipe calling for crushed pineapple.

Melinda Taggart
Shreveport, Louisiana

ZUCCHINI RELISH
6 pints.

10 cups sliced zucchini	2 teaspoons celery seeds
4 cups chopped onions	1 teaspoon cornstarch
3 teaspoons salt	1 teaspoon nutmeg
3 cups sugar	1 red pepper, seeded, chopped
2½ cups vinegar (5% acidity)	1 green pepper, seeded, chopped
1 teaspoon turmeric	

Combine zucchini, onions, and salt; let stand overnight; drain. Add remaining ingredients; simmer 30 minutes. Ladle into hot sterilized jars; seal.

In memory of Agnes A. McKinley
Velma Jones

GRANOLA
6 cups.

2 cups regular oats	½ cup firmly packed brown sugar
1 cup wheat germ	⅓ cup water
½ cup flaked coconut	2 tablespoons honey
½ cup sliced almonds	⅓ cup oil
½ cup dry-roasted sunflower seeds	½ teaspoon vanilla
½ cup chopped dates	¾ cup raisins
2 tablespoons sesame seeds	

Thoroughly mix first 7 ingredients in a large bowl. In separate bowl combine remaining ingredients except raisins; pour over oats mixture; mix well. Spread evenly in a lightly greased 10 × 15-inch jelly roll pan; bake at 300° for 40 minutes, stirring every 10 minutes. Remove from oven; add raisins; mix well; cool. Store in airtight container.

Rhoda Smith

PRUNE PICKLES
2 cups.

1 pound dried, pitted prunes	1 teaspoon cloves
1 cup vinegar	1 teaspoon cinnamon
1 cup sugar	

In a sauce pan combine all ingredients; bring to a boil; remove from heat; cool. Return to heat; bring to a boil a second time; remove from heat immediately; cool. Refrigerate, covered. Make a nice addition to relish plate.

Irene Slaton Zachry
Oklahoma City, Oklahoma

All-Purpose Creole Seasoning 72
Almond Bark Candy 293
Almond Butter Beverage Mix 34
Anadama (Squaw) Bread 248
Angel Graham Bars 309
Antipasto 8
APPETIZERS
Dips
  Antipasto 8
  Baked Beef Dip 9
  Broccoli Dip (Microwave) 9
  Caracas 10
  Chilled Crab Dip 11
  Curry Dip 11
  Dill Dip in Pumpernickel 11
  Fresh Fruit Dip 12
  Guacamole 12
  Hot Artichoke Dip 8
  Hot Crab Dip 12
  Hot Tuna Dip 16
  Low Calorie Dip 9
  Party Shrimp Dip 14
  Red Fruit Dip 13
  Salsa 13
  Shrimp Dip 13
  Spicy Cheese Dip 10
  Spinach Dip 14
  Taco Dip 15
  Tex-Mex Dip 15
Hors D'oeuvres
  Avocados with Hot
    Cocktail Sauce 16
  Beef and Chicken Fondue 21
  Cheddar-Nut Wafers 24
  Cheese and Bacon Potato
    Rounds 18
  Cheese and Sausage Rolls 25
  Cheese Petit Fours 22
  Cheese Puffs 23
  Cheese Straws 7
  Chicken Little Fingers 18
  Cocktail Meatballs 19
  Crusty Dill Spears 17
  Deviled Cheese Crackers 24
  Glazed Ham Balls 20
  Ham and Cheese Pinwheels 26
  Ham Rolls 25
  Hot Pepper Pecans 26
  Marinated Broccoli or
    Cauliflower 17
  Meat Pies 20
  Nut Sticks 23
  Olive Cheese Balls 19
  Orange Pecans 27
  Oyster Crackers 23
  Sausage Stuffed Mushrooms 22
Spreads
  "Plains Special" Cheese Ring 29
  Artichoke Heart Spread 27

Boursin Cheese 28
Cheese Logs 30
Cheese Roll 31
Cheesy-Bacon Sour Cream
  Spread 29
Chicken Pecan Log 31
Cucumber Spread 32
Dried Beef Cheese Spread 28
Garlic Cheese Rolls 28
Monterey Jack Cheese
  Spread 30
"Plains Special" Cheese Ring 29
Salmon Ball 32
Shrimp Mold 31
Apple Bread, Cheddar- 227
Apple Butter 342
Apple Cake, Fresh 265
Apple Cider, Spiced 36
Apple Divinity 250
Apple Fritters 251
Apple Lemon Pie 317
Apple or Pear Bread with Brown
  Sugar Topping 233
Apple Pecan Pie 317
Apple Pie Filling, Canned 343
Apple Pie, Green 318
Apple Pie, Sour Cream 318
Apple Pudding with Brandy
  Sauce, Baked 254
Apple Squares, Glazed 251
Apples, Baked 250
Apples, Candied 250
Applesauce Cake 265
Applesauce Pancakes 223
Apricot Bread 238
Apricot Nectar Cake 266
Apricot Pie, Mimi's 319
Apricot Salad 179
Apricot Tarts 319
Apricot-Walnut Conserve 342
Arkansas Mincemeat Cake 281
Arkansas Rice Casserole 63
Artichoke Dip, Hot 8
Artichoke Heart Spread 27
Artichokes and Mushrooms 194
Asparagus Casserole 194
Avocado Salad 169
Avocados with Hot Cocktail Sauce 16
Bacon Spaghetti 53
"Baconized" Cornbread 228
Baja California Chicken 112
Baked Alaska Pie 336
Baked Apple Pudding with
  Brandy Sauce 254
Baked Apples 250
Baked Beef Dip 9
Baked Chicken Breasts
  with Stuffing 139
Baked Chicken Italian 117

Baked Chicken Parmesan 121
Baked Fish 156
Baked Fudge 294
Baked Pasta, Cheese and Chicken 67
Baked Pheasants 154
Baked Rice 64
Baked Tuna with Biscuits 162
Banana Nut Cake 266
Banana Nut Cookies 301
Banana Nut Dressing 192
Banana Pudding, Grandma
   Revils' 255
Banana-Lemon Tea Bread 233
Banana-Strawberry Salad, Frozen ... 183
Bananas Foster 260
Barbecued Beef Brisket 78
Barbecued Beef Roast 78
Barbecued Meatloaf 86
Barbecued Pork Chops 102
Barbecued Shredded Beef 50
Barbecued Shrimp 163
Basic Crepe Batter 230
Basic Ice Cream 262
Basic Roll Dough 238
Basic Tempura 165
Basic White Sauce 218
Batter, Catfish 166
Bea's Salad Dressing 192
Bean Soup, Millie Wood's 42
Bean Soup, Southern 41
Beans and Cornbread Casserole,
   Spicy 196
Beans and Rice, Red 195
Beans, Old Hickory Barbecued 195
Beans, Pasta with 61
"Beats-All" Beets 196
Beef and Biscuits 81
Beef and Chicken Fondue 21
Beef and Zucchini 93
Beef Balls, Olive 19
Beef Burgundy 70
Beef Casserole, French 71
Beef Dip, Baked 9
Beef In Casserole 90
Beef Internationale 74
Beef Roast, Barbecued 78
Beef Roast, Charcoal-Water
   Smoked 79
Beef Roulades 71
Beef Sandwiches 51
Beef Sandwiches, Pineapple-
   Barbecued 50
Beef Stew, Oven 77
Beef Stroganoff 75
Beef Stroganoff Casserole, Ground ... 88
Beef, Barbecued Shredded 50
Beef, Braised 70
Beef-Corn Casserole, Mexican 82
Beef-Green Bean-Potato Casserole ... 92

Beets, "Beats-All" 196
Beignets 238
Ben Lomond Barbecued Liver 79
Best Ever Cookies 310
BEVERAGES
   Almond Butter Beverage Mix 34
   Cindy's Coffee 35
   Citric Acid Punch 38
   Dottie Lou's Tea 35
   Easy Punch 38
   Exotic Coffee 34
   Fruit Flip Punch 37
   Hot Chocolate Mix 34
   Hot Spiced Tea 37
   Lime Light Punch 39
   Mexican Punch 39
   Old-Fashioned Egg Nog 35
   Pink Party Punch 40
   Raspberry Fizz 37
   Spiced Apple Cider 36
   Spiced Peach Punch 36
   Spiced Percolator Punch 36
   Spring Tonic 33
   Strawberry Breakfast Shake 40
   Sunshine Shake 40
Biscuit Nugget Chicken 141
Biscuits, Buttermilk 227
Biscuits, Sweet Potato 228
Black Walnut Cake 292
Black Walnut-Prune Bread 235
Blackberry Cake 290
Blanche's Pear Mincemeat 347
Blender Whole Wheat Pancakes 224
Bleu Cheese Dressing 191
Blond Brownies 304
Blueberry Chiffon Pie 321
Blueberry Coffee Cake 220
Blueberry Gingerbread 232
Blueberry Pie, Marion Benson's 320
Blueberry Salad 180
Blueberry Torte 252
Blueberry-Apple Coffee Cake 220
Bo Pilgrim's Italian Chicken
   Medley 117
Bob Brookes' Cheesecake 267
Bourbon Nut Log 297
Boursin Cheese 28
Braised Beef 70
Braised Cucumbers 200
Braised Short Ribs 73
Braised Veal 108
Bran Muffins, Ever-Ready 224
Brandied Fruit Starter 343
Bread Pudding, Luise's 261
BREADS
  Breakfast
     Applesauce Pancakes 223
     Blender Whole Wheat
       Pancakes 224

Blueberry Coffee Cake 220
Blueberry-Apple Coffee
  Cake 220
Cinnamon Pancakes 223
Cranberry Yogurt Coffee
  Cake 221
Grandma Chetterbox's
  Flap-Jacks 222
Streusel Coffee Cake 221
Waffles 222

Muffins
Ever-Ready Bran Muffins 224
Ham and Sausage Muffins 225
Peach Muffins 226
Spiced Cheese Muffins 225
Williamsburg Sweet Potato
  Muffins 226

Quick
Apple or Pear Bread with
  Brown Sugar Topping 233
"Baconized" Cornbread 228
Banana-Lemon Tea Bread 233
Basic Crepe Batter 230
Black Walnut-Prune Bread 235
Blueberry Gingerbread 232
Buttermilk Biscuits 227
Cheddar-Apple Bread 227
Cornbread Dressing 229
Cranberry Bread 230
Date Scones 236
Date-Nut Bread 231
Fluffy Cornbread 228
Hush Puppies 232
Jalapeño Cornbread 229
Lemon-Glazed Plum Bread 235
Old-Fashioned Cake
  Doughnuts 231
Old-Fashioned Stone-Ground
  Cornbread 219
Persimmon Bread 234
Pumpkin Bread 236
Pumpkin Scones 237
Sweet Potato Biscuits 228
Sweet Potato Bread 234
Vegetable Bubble Bread 227
Zucchini Bread 237

Yeast
Anadama (Squaw) Bread 248
Apricot Bread 238
Basic Roll Dough 239
Beignets 238
Brown Bread 243
Carmel's Rolls 241
Cream Cheese Braid 244
Dilly Bread 243
German Bread 245
Golden Bubble Ring 245
Honey Wheat Bread 246
Irish Soda Bread 246

Moravian Sugar Cake 247
Mother's Rolls 240
Oatmeal Bread 247
One-Rise Cinnamon Rolls 241
Red Apple Inn Rolls 242
Refrigerator Yeast Rolls 242
Breakfast Casserole 54
Breakfast Tacos 55
Breast of Chicken Supreme 127
Breast of Turkey with Apple
  Raisin Sauce 148
Brisket, Barbecued Beef 78
Broccoli Casserole For A Crowd 197
Broccoli Dip (Microwave) 9
Broccoli Rice Salad 171
Broccoli Soup 42
Brown Bread 243
Brown Sugar Cookies 301
Brown Sugar Kisses 301
Brownie Alaskas 336
Brownie Fudge Squares 305
Brownies, Blond 304
Brownies, Elegant Frosted 305
Buckeye Balls 296
Butterfinger Ice Cream 263
Buttermilk Biscuits 227
Buttermilk Pie, Old Time 320
Buttermilk Pralines 298
Cabbage Rolls 198
Cabbage, Sweet and Sour Red 197
California Chicken Breasts 113
Candied Apples 250
Canned Apple Pie Filling 343
Canned Green Beans 341
Caracas 10
Caramel Crunch 300
Caramel Nut Pie 321
Carmel's Rolls 241
Carrot Cake 267
Carrot Cookies, Frosted 303
Carrot-Coconut Cake 269
Carrots Flambe 198
Carrots, Lo-Cal 199
Cashew Stuffed Shrimp with
  Lemon Sauce 161
Cassoulet 114
Catfish Batter 166
Catfish Fry with Tartar Sauce,
  Crispy 156
Cauliflower French-Style, Cold 173
Cauliflower Soup, Cream of 43
Cauliflower, Creamy 199
Charcoal-Water Smoked Beef
  Roast 79
Cheddar Turkey Casserole 150
Cheddar-Apple Bread 227
Cheddar-Nut Wafers 24
Cheese and Bacon Potato Rounds, ... 18
Cheese and Sausage Rolls 25

Entry	Page
Cheese Balls, Olive	19
Cheese Dip, Spicy	10
Cheese Grits	58
Cheese Logs	30
Cheese Muffins, Spiced	225
Cheese Petit Fours	22
Cheese Potatoes	209
Cheese Puffs	23
Cheese Ring, "Plains Special"	29
Cheese Roll	31
Cheese Rolls, Garlic	28
Cheese Soup	43
Cheese Spread, Dried Beef	28
Cheese Spread, Monterey Jack	30
Cheese Straws	7
Cheeseburgers To Go	51
Cheesecake Cookies	303
Cheesecake with Raspberry Sauce, Deluxe	268
Cheesecake, Bob Brookes'	267
Cheesy-Bacon Sour Cream Spread	29
Cherries In The Snow	323
Cherry Bar Cake, Chocolate	274
Cherry Chicken	114
Cherry Cobbler	322
Cherry Dump Cake	270
Cherry Pudding	256
Chess Pie	324
Chess Pie, Chocolate	325
Chess Pie, Pineapple	324
Chess Pie, Southern	324
Chicken a la King	128
Chicken and Rice, Scalloped	134
Chicken and Wild Rice Casserole	134
Chicken Breasts with Stuffing, Baked	139
Chicken Breasts, California	113
Chicken Breasts, Herbed	116
Chicken Breasts, Russian	124
Chicken Cacciatore	145
Chicken Cacciatore, Low Calorie	144
Chicken Casserole For A Crowd	135
Chicken Casserole with Cornbread Stuffing	140
Chicken Casserole, Crunchy	136
Chicken Casserole, Party	137
Chicken Corn Soup	44
Chicken Curry	141
Chicken Dip'n Sauces	151
Chicken Divan	120
Chicken Drumettes Teriyaki	115
Chicken Fritters	151
Chicken In Chili-Tomato Sauce	115
Chicken In Wine Sauce	130
Chicken Italian, Baked	117
Chicken Little Fingers	18
Chicken Loaf with Lemon Sauce	128
Chicken Loaf with Mushroom Sauce, Hot	129
Chicken Marengo	118
Chicken Mayonnaise	186
Chicken Medley, Bo Pilgrim's Italian	117
Chicken Normandy	142
Chicken Oriental, Peanut	122
Chicken Parmesan, Baked	121
Chicken Pecan Log	31
Chicken Pie, Jim's Favorite	143
Chicken Potato Salad	187
Chicken Rice Casserole	133
Chicken Rosalie	124
Chicken Salad	187
Chicken Salad Deluxe, Hot	186
Chicken Salad with Honey Mustard Vinaigrette	185
Chicken San José	126
Chicken Spaghetti	147
Chicken Spectacular	136
Chicken Squares	138
Chicken Stuff, Nancy's	132
Chicken Supreme, Breast of	127
Chicken Surprise	131
Chicken Sweet'n Hot	132
Chicken Tetrazzini, Easy	145
Chicken Tetrazzini, Party	146
Chicken Turnovers, Hot	139
Chicken with Artichokes	112
Chicken with Mustard Sauce, Peanut	121
Chicken with Onion Gravy, Fried	143
Chicken with Vegetables, Scalloped	125
Chicken, Baja California	112
Chicken, Biscuit Nugget	141
Chicken, Cherry	114
Chicken, Country Captain	125
Chicken, Curried	144
Chicken, Curried Mango	118
Chicken, Easy Bake	130
Chicken, Huntington	135
Chicken, Italian	116
Chicken, Minty	119
Chicken, Oven Barbecued	130
Chicken, Oven-Fried Sesame	126
Chicken, Paprika	120
Chicken, Peachy Keen	140
Chicken, Polynesian	122
Chicken, Poppy Seed	123
Chicken, Relaxing	123
Chicken, Saturday	131
Chicken, Sherried	127
Chicken, Southern Fried	111
Chicken, Stir-Fry	148
Chicken, Sweet and Sour	113
Chicken-Rice Bake, Quick	137
Chicken-Spaghetti Casserole	146
Chili Cornbread, Upside Down	91
Chili, Wild Hog	88

Chilies Rellenos, Easy 59
Chilled Crab Dip 11
Chinese Salad 184
Chocolate Cake, Foolproof
   Buttermilk 269
Chocolate Cherry Bar Cake 274
Chocolate Chess Pie 325
Chocolate Chip Cookies, Famous
   Amos (Raisin-Filled) 307
Chocolate Chip Pie 326
Chocolate Cookies, Easy 306
Chocolate Cream Cake 272
Chocolate Dessert, Party 253
Chocolate Four-Layer Dessert 251
Chocolate Fudge Sauce 261
Chocolate Meringue Pie 327
Chocolate Mix, Hot 34
Chocolate Peanut Butter Cookies 315
Chocolate Peanut Clusters,
   Mimi Matteson's 296
Chocolate Pie, Microwave 326
Chocolate Torte, Mother's
   German 270
Chow-Chow 344
Chowder, Clam 44
Chowder, Crab-Corn 45
Christmas Fruit Cookies 304
Cider, Spiced Apple 36
Cindy's Coffee 35
Cinnamon Pancakes 223
Citric Acid Punch 38
Clam Chowder 44
Cobbler, Cherry 322
Cobbler, Peach 332
Cocktail Meatballs 19
Coconut Bars 309
Coconut Cake 276
Coconut Cream Pie 328
Coffee Cake, Blueberry 220
Coffee Cake, Blueberry-Apple 220
Coffee Cake, Cranberry Yogurt 221
Coffee Cake, Streusel 221
Coffee, Cindy's 35
Coffee, Exotic 34
Coke Salad 178
Cola Cake 273
Cold Cauliflower French-Style 173
Cole Slaw Dressing 190
Confetti Cottage Cheese Salad 172
Conserve, Apricot-Walnut 342
Cookies 307
Cora Locke's Spice Cake 291
Corn Chowder, Crab 45
Corn Fritters 200
Corn Pudding 201
Corn Relish 344
Corn Soup, Chicken 44
Corn, Fried 200
Corn, Pepper 201
Corn, Scalloped 202
Cornbread Dressing 229
Cornbread Dumplings, Turnip
   Greens with 216
Cornbread Souffle 59
Cornbread, "Baconized" 228
Cornbread, Fluffy 228
Cornbread, Jalapeño 229
Cornbread, Sour Cream Jalapeño ... 229
Cornbread, Old-Fashioned
   Stone-Ground 219
Cottage Cheese Salad, Confetti 172
Country Captain Chicken 125
Country Ham and Red-Eye Gravy ... 104
Country Potatoes 209
County Fair Special 133
Crab Dip, Chilled 11
Crab Dip, Hot 12
Crab Louis 188
Crab Meat Au Gratin 157
Crab Muffins 157
Crab Quiche 57
Crab-Corn Chowder 45
Crackers, Deviled Cheese 24
Crackers, Oyster 23
Cranberry Bread 230
Cranberry Casserole 182
Cranberry Ring 181
Cranberry Yogurt Coffee Cake 221
Cream Cheese Braid 244
Cream Cheese Pound Cake 291
Cream of Cauliflower Soup 43
Cream of Rice Pudding 258
Creamy Cabbage and Apple Slaw ... 169
Creamy Cauliflower 199
Creamy Pumpkin Pie 337
Crepe, Basic Batter 230
Crepes with Chicken, Cheese,
   Jalapeño Filling 147
Crispy Catfish Fry with
   Tartar Sauce 156
Crock Pot Meatloaf 87
Crunchy Chicken Casserole 136
Crust For Fried Pies 338
Crust, Easy Pie 338
Crust, Never-Fail Flaky Pie 338
Crust, Oatmeal Pie 339
Crust, Peanut Butter-Graham
   Cracker Pie 339
Crusty Dill Spears 17
Cube Steaks Diane 73
Cucumber Pickles 345
Cucumber Ring Supreme 177
Cucumber Spread 32
Cucumbers, Braised 200
Curried Chicken 144
Curried Mango Chicken 118
Curried Rice 64
Curry Dip 11

Curry, Jack's Favorite 150
Custard Pie 328
Date Pinwheel Cookies 311
Date Pudding 256
Date Scones 236
Date-Nut Bread 231
Deluxe Cheesecake with
   Raspberry Sauce 268
Deluxe Macaroni and Cheese 62
DESSERTS
   Apple Divinity 250
   Apple Fritters 251
   Baked Apples 250
   Baked Apple Pudding with
      Brandy Sauce 254
   Bananas Foster 260
   Basic Ice Cream 262
   Blueberry Torte 252
   Butterfinger Ice Cream 263
   Candied Apples 250
   Cherry Pudding 256
   Chocolate Four-Layer Dessert 252
   Chocolate Fudge Sauce 261
   Cream of Rice Pudding 258
   Date Pudding 256
   Fresh Strawberry Mousse 259
   Frozen Fruit Cups 260
   Fruit Compote 253
   Fruity Cheesecake Cups 260
   Glazed Apple Squares 251
   Grandma Revils' Banana
      Pudding 255
   Harlan's Ice Cream 262
   Homemade Ice Cream 263
   Lemon Ice Cream 263
   Luise's Bread Pudding 261
   Mom's Lemon Sherbet 264
   Old-Fashioned Raisin Pudding 258
   Orange Pudding 257
   Oreo Cookie Dessert 259
   Party Chocolate Dessert 253
   Peach Dumplings 261
   Pecan Delight 254
   Persimmon Pudding 258
   Scalloped Pineapple 255
   Strawberry-Banana-Nut
      Ice Cream 264
   Theodore Roosevelt's
      Indian Pudding 257
Cakes
   Applesauce Cake 265
   Apricot Nectar Cake 266
   Arkansas Mincemeat Cake 281
   Banana Nut Cake 266
   Black Walnut Cake 292
   Bob Brookes' Cheesecake 267
   Carrot Cake 267
   Carrot-Coconut Cake 269
   Cherry Dump Cake 270

Chocolate Cherry Bar Cake 274
Chocolate Cream Cake 272
Coconut Cake 276
Cola Cake 273
Cora Locke's Spice Cake 291
Cream Cheese Pound Cake 291
Deluxe Cheesecake with
   Raspberry Sauce 268
Five Flavor Buttermilk
   Pound Cake 289
Foolproof Buttermilk
   Chocolate Cake 269
Fresh Apple Cake 265
Friendship Cake 277
Fruit Cake 278
Fruit Cocktail Cake 277
Fudge Cake 271
Fudge Cake of 1920 272
Hawaiian Pineapple Cake 287
Heavenly Pineapple Cake 285
Hummingbird Cake 286
Iron Skillet Upside Down
   Cake 249
Italian Cream Cake 275
Jam Cake 282
Lemon Fruit Cake 279
Lemon Lovers' Delight 276
Lemon Pound Cake 289
Mother's German Chocolate
   Torte 270
Mound Cake 282
Peanut Butter Cake 283
Pear Fruit Cake 279
Persimmon Cake 283
Pineapplesheet Cake 285
Piña Colada Cake 284
Poppy Seed Cake 286
Pumpkin Pie Cake 287
Pumpkin Walnut Cake 288
Rum Cake 290
Scotch Fudge 271
Vanilla Wafer Fruit Cake 280
Whipping Cream Pound
   Cake 288
White Fruit Cake 280
Candies
   Almond Bark Candy 293
   Baked Fudge 294
   Bourbon Nut Log 297
   Buckeye Balls 296
   Buttermilk Pralines 298
   Caramel Crunch 300
   Easy Divinity 293
   Fast Chocolate Fudge 295
   Lazy Millionaires 297
   Mimi Matteson's Chocolate
      Peanut Clusters 296
   Never Say "Never Fail"
      Divinity 293

Peanut Brittle 298
Peanut Butter Fudge 295
Pecan Clusters 297
Peppermint Bark 299
Reese Cups 295
Rocky Road............................. 300
Rocky Road Bars..................... 299
Sees Fudge............................. 294

Cookies
Angel Graham Bars................. 309
Banana Nut Cookies................ 301
Best Ever Cookies 310
Blond Brownies 304
Brown Sugar Cookies 301
Brown Sugar Kisses................. 301
Brownie Fudge Squares........... 305
Cheesecake Cookies................ 303
Chocolate Peanut Butter
   Cookies 315
Christmas Fruit Cookies 304
Coconut Bars 309
Date Pinwheel Cookies 311
Drop Sugar Cookies 314
Easy Chocolate Cookies 306
Elegant Frosted Brownies 305
Famous Amos (Raisin-Filled)
   Chocolate Chip Cookies....... 307
Frosted Carrot Cookies 303
Germantown Oatmeal
   Cookies 310
Grapenut Cookies................... 311
Lemon Bars 312
Magic Cookie Bars 306
Magic Granola Bars................. 308
Neither Cake Nor Candy 307
Old-Fashioned Tea Cakes........ 316
Orange Chews........................ 312
Pecan Sandies 313
Pineapple Cookies 315
Ranger Macaroons.................. 302
Rice Krispie and Corn
   Flake Treat......................... 313
Sand Tarts 316
Stir and Spoon Fudge Drops.... 308
Sugar Cookies 314
Swedish Shortbread Cookies ... 316
Vanilla Crisps 302

Pies
Apple Lemon Pie 317
Apple Pecan Pie...................... 317
Apricot Tarts........................... 319
Baked Alaska Pie 336
Blueberry Chiffon Pie 321
Caramel Nut Pie...................... 321
Cherries In The Snow 323
Cherry Cobbler 322
Chess Pie 324
Chocolate Chess Pie 325
Chocolate Chip Pie.................. 326

Chocolate Meringue Pie........... 327
Coconut Cream Pie 328
Creamy Pumpkin Pie................ 337
Crust For Fried Pies 338
Custard Pie 328
Drum Roll Pie.......................... 327
Easy Pie Crust........................ 338
Gold Brick Pie 325
Green Apple Pie...................... 318
Lemon Meringue Pie 329
Luscious Lemon Pie 329
Marion Benson's Blueberry
   Pie...................................... 320
Microwave Chocolate Pie 326
Million Dollar Pie..................... 334
Mimi's Apricot Pie................... 319
Muscadine and Pecan Pie 330
Never-Fail Flaky Pie Crust....... 338
No-Bake Regal Cheese Pie 322
Oatmeal Pie Crust................... 339
Old Time Buttermilk Pie.......... 320
Old-Fashioned Lemon
   Meringue Pie 330
Osgood Pie............................. 331
Out of This World Pie 323
Party Peach Pie...................... 331
Peach Cobbler........................ 332
Peanut Butter Pie 332
Peanut Butter-Graham Cracker
   Pie Crust 339
Pear Mince Pie 336
Pecan Pie 333
Pecan-Cream Cheese Pie 333
Pecan-Sour Cream Pie............ 334
Pineapple Chess Pie 324
Sour Cream Apple Pie 318
Sour Cream Raisin Pie............. 335
Southern Chess Pie 324
Sweet Potato Pie..................... 336
Tiny Russian Mint Pies 335
Vanilla Pie.............................. 337

Sauces
Apple Pudding with
   Brandy Sauce 254
Chocolate Fudge Sauce 261
Deluxe Cheesecake with
   Raspberry Sauce 268
Deviled Cheese Crackers 24
Dill Dip In Pumpernickel 11
Dill Spears, Crusty............................ 17
Dilled Okra..................................... 345
Dilly Bread 243
Dirty Rice Dressing 65
Divinity, Easy.................................. 293
Divinity, Never Say "Never Fail".... 293
Don't-Cook-the-Pasta Manicotti 91
Dottie Lou's Tea................................ 35
Doughnuts, Old-Fashioned Cake 231
Dove or Duck, Grilled 152

Dressing, Cornbread 229
Dressing, Dirty Rice 65
Dried Beef Cheese Spread 28
Drop Sugar Cookies 314
Drum Roll Pie 327
Duck, Grilled Dove or 152
Duck, Roast Wild 153
Dumplings, Peach 261
Easy Bake Chicken 130
Easy Chicken Tetrazzini 145
Easy Chilies Rellenos 59
Easy Chocolate Cookies 306
Easy Divinity 293
Easy Gumbo 45
Easy Meatless Tomato Sauce 85
Easy Pie Crust 338
Easy Punch 38
Egg Nog, Old-Fashioned 35
Eggplant Casserole, Golden 204
Eggplant Fritters 203
Eggplant, Franke's Scalloped 204
Eggplant, Fried 203
EGGS AND CHEESE
    Breakfast Casserole 54
    Breakfast Tacos 55
    Cheese Grits 58
    Cornbread Souffle 59
    Crab Quiche 57
    Easy Chilies Rellenos 59
    Hot Cheese Strata 59
    Olive Quiche 57
    Sausage and Egg Casserole 55
    Spinach Quiche 58
    Suppertime Eggs 56
    24-Hour Omelet 54
    With-It Deviled Eggs 60
    Zucchini Omelet 56
El Paso Beef 87
Elegant Frosted Brownies 305
Enchiladas 80
Enchiladas, White 81
Ever-Ready Bran Muffins 224
Exotic Coffee 34
Famous Amos (Raisin-Filled)
    Chocolate Chip Cookies 307
Fast Chocolate Fudge 295
Fettuccini with Ham, Peas
    & Cheese 60
Filleted Fish A La Microwave 158
Fisherman's Catch 155
Fish, Baked Fish 156
Five Flavor Buttermilk
    Pound Cake 289
Fizz, Raspberry 37
Flap-Jacks, Grandma
    Chetterbox's 222
Fluffy Cornbread 228
Foolproof Buttermilk
    Chocolate Cake 269

Franke's Scalloped Eggplant 204
French Beef Casserole 71
French Fried Liver 79
Fresh Apple Cake 265
Fresh Fruit Dip 12
Fresh Lemon Rice 66
Fresh Strawberry Mousse 259
Fried Chicken with Onion Gravy 143
Fried Corn 200
Fried Eggplant 203
Fried Green Tomatoes 215
Fried Quail 154
Fried Venison Steak 69
Friendship Cake 277
Fritters, Apple 251
Frosted Carrot Cookies 303
Frozen Banana-Strawberry Salad ... 183
Frozen Fruit Cups 260
Frozen Fruit Salad 183
Fruit Cake 278
Fruit Cake, Lemon 279
Fruit Cake, Pear 279
Fruit Cake, Vanilla Wafer 280
Fruit Cake, White 280
Fruit Cocktail Cake 277
Fruit Compote 253
Fruit Cookies, Christmas 304
Fruit Cups, Frozen 260
Fruit Dip, Fresh 12
Fruit Dip, Red 13
Fruit Flip Punch 37
Fruit Salad with Pineapple
    Dressing, Turkey 184
Fruit Salad, Frozen 183
Fruit Salad, Hot 182
Fruity Cheesecake Cups 260
Fudge Cake 271
Fudge Cake of 1920 272
Fudge Drops, Stir and Spoon 308
Fudge, Baked 294
Fudge, Fast Chocolate 295
Fudge, Peanut Butter 295
Fudge, Sees 294
GAME
    Baked Pheasants 154
    Fried Quail 154
    Fried Venison Steak 69
    Grilled Dove Or Duck 152
    Roast Wild Duck 153
    Skillet BBQ Venison 110
    Smothered Venison 110
    Squirrel Stew 109
    Wild Duck Gumbo 153
Garlic Cheese Rolls 28
German Bread 245
German Cole Slaw 174
German Sauerkraut 214
Germantown Oatmeal Cookies 311
Gingerbread, Blueberry 232

Glazed Apple Squares	251
Glazed Ham	97
Glazed Ham Balls	20
Gold Brick Pie	325
Golden Bubble Ring	245
Golden Eggplant Casserole	204
Golden Ham Casserole	103
Gorditos	89
Goulash, Hungarian	74
Grandma Chetterbox's Flap-Jacks	222
Grandma Revils' Banana Pudding	255
Granola	351
Grapenut Cookies	311
Green and White Vegetable Salad	172
Green Apple Pie	318
Green Bean Casserole	205
Green Bean Casserole, Original	205
Green Beans, Canned	341
Green Beans, Pickled	348
Green Chili Rice	66
Green Noodles	62
Grillades	72
Grilled Dove Or Duck	152
Grits, Cheese	58
Grits, Garlic Cheese	58
Ground Beef Stroganoff Casserole	88
Guacamole	12
Guacamole Dressing	190
Gumbo, Easy	45
Gumbo, Wild Duck	153
Hacienda Bake	92
Ham and Cheese Pinwheels	26
Ham and Red-Eye Gravy, Country	104
Ham and Sausage Muffins	225
Ham Balls, Glazed	20
Ham Casserole, Golden	103
Ham Ring with Cherry Sauce	96
Ham Rolls	25
Ham Rolls	99
Ham Sandwiches, Hot	52
Ham, Glazed	97
Ham-Sausage Loaf	97
Harlan's Ice Cream	262
Hawaiian Pineapple Cake	287
Heavenly Pineapple Cake	285
Herbed Chicken Breasts	116
Hollandaise Sauce	218
Homemade Ice Cream	263
Hominy Casserole	202
Honey Mustard	349
Honey Watermelon Rind Preserves	345
Honey Wheat Bread	246
Hoppin' John	206
Hot Artichoke Dip	8
Hot Cheese Strata	59
Hot Chicken Loaf with Mushroom Sauce	129
Hot Chicken Salad Deluxe	186
Hot Chicken Turnovers	139
Hot Chocolate Mix	34
Hot Crab Dip	12
Hot Dog Casserole	107
Hot Dog Relish	346
Hot Fruit Salad	182
Hot Ham Sandwiches	52
Hot Pepper Pecans	26
Hot Spiced Tea	37
Hot Tuna Dip	16
Hummingbird Cake	286
Hungarian Goulash	74
Huntington Chicken	135
Hush Puppies	232
Ice Cream, Basic	262
Ice Cream, Butterfinger	263
Ice Cream, Harlan's	262
Ice Cream, Homemade	263
Ice Cream, Lemon	263
Ice Cream, Strawberry-Banana-Nut	264
Idaho Potato Salad	171
Indian Country Casserole	65
Indian Pudding, Theodore Roosevelt's	257
Irish Soda Bread	246
Iron Skillet Upside Down Cake	249
It's Pecan Season	346
Italian Casserole	84
Italian Chicken	116
Italian Cream Cake	275
Italian Dressing	189
Italian Sausage Supper	104
Jack's Favorite Curry	150
Jalapeño Cornbread	229
Jam Cake	282
Jim's Favorite Chicken Pie	143
Just Peachy Limas	206
King Ranch Casserole	138
Lamb Stew	95
Lasagna	90
Lazy Millionaires	297
Le French Salad Dressing	189
Leg of Lamb, Rolled Roast	95
Lemon Bars	312
Lemon Buttermilk Pie, Old Time	320
Lemon Fruit Cake	279
Lemon Ice Cream	263
Lemon Lovers' Delight	276
Lemon Meringue Pie	329
Lemon Meringue Pie, Old-Fashioned	330
Lemon Pie, Luscious	329
Lemon Pound Cake	289
Lemon Tea Bread, Banana-	233
Lemon-Glazed Plum Bread	235

Lentil Soup 46
Lettuce Salad, Wilted 167
Limas, Just Peachy 206
Lime Light Punch 39
Liver and Onions 80
Liver, Ben Lomond Barbecued 79
Liver, French Fried 79
Lo-cal Carrots 199
Low Calorie Chicken Cacciatore 144
Low Calorie Dip 9
Low-Calorie Veal Scallopini 109
Luise's Bread Pudding 261
Luscious Lemon Pie 329
Maraconi and Cheese, Deluxe 62
Macaroni Salad 175
Macaroni-Ham Casserole 61
Magic Cookie Bars 306
Magic Granola Bars 308
Mama Nina's Pimento Cheese 51
Manicotti, Don't-Cook-the-Pasta 91
Marinated Broccoli Or Cauliflower 17
Marinated Vegetables 176
Marion Benson's Blueberry Pie 320
May's Okra Casserole 207
Mayonnaise, Prize-Winning
   Homemade 191
Maytime Muffuletta Mix 52
Meat Balls, Swedish 86
Meat Pies 20
Meatball Soup, Polish 47
Meatballs with Sweet and Sour
   Sauce, Oriental 85
Meatballs, Cocktail 19
Meatloaf, Barbecued 86
Meatloaf, Crock Pot 87
MEATS
  Beef
    Barbecued Beef Brisket 78
    Barbecued Beef Roast 78
    Barbecued Meatloaf 86
    Beef and Biscuits 81
    Beef and Zucchini 93
    Beef Burgundy 70
    Beef In Casserole 90
    Beef Internationale 74
    Beef Roulades 71
    Beef Stroganoff 75
    Beef-Green Bean-Potato
      Casserole 92
    Ben Lomond Barbecued Liver ... 79
    Braised Beef 70
    Braised Short Ribs 73
    Charcoal-Water Smoked
      Beef Roast 79
    Crock Pot Meatloaf 87
    Cube Steaks Diane 73
    Don't-Cook-the-Pasta
      Manicotti 91
    El Paso Beef 87

Enchiladas 80
French Beef Casserole 71
French Fried Liver 79
Gorditos 89
Grillades 72
Ground Beef Stroganoff
   Casserole 88
Hacienda Bake 92
Hungarian Goulash 74
Italian Casserole 84
Lasagna 90
Liver and Onions 80
Mexican Beef-Corn Casserole 82
Mexican Spaghetti Sauce 83
Old-Fashioned Swiss Steak 77
Oriental Meatballs with Sweet
   and Sour Sauce 85
Oven Beef Stew 77
Shish Kebabs 76
Sicilian Spaghetti Sauce 84
Smothered Steak 76
Super Mexican Casserole 93
Swedish Meat Balls 86
Sweet and Sour Roast 75
Taco From The Oven 83
Tamale Pie 82
Tortellini 89
Upside Down Chili Cornbread 91
White Enchiladas 81
Wild Hog Chili 88
Lamb
  Lamb Stew 95
  Rolled Roast Leg of Lamb 95
Pork
  Barbecued Pork Chops 102
  Country Ham and
    Red-eye Gravy 104
  Glazed Ham 97
  Golden Ham Casserole 103
  Ham Ring with Cherry Sauce 96
  Ham Rolls 99
  Ham-Sausage Loaf 97
  Hot Dog Casserole 107
  Italian Sausage Supper 104
  Orange-Glazed Pork Chops 100
  Oven "Boiled" Dinner 105
  Pat McGoldrick's One-Stop
    Chops 100
  Pizza 106
  Pork Chop Dinner 102
  Pork Chop Skillet Meal 101
  Pork Chop-Noodle Casserole 99
  Pork Chops and
    Cream Gravy 103
  Pork in Sweet and
    Sour Sauce 98
  Sausage and Peppers 106
  Sausage Supper Dish 105
  Sausage-Apple Bake 98

Sausage-Rice Casserole 104
Spaghetti with Wiener Sauce ... 107
Sweet and Sour Pork Roast 96
Sweet and Sour Wieners 101
Tasty Pork Tenders 101
Veal
Braised Veal 108
Low-Calorie Veal Scallopini 109
Veal Parmesan 108
Mexican Beef-Corn Casserole 82
Mexican Punch 39
Mexican Red Sauce 94
Mexican Spaghetti Sauce 83
Mickey's Shrimp Creole 164
Microwave Chocolate Pie 326
Microwave Potato Soup 48
Millie Wood's Bean Soup 42
Million Dollar Pie 334
Millionaires, Lazy 296
Mimi Matteson's Chocolate
 Peanut Clusters 296
Mimi's Apricot Pie 319
Mimi's Waldorf Salad 181
Mincemeat Cake, Arkansas 281
Mint Pies, Tiny Russian 335
Minty Chicken 119
Mom's Lemon Sherbet 264
Monterey Jack Cheese Spread 30
Moravian Sugar Cake 247
Mornay Sauce 152
Mother's German Chocolate
 Torte 270
Mother's Rolls 240
Mound Cake 282
Mousse, Fresh Strawberry 259
Muffuletta Mix, Maytime 52
Muscadine and Pecan Pie 330
Mushrooms, Sausage Stuffed 22
Mustard, Honey 349
My Zucchini 217
Nancy's Chicken Stuff 132
Neither Cake Nor Candy 307
Never Say "Never Fail" Divinity 293
Never-Fail Flaky Pie Crust 338
Ninfa's Mexican Green Sauce 94
No-Bake Regal Cheese Pie 322
Noodles, Green 62
Nut Log, Bourbon 297
Nut Sticks 23
Oatmeal Bread 247
Oatmeal Cookies, Germantown 310
Oatmeal Pie Crust 339
Okra and Tomatoes 207
Okra Casserole, May's 207
Okra, Dilled 345
Old Hickory Barbecued Beans 195
Old Time Buttermilk Pie 320
Old-Fashioned Cake Doughnuts 231
Old-Fashioned Egg Nog 35

Old-Fashioned Lemon
 Meringue Pie 330
Old-Fashioned Raisin Pudding 258
Old-Fashioned Stone-Ground
 Cornbread 219
Old-Fashioned Swiss Steak 77
Old-Fashioned Tea Cakes 316
Old-Fashioned Turnips 215
Olive Cheese Balls 19
Olive Quiche 57
Omelet, 24-Hour 54
Omelet, Zucchini 56
One-Rise Cinnamon Rolls 241
Onion Custard, Spanish 208
Onion Patties 208
Onion Wine Soup 46
Orange Chews 312
Orange Pecans 27
Orange Pudding 257
Orange-Glazed Pork Chops 100
Oreo Cookie Dessert 259
Oriental Meatballs with Sweet
 and Sour 85
Original Green Bean Casserole 205
Osgood Pie 331
Out of This World Pie 323
Oven "Boiled" Dinner 105
Oven Barbecued Chicken 130
Oven Beef Stew 77
Oven-Fried Sesame Chicken 126
Oyster Crackers 23
Oyster Stew 47
Paella Española 119
Paella, Shrimp 163
Pancakes, Applesauce 223
Pancakes, Blender Whole Wheat 224
Pancakes, Cinnamon 223
Paprika Chicken 120
Party Chicken Casserole 137
Party Chicken Tetrazzini 146
Party Chocolate Dessert 253
Party Peach Pie 331
Party Shrimp Dip 14
PASTA
Bacon Spaghetti 53
Baked Pasta, Cheese
 and Chicken 67
Deluxe Macaroni and Cheese 62
Fettuccini with Ham, Peas
 & Cheese 60
Green Noodles 62
Macaroni-Ham Casserole 61
Pasta Fazuli (Pasta with Beans) 61
Pizza Casserole 63
Pat McGoldrick's One-stop Chops ... 100
Peach Cobbler 332
Peach Dumplings 261
Peach Honey 347
Peach Muffins 226

Peach Pie, Party 331
Peach Salad, Spicy 185
Peachy Keen Chicken 140
Peanut Brittle 298
Peanut Butter Cake 283
Peanut Butter Cookies, Chocolate... 315
Peanut Butter Fudge......................... 295
Peanut Butter Pie 332
Peanut Butter-Graham Cracker
  Pie Crust....................................... 339
Peanut Chicken Oriental 122
Peanut Chicken with Mustard
  Sauce.. 121
Peanut Clusters, Mimi Matteson's
  Chocolate..................................... 296
Pear Bread with Brown Sugar
  Topping 233
Pear Fruit Cake 279
Pear Marmalade, Tommie's 347
Pear Mince Pie 336
Pear Mincemeat, Blanche's 347
Pear Relish 348
Peas, Purple Hull.............................. 209
Pecan Clusters.................................. 297
Pecan Delight 254
Pecan Pie 333
Pecan Sandies 313
Pecan Surprise Bars 312
Pecan-Cream Cheese Pie 333
Pecan-Sour Cream Pie 334
Pecans, Hot Pepper............................ 26
Pecans, Orange 27
Pecans, Storage 346
Pepper Corn...................................... 201
Peppermint Bark 299
Persimmon Bread 234
Persimmon Cake............................... 283
Persimmon Pudding 258
Pheasants, Baked 154
Picante Sauce 348
Pickled Green Beans........................ 348
Pickles, Cucumber 345
Pickles, Prune................................... 352
Pimento Cheese, Mama Nina's.......... 51
Pineapple Cake, Hawaiian 287
Pineapple Cake, Heavenly 285
Pineapple Chess Pie 324
Pineapple Cookies 315
Pineapple Sheet Cake....................... 285
Pineapple, Mock Crushed 350
Pineapple, Scalloped........................ 255
Pineapple-Barbecued Beef
  Sandwiches 50
Pink Party Punch................................ 40
Pizza.. 106
Pizza Casserole 63
Piña Colada Cake 284
"Plains Special" Cheese Ring 29
Plum Bread, Lemon-Glazed 235

Poke Sallet 193
Polish Meatball Soup 47
Polynesian Chicken.......................... 122
Poppy Seed Cake 286
Poppy Seed Chicken......................... 123
Poppy Seed Dressing 189
Pork Chop Dinner 102
Pork Chop Skillet Meal 101
Pork Chop-Noodle Casserole 99
Pork Chops and Cream Gravy 103
Pork Chops, Barbecued 102
Pork Chops, Orange-Glazed............ 100
Pork In Sweet and Sour Sauce.......... 98
Pork Roast, Sweet and Sour 96
Potato Casserole............................... 210
Potato Rounds, Cheese and Bacon.... 18
Potato Salad...................................... 170
Potato Salad, Chicken...................... 187
Potato Salad, Idaho 171
Potato Soup 48
Potato Soup, Microwave 48
Potatoes, Cheese 209
Potatoes, Quarter-Baked.................. 210
Potatoes, Country............................. 209
POULTRY
  Baja California Chicken................ 112
  Baked Chicken Breasts with
    Stuffing 139
  Baked Chicken Italian 117
  Baked Chicken Parmesan............. 121
  Biscuit Nugget Chicken 141
  Bo Pilgrim's Italian Chicken
    Medley.. 117
  Breast of Chicken Supreme......... 127
  Breast of Turkey with Apple
    Raisin Sauce.............................. 148
  California Chicken Breasts 113
  Cassoulet 114
  Cheddar Turkey Casserole.......... 150
  Cherry Chicken 114
  Chicken A La King....................... 128
  Chicken and Wild Rice
    Casserole 134
  Chicken Cacciatore 145
  Chicken Casserole
    For A Crowd 135
  Chicken Casserole with
    Cornbread Stuffing 140
  Chicken Curry.............................. 141
  Chicken Dip'n Sauces.................. 151
  Chicken Divan.............................. 120
  Chicken Drumettes Teriyaki........ 115
  Chicken Fritters 151
  Chicken In Chili-tomato Sauce..... 115
  Chicken In Wine Sauce 130
  Chicken Loaf with
    Lemon Sauce 128
  Chicken Marengo 118
  Chicken Normandy 142

Chicken Rice Casserole 133
Chicken Rosalie........................... 124
Chicken San José 126
Chicken Spaghetti 147
Chicken Spectacular.................... 136
Chicken Squares 138
Chicken Surprise 131
Chicken Sweet'n Hot................... 132
Chicken with Artichokes............... 112
Chicken-Spaghetti Casserole 146
Country Captain Chicken 125
County Fair Special..................... 133
Crepes with Chicken, Cheese,
   Jalapeño Filling 147
Crunchy Chicken Casserole......... 136
Curried Chicken 144
Curried Mango Chicken............... 118
Easy Bake Chicken 130
Easy Chicken Tetrazzini 145
Fried Chicken with
   Onion Gravy............................ 143
Herbed Chicken Breasts.............. 116
Hot Chicken Loaf with
   Mushroom Sauce..................... 129
Hot Chicken Turnovers 139
Huntington Chicken..................... 135
Italian Chicken 116
Jack's Favorite Curry................... 150
Jim's Favorite Chicken Pie 143
King Ranch Casserole 138
Low Calorie Chicken
   Cacciatore 144
Minty Chicken............................. 119
Nancy's Chicken Stuff 132
Oven Barbecued Chicken............ 130
Oven-Fried Sesame Chicken....... 126
Paella Española 119
Paprika Chicken 120
Party Chicken Casserole 137
Party Chicken Tetrazzini 146
Peachy Keen Chicken 140
Peanut Chicken Oriental 122
Peanut Chicken with
   Mustard Sauce 121
Polynesian Chicken 122
Poppy Seed Chicken 123
Quick Chicken-Rice Bake 137
Relaxing Chicken 123
Russian Chicken Breasts 124
Saturday Chicken........................ 131
Scalloped Chicken and Rice 134
Scalloped Chicken
   with Vegetables 125
Sherried Chicken........................ 127
Southern Fried Chicken............... 111
Stir-Fry Chicken 148
Sweet and Sour Chicken 113
Turketti....................................... 149
Turkey-Rice Casserole 149

Pound Cake, Cream Cheese 291
Pound Cake, Five Flavor
   Buttermilk................................. 289
Pound Cake, Lemon 289
Pound Cake, Whipping Cream 288
Pralines, Buttermilk 298
Preserved Children 345
PRESERVING
   Apple Butter.............................. 342
   Apricot-Walnut Conserve 342
   Blanche's Pear Mincemeat 347
   Brandied Fruit Starter 343
   Canned Apple Pie Filling............ 343
   Canned Green Beans 341
   Chow-Chow............................... 344
   Corn Relish............................... 344
   Cucumber Pickles 345
   Dilled Okra 345
   Granola..................................... 351
   Honey Mustard 349
   Honey Watermelon
      Rind Preserves 346
   Hot Dog Relish.......................... 346
   It's Pecan Season...................... 346
   Peach Honey 347
   Pear Relish 348
   Picante Sauce 348
   Pickled Green Beans 348
   Preserved Children.................... 345
   Prune Pickles 352
   Ripe Tomato Relish................... 349
   Taco Sauce 349
   Tommie's Pear Marmalade 347
   Yellow Squash Relish 350
   Zucchini Relish 351
   Zucchini-Pineapple 350
Preserves, Honey Watermelon
   Rind... 346
Pretzel Salad 179
Prize-Winning Homemade
   Mayonnaise.............................. 191
Prune Bread, Black Walnut-............ 235
Prune Pickles 352
Pudding with Brandy Sauce,
   Baked Apple............................. 254
Pudding, Cherry 256
Pudding, Cream of Rice 258
Pudding, Date 256
Pudding, Grandma Revils'
   Banana 255
Pudding, Luise's Bread 261
Pudding, Old-Fashioned Raisin 258
Pudding, Orange 257
Pudding, Persimmon 258
Pudding, Theodore Roosevelt's
   Indian 257
Pumpkin Bread.............................. 236
Pumpkin Pie Cake 287
Pumpkin Pie, Creamy 337

Pumpkin Scones	237
Pumpkin Walnut Cake	288
Punch, Citric Acid	38
Punch, Easy	38
Punch, Fruit Flip	37
Punch, Lime Light	39
Punch, Mexican	39
Punch, Pink Party	40
Punch, Spiced Peach	36
Punch, Spiced Percolator	36
Purple Hull Peas	209
Quail, Fried	154
Quarter-Baked Potatoes	210
Quiche, Crab	57
Quiche, Olive	57
Quiche, Spinach	58
Quick Chicken-Rice Bake	137
Raisin Pie, Sour Cream	335
Raisin Pudding, Old-Fashioned	258
Ranger Macaroons	302
Raspberry Fizz	37
Red Apple Inn Rolls	242
Red Beans and Rice	195
Red Fruit Dip	13
Reese Cups	295
Refrigerator Yeast Rolls	242
Relaxing Chicken	123
Relish, Corn	344
Relish, Hot Dog	346
Relish, Pear	348
Relish, Ripe Tomato	349
Relish, Yellow Squash	350
Relish, Zucchini	351
Rice Krispie and Corn Flake Treat	313
Rice Pudding, Cream of	258
RICE	
Arkansas Rice Casserole	63
Baked Rice	64
Curried Rice	64
Dirty Rice Dressing	65
Fresh Lemon Rice	66
Green Chili Rice	66
Indian Country Casserole	65
Shrimp Fried Rice	67
Rice-a-Roni Salad	177
Ripe Tomato Relish	349
Roast Wild Duck	153
Roast, Sweet and Sour	75
Rocky Road	300
Rocky Road Bars	299
Roll Dough, Basic	239
Rolled Roast Leg of Lamb	95
Rolls, Carmel's	241
Rolls, Cinnamon	240
Rolls, Mother's	240
Rolls, One-Rise Cinnamon	241
Rolls, Red Apple Inn	242
Rolls, Refrigerator Yeast	242

Rum Cake	290
Russian Chicken Breasts	124
SALAD DRESSINGS	
Banana Nut Dressing	192
Bea's Salad Dressing	192
Bleu Cheese Dressing	191
Chicken Salad with Honey Mustard Vinaigrette	185
Cole Slaw Dressing	190
Crab Louis	188
Guacamole Dressing	190
Italian Dressing	189
Le French Salad Dressing	189
Poppy Seed Dressing	189
Prize-Winning Homemade Mayonnaise	191
Spinach Salad with Mustard Dressing	170
Thousand Island Dressing	190
Turkey Fruit Salad with Pineapple Dressing	184
Salad Ring	176
SALADS	
Fruit	
Apricot Salad	179
Blueberry Salad	180
Coke Salad	178
Cranberry Casserole	182
Cranberry Ring	181
Frozen Banana-Strawberry Salad	183
Frozen Fruit Salad	183
Hot Fruit Salad	182
Mimi's Waldorf Salad	181
Pretzel Salad	179
Spicy Peach Salad	185
Strawberry Crown Salad	180
Sunshine Salad	178
Poultry	
Chicken Mayonnaise	186
Chicken Potato Salad	187
Chicken Salad	187
Chicken Salad with Honey Mustard Vinaigrette	185
Chinese Salad	184
Hot Chicken Salad Deluxe	186
Turkey Fruit Salad with Pineapple Dressing	184
Seafood	
Crab Louis	188
Summer Meal-in-a-Dish	168
Tuna Macaroni Salad	188
Vegetable	
Avocado Salad	169
Broccoli Rice Salad	171
Cold Cauliflower French-Style	173
Confetti Cottage Cheese Salad	172

Creamy Cabbage and
    Apple Slaw 169
Cucumber Ring Supreme 177
German Cole Slaw 174
Green and White
    Vegetable Salad.................... 172
Idaho Potato Salad 171
Macaroni Salad 175
Marinated Vegetables 176
Potato Salad............................. 170
Rice-a-Roni Salad 177
Salad Ring................................ 176
Sliced Tomatoes Vinaigrette 174
Spinach Salad with
    Mustard Dressing.................. 170
Tossed Salad Supreme 173
24-hour Vegetable Salad 168
Wilted Lettuce Salad 167
Salmon Ball 32
Salmon Croquettes 159
Salmon Loaf 158
Salmon Loaf with Sauce Verte 160
Salsa.. 13
Sand Tarts 316

SANDWICHES
Barbecued Shredded Beef............ 50
Beef Sandwiches 51
Cheeseburgers To Go 51
Hot Ham Sandwiches................... 52
Mama Nina's Pimento Cheese....... 51
Maytime Muffuletta Mix 52
Pineapple-Barbecued Beef
    Sandwiches 50
Saturday Chicken 131

SAUCES
Dessert
Baked Apple Pudding with
    Brandy Sauce 254
Chocolate Fudge Sauce 261
Deluxe Cheesecake with
    Raspberry Sauce 268

Meat
All-purpose Creole Seasoning 72
Breast of Turkey with
    Apple Raisin Sauce............... 148
Brown Mushroom Sauce............ 21
Chicken Dip'n Sauces............. 151
Chicken Loaf with
    Lemon Sauce...................... 128
Country Ham and Red-Eye
    Gravy 104
Easy Meatless Tomato Sauce 85
Ham Ring with Cherry Sauce 96
Herb Basting Sauce................. 116
Hot Chicken Loaf with
    Mushroom Sauce 129
Mexican Red Sauce 94
Mexican Spaghetti Sauce........... 83
Mornay Sauce 152

Ninfa's Mexican Green Sauce 94
Oriental Meatballs with
    Sweet and Sour Sauce 85
Pork In Sweet and
    Sour Sauce 98
Plum Sauce 18
Salsa.. 13
Sicilian Spaghetti Sauce............. 84
Sour Cream Curry Sauce 21
Spaghetti with Wiener Sauce... 107

Vegetable
Basic White Sauce................. 218
Hollandaise Sauce 218
Spanish Onion Custard 208
Sauerkraut, German 214
Sausage and Egg Casserole............... 55
Sausage and Peppers..................... 106
Sausage Muffins, Ham and............ 225
Sausage Rolls, Cheese and........... 25
Sausage Stuffed Mushrooms 22
Sausage Supper Dish 105
Sausage Supper, Italian 104
Sausage-Apple Bake 98
Sausage-Rice Casserole.................. 104
Scalloped Chicken and Rice............ 134
Scalloped Chicken
    with Vegetables..................... 125
Scalloped Corn 202
Scalloped Pineapple......................... 255
Scones, Date................................... 236
Scones, Pumpkin 237
Scotch Fudge................................. 271

SEAFOOD
Baked Fish................................. 156
Baked Tuna with Biscuits 162
Barbecued Shrimp 163
Basic Tempura............................ 165
Cashew Stuffed Shrimp with
    Lemon Sauce 161
Catfish Batter............................. 166
Crab Meat Au Gratin 157
Crab Muffins 157
Crispy Catfish Fry with
    Tartar Sauce 156
Filleted Fish A La Microwave 158
Fisherman's Catch...................... 155
Mickey's Shrimp Creole 164
Salmon Croquettes..................... 159
Salmon Loaf 158
Salmon Loaf with Sauce Verte 160
Shrimp Cocktail Sauce 166
Shrimp Curry 165
Shrimp Paella 163
Shrimp Puffs 164
Shrimp Stir-Fry with
    Vegetables 162
Shrimp Victoria 160
Sole Au Gratin 159
Sees Fudge................................ 294

Shake, Strawberry Breakfast 40
Shake, Sunshine 40
Sherbet, Mom's Lemon................... 264
Sherried Chicken 127
Shish Kebabs 76
Short Ribs, Braised 73
Shrimp Cocktail Sauce.................... 166
Shrimp Creole, Mickey's 164
Shrimp Curry 165
Shrimp Dip 13
Shrimp Dip, Party.............................. 14
Shrimp Fried Rice.............................. 67
Shrimp Mold 31
Shrimp Paella 163
Shrimp Puffs.................................... 164
Shrimp Stir-Fry with Vegetables...... 162
Shrimp Victoria............................... 160
Shrimp with Lemon Sauce,
   Cashew Stuffed........................... 161
Shrimp, Barbecued 163
Sicilian Spaghetti Sauce 84
Skillet BBQ Venison........................ 110
Slaw, Creamy Cabbage
   and Apple................................... 169
Slaw, German Cole 174
Sliced Tomatoes Vinaigrette 174
Smothered Steak 76
Smothered Venison......................... 110
Sole au Gratin 159

SOUPS
   Broccoli Soup 42
   Cheese Soup.................................. 43
   Chicken Corn Soup 44
   Clam Chowder 44
   Crab-Corn Chowder 45
   Cream of Cauliflower Soup 43
   Easy Gumbo 45
   Lentil Soup 46
   Microwave Potato Soup 48
   Millie Wood's Bean Soup 42
   Onion Wine Soup 46
   Oyster Stew 47
   Polish Meatball Soup.................... 47
   Potato Soup.................................. 48
   Southern Bean Soup 41
   Spicy Tortilla Soup 49
   Squash Soup................................. 49
   Univith Soup 42
Sour Cream Apple Pie..................... 318
Sour Cream Raisin Pie 335
Sour Cream Spread,
   Cheesy-Bacon 29
Southern Bean Soup 41
Southern Chess Pie.......................... 324
Southern Fried Chicken 111
Spaghetti Casserole, Chicken- 146
Spaghetti Sauce, Mexican 83
Spaghetti Sauce, Sicilian 84
Spaghetti with Wiener Sauce 107

Spaghetti, Bacon................................ 53
Spaghetti, Chicken........................... 147
Spanish Onion Custard 208
Speedy Spinach 211
Spice Cake, Cora Locke's................ 291
Spicy Peach Salad 185
Spiced Apple Cider............................ 36
Spiced Cheese Muffins 225
Spiced Peach Punch 36
Spiced Percolator Punch 36
Spicy Beans and Cornbread
   Casserole 196
Spicy Cheese Dip............................... 10
Spicy Sweet Potato Casserole......... 214
Spicy Tortilla Soup 49
Spinach Dip 14
Spinach Quiche.................................. 58
Spinach Salad with
   Mustard Dressing 170
Spinach Squares 211
Spinach, Speedy 211
Spring Tonic 33
Squash Casserole, Yellow 212
Squash Fritters 213
Squash Soup...................................... 49
Squash, Stir-Fry 212
Squash, Stuffed Summer................. 213
Squash-Carrot Casserole................. 212
Squirrel Stew................................... 109
Steak, Old-Fashioned Swiss.............. 77
Steak, Smothered 76
Stir and Spoon Fudge Drops........... 308
Stir-Fry Chicken.............................. 148
Stir-Fry Squash 212
Strawberry Breakfast Shake 40
Strawberry Crown Salad................. 180
Strawberry-Banana-Nut
   Ice Cream 264
Straws, Cheese 7
Streusel Coffee Cake 221
Stuffed Summer Squash.................. 213
Sugar Cookies 314
Sugar Cookies, Drop....................... 314
Summer Meal-in-a-Dish 168
Sunshine Salad 178
Sunshine Shake 40
Super Mexican Casserole.................. 93
Suppertime Eggs................................ 56
Swedish Meat Balls 86
Swedish Shortbread Cookies........... 316
Sweet and Sour Chicken................. 113
Sweet and Sour Pork Roast 96
Sweet and Sour Red Cabbage......... 197
Sweet and Sour Roast....................... 75
Sweet and Sour Wieners................. 101
Sweet Potato Biscuits...................... 228
Sweet Potato Bread......................... 234
Sweet Potato Casserole 214
Sweet Potato Casserole, Spicy........ 214

Entry	Page
Sweet Potato Muffins, Williamsburg	226
Sweet Potato Pie	336
Taco Dip	15
Taco From The Oven	83
Taco Sauce	349
Tacos, Breakfast	55
Tamale Pie	82
Tarts, Apricot	319
Tasty Pork Tenders	101
Tea Cakes, Old-Fashioned	316
Tea, Dottie Lou's	35
Tea, Hot Spiced	37
Tempura, Basic	165
Tex-Mex Dip	15
Theodore Roosevelt's Indian Pudding	257
This Can't Be Turnips	216
Thousand Island Dressing	190
Tiny Russian Mint Pies	335
Tomato Casserole	215
Tomatoes Vinaigrette, Sliced	174
Tomatoes, Fried Green	215
Tommie's Pear Marmalade	347
Tortellini	89
Tossed Salad Supreme	173
Tuna Dip, Hot	16
Tuna Macaroni Salad	188
Tuna with Biscuits, Baked	162
Turketti	149
Turkey Casserole, Cheddar	150
Turkey Fruit Salad with Pineapple Dressing	184
Turkey with Apple Raisin Sauce, Breast of	148
Turkey-Rice Casserole	149
Turnip Greens with Cornbread Dumplings	216
Turnips, Old-Fashioned	215
Turnips, This Can't Be	216
24-Hour Omelet	54
24-Hour Vegetable Salad	168
Univith Soup	42
Upside Down Chili Cornbread	91
Vanilla Crisps	302
Vanilla Pie	337
Vanilla Wafer Fruit Cake	280
Veal Parmesan	108
Veal Scallopini, Low Calorie	109
Veal, Braised	108
Vegetable Bubble Bread	227
Vegetable Salad, 24-Hour	168
Vegetable Salad, Green and White	172
VEGETABLES	
Artichokes and Mushrooms	194
Asparagus Casserole	194
"Beats-All" Beets	196
Braised Cucumbers	200
Broccoli Casserole For A Crowd	197
Cabbage Rolls	198
Carrots Flambe	198
Cheese Potatoes	209
Corn Fritters	200
Corn Pudding	201
Country Potatoes	209
Creamy Cauliflower	199
Eggplant Fritters	203
Franke's Scalloped Eggplant	204
Fried Corn	200
Fried Eggplant	203
Fried Green Tomatoes	215
German Sauerkraut	214
Golden Eggplant Casserole	204
Green Bean Casserole	205
Hominy Casserole	202
Hoppin' John	206
Just Peachy Limas	206
Lo-Cal Carrots	199
May's Okra Casserole	207
My Zucchini	217
Okra and Tomatoes	207
Old Hickory Barbecued Beans	195
Old-Fashioned Turnips	215
Onion Patties	208
Original Green Bean Casserole	205
Pepper Corn	201
Poke Sallet	193
Potato Casserole	210
Purple Hull Peas	209
Quarter-Baked Potatoes	210
Red Beans and Rice	195
Scalloped Corn	202
Spanish Onion Custard	208
Speedy Spinach	211
Spicy Beans and Cornbread Casserole	196
Spicy Sweet Potato Casserole	214
Spinach Squares	211
Squash Fritters	213
Squash-Carrot Casserole	212
Stir-Fry Squash	212
Stuffed Summer Squash	213
Sweet and Sour Red Cabbage	197
Sweet Potato Casserole	214
This Can't Be Turnips	216
Tomato Casserole	215
Turnip Greens with Cornbread Dumplings	216
Yellow Squash Casserole	212
Zucchini Medley	217
Vegetables, Marinated	176
Venison, Skillet BBQ	110
Venison, Smothered	110
Venison Steak, Fried	69
Waffles	222
Waldorf Salad, Cranberry	181

Waldorf Salad, Mimi's 181
Walnut Cake, Black 292
Whipping Cream Pound Cake 288
White Enchiladas 81
White Fruit Cake 280
Wieners, Sweet and Sour 101
Wild Duck Gumbo 153
Wild Hog Chili 88
Williamsburg Sweet Potato
 Muffins 226
Wilted Lettuce Salad 167
With-it Deviled Eggs 60
Yellow Squash Casserole 212
Yellow Squash Relish 349
Zucchini Bread 237
Zucchini Medley 217
Zucchini Omelet 56
Zucchini, Relish 351
Zucchini, My 217
Zucchini-Pineapple 350

Sevier County Cookbook Committee
P. O. Box 66
Lockesburg, Arkansas 71846

Please send me _____ copies of CELEBRATION, **A Taste of Arkansas** at $13.95 per copy. Add $2.25 per copy for postage and handling. Enclosed is my check (   ) or money order (   ) for $ _____ .

Make checks payable to CELEBRATION.

Name _____

Address _____

City: _____ State: _____ Zip: _____

Sevier County Cookbook Committee
P. O. Box 66
Lockesburg, Arkansas 71846

Please send me _____ copies of CELEBRATION, **A Taste of Arkansas** at $13.95 per copy. Add $2.25 per copy for postage and handling. Enclosed is my check (   ) or money order (   ) for $ _____ .

Make checks payable to CELEBRATION.

Name _____

Address _____

City: _____ State: _____ Zip: _____

Sevier County Cookbook Committee
P. O. Box 66
Lockesburg, Arkansas 71846

Please send me _____ copies of CELEBRATION, **A Taste of Arkansas** at $13.95 per copy. Add $2.25 per copy for postage and handling. Enclosed is my check (   ) or money order (   ) for $ _____ .

Make checks payable to CELEBRATION.

Name _____

Address _____

City: _____ State: _____ Zip: _____